Childhood and Consumer Culture

Studies in Childhood and Youth
Series Editors: **Allison James** and **Adrian L. James**

Titles include:

Kate Bacon
TWINS IN SOCIETY
Parents, Bodies, Space and Talk

David Buckingham and Vebjørg Tingstad (*editors*)
CHILDHOOD AND CONSUMER CULTURE

Allison James, Anne Trine Kjørholt and Vebjørg Tingstad (*editors*)
CHILDREN, FOOD AND IDENTITY IN EVERYDAY LIFE

Studies in Childhood and Youth
Series Standing Order ISBN 978–0–230–21686–0 hardback
(outside North America only)

You can receive future titles in this series as they are published by placing a standing order. Please contact your bookseller or, in case of difficulty, write to us at the address below with your name and address, the title of the series and the ISBN quoted above.

Customer Services Department, Macmillan Distribution Ltd, Houndmills, Basingstoke, Hampshire RG21 6XS, England

Childhood and Consumer Culture

Edited by

David Buckingham
Institute of Education, University of London, UK

and

Vebjørg Tingstad
Norwegian University of Science and Technology, Norway

First published 2010 by
PALGRAVE MACMILLAN

Palgrave Macmillan in the UK is an imprint of Macmillan Publishers Limited,
registered in England, company number 785998, of Houndmills, Basingstoke,
Hampshire RG21 6XS.

Palgrave Macmillan in the US is a division of St Martin's Press LLC,
175 Fifth Avenue, New York, NY 10010.

Palgrave Macmillan is the global academic imprint of the above companies
and has companies and representatives throughout the world.

Palgrave® and Macmillan® are registered trademarks in the United States,
the United Kingdom, Europe and other countries.

ISBN 978–0–230–22783–5   hardback

This book is printed on paper suitable for recycling and made from fully
managed and sustained forest sources. Logging, pulping and manufacturing
processes are expected to conform to the environmental regulations of the
country of origin.

A catalogue record for this book is available from the British Library.

Library of Congress Cataloging-in-Publication Data

Childhood and consumer culture / [edited by] David Buckingham,
    Vebjørg Tingstad.
      p. cm.
    ISBN 978–0–230–22783–5 (hardback)
    1. Child consumers. 2. Consumption (Economics)––Sociological aspects.
      I. Tingstad, Vebjørg. II. Buckingham, David, 1954-
    HF5415.32.C46 2010
      306.3083—dc22   2010012007

10 9 8 7 6 5 4 3 2 1
19 18 17 16 15 14 13 12 11 10

Printed and bound in Great Britain by
CPI Antony Rowe, Chippenham and Eastbourne

Contents

List of Tables, Figures and Illustrations   vii

Acknowledgements   viii

Notes on Contributors   ix

Introduction   1
David Buckingham and Vebjørg Tingstad

Part I   History of Children's Consumption

1   Valves of Adult Desire: The Regulation and Incitement
    of Children's Consumption   17
    Gary Cross

2   Proper Toys for Proper Children: A Case Study of the
    Norwegian Company A/S Riktige Leker (Proper Toys)   31
    Tora Korsvold

3   The Books That Sing: The Marketing of Children's
    Phonograph Records, 1890–1930   46
    Jacob Smith

**Part II   Theory and Method in Research on Children's
Consumption**

4   Commercial Enculturation: Moving Beyond Consumer
    Socialization   63
    Daniel Thomas Cook

5   Subjectivities of the Child Consumer: Beings and Becomings   80
    Barbro Johansson

6   Researching Things, Objects and Gendered
    Consumption in Childhood Studies   94
    Claudia Mitchell

Part III   Practices of Contemporary Marketers

7   Children's Virtual Worlds: The Latest Commercialization
    of Children's Culture   113
    Janet Wasko

 8 Creating Long-lasting Brand Loyalty – or a
    Passing "Craze"?: Lessons from a "Child Classic"
    in Norway   130
    Ingunn Hagen and Øivind Nakken

 9 The Cute, the Spectacle and the Practical: Narratives of
    New Parents and Babies at The Baby Show   146
    Lydia Martens

Part IV Social Contexts of Children's Consumption

10 The Stuff at Mom's House and the Stuff at Dad's House:
    The Material Consumption of Divorce for Adolescents   163
    Caitlyn Collins and Michelle Janning

11 The Dao of Consumer Socialization: Raising Children
    in the Chinese Consumer Revolution   178
    Randi Wærdahl

12 "Those Who Have Less Want More. But Does It Make
    Them Feel Bad?": Deprivation, Materialism and
    Self-Esteem in Childhood   194
    Agnes Nairn, Paul Bottomley and Johanne Ormrod

Part V Childhood Identities and Consumption

13 Branded Selves: How Children Relate to Marketing
    on a Social Network Site   211
    Håvard Skaar

14 "Hello – We're Only in the Fifth Grade!!":
    Children's Rights, Inter-generationality and Constructions of
    Gender in Public Discourses About Childhood   228
    Mari Rysst

15 "One Meets Through Clothing": The Role of Fashion
    in the Identity Formation of Former Soviet Union
    Immigrant Youth in Israel   244
    Dafna Lemish and Nelly Elias

Index   259

List of Tables, Figures and Illustrations

Tables

12.1 Youth materialism by SES   201

12.2 Materialism and attitude to parents by SES   203

13.1 Production modes   219

Figures

8.1 Dynamics of brand loyalty   142

11.1 Sources of information and influence on children's
consumer choices   182

11.2 Children and their knowledge about consumption   185

Illustrations

6.1 Bride doll   103

8.1 Captain Sabertooth with his sword   143

Acknowledgements

Grateful acknowledgements are made to Claudia Mitchell and Lewis Wosu, McGill University, for permission to reproduce the picture of the Bride Doll; Nicolai Prebensen for permission to reproduce the picture of Captain Sabertooth with his sword; and to Taylor & Francis Ltd, *Journal of Children and Media* for permission to reproduce Jacob Smith's article *The Books that Sing: The Marketing of Children's Phonograph Records, 1890–1930* (2009), Håvard Skaar's article *Branded Selves: How Children Relate to Marketing on a Social Network Site* (2009) and parts of David Buckingham's article *Selling Childhood? Children and Consumer Culture* (2007).

Notes on Contributors

Daniel Thomas Cook is an Associate Professor of Childhood Studies and Sociology at Rutgers University, Camden, New Jersey, USA. He is editor of *Symbolic Childhood* (2002) and author of *The Commodification of Childhood* (2004) as well as a number of articles and book chapters on childhood, consumer society, leisure and urban culture. Cook serves as an editor of *Childhood: A Journal of Global Child Research*.

Paul Bottomley is a distinguished Senior Research Fellow at Cardiff Business School. His current research interests are in the areas of brand management, consumers' connections with brands, and materialism. His previous work has been published in leading marketing journals including *Journal of Marketing Research, Marketing Science,* and *International Journal of Research in Marketing*.

David Buckingham is a Professor of Education, and Director of the Centre for the Study of Children, Youth and Media at the Institute of Education, University of London; and a Visiting Professor at the Centre for Child Research, NTNU Trondheim, Norway. His research focuses on children and young people's interactions with electronic media, and on media education. Among his most recent publications are *Beyond Technology: Children's Learning in the Age of Digital Culture, Video Culture: Media Technology and Amateur Creativity* (Palgrave, 2009) and *Youth, Identity and Digital Media*.

Caitlyn Collins is a graduate of Whitman College in Walla Walla, Washington, USA and is currently following a PhD programme in sociology at the University of Texas in Austin. Her most recent research focuses on material culture associated with childhood and divorce, and her interests lie in studies of the family, education, culture, and international issues.

Gary Cross is a Distinguished Professor of Modern History at Pennsylvania State University. Germane books include *Kids' Stuff: Toys and the Changing World of Modern Childhood ; An All-Consuming Century: Why Commercialism Won in Modern America; The Cute and the Cool: Wondrous Innocence and American Children's Culture;* and *Men to Boys: The Making of Modern Immaturity*.

Nelly Elias is a Senior Lecturer and a Chair of the Department of Communication Studies, Ben-Gurion University of the Negev, Israel. Her research interests are in the area of mass communication and immigration. Her most recent studies focus on the roles of mass media in the lives of immigrant children and adolescents in Israel and Germany and on the transnational virtual communities established by immigrants from the FSU. She has various academic publications in the fields of mass media and immigrant integration, including a book entitled *Coming Home: Media and Returning Diaspora in Israel and Germany* (2008).

Michelle Janning is an Associate Professor, Chair of Sociology and Garrett Fellow at Whitman College in Walla Walla, Washington, USA. She has served as guest editor of *Journal of Family Issues* for an issue entitled "Spaces and Places of Family Life: Cultural and Popular Cultural Representations of Homes and Families". Her recent publications focus on areas of work and family boundary permeability, gender and decorating, television viewing habits, material culture in families and homes, spousal support and shared paid work, and gender and sports.

Ingunn Hagen is a Professor in the Department of Psychology at the Norwegian University of Science and Technology (NTNU). Her research focuses on media reception, political communication, consumption of popular culture, young people and media, and children, commercialization and consumption. Her authored and edited books include: *Mediegenerasjonen. Barn og unge i det nye medielandskapet (The Media Generation. Children and Young People in the New Media Landscape*, with Thomas Wold); *Medias Publikum: Frå mottakar til brukar? (Media Audiences. From Receiver to User?*); and (with Janet Wasko) *Consuming Audiences: Production and Reception in Media Research.* She has published articles in a number of books and journals, both in English and Norwegian.

Barbro Johansson is an Associate Professor of Ethnology and researcher at the Centre for Consumer Science at School of Business, Economics and Law, University of Gothenburg. Her research area is children and childhood, with a focus on consumption, food, children's rights and childhood theory. Recent publications are *Nordic children's foodscapes: Images and reflections (Food, Culture and Society*, 2009) and *Fashion and style in a commercial and cultural borderland.* (in Brembeck, H., K. M. Ekström and M. Mörck (eds) 2007: *Little Monsters, (De)coupling Assemblages of Consumption*).

Tora Korsvold is dr.art. and a senior research fellow at the Norwegian Centre for Child Research, NTNU Trondheim, Norway. Her main research fields are the history of the welfare state, children and childhood. Recent publications are *Barns verdi* (*Childrens' value*) (2006) and *Barn og barndom i velferdsstatens småbarnspolitikk* (*The welfare politics for small children*, 2008). Among publications in English are *Childcare and childcare dilemmas* (Palgrave) and *In the Best Interests of the Child* . She is co-editor of the Nordic journal *Barn*.

Dafna Lemish is a Professor of Communication at Tel Aviv University and founding editor of the *Journal of Children and Media*. Her research interests include the roles of media in children's lives and gender representation. Her recent books include *Screening gender on children's television: The views of producers around the world* (forthcoming 2010); *The wonder phone in the land of miracles: Mobile telephony in Israel* (with Cohen and Schejter 2008) *Children and television: A global perspective* (2007); and *Children and media in times of war and conflic* (edited with Götz, 2007).

Lydia Martens is Senior Lecturer in Sociology at Keele University (UK). She has been researching children, families and consumer culture and has conducted fieldwork at The Baby Show and other market encounter platforms. She is currently writing a book on this project. Her publications include *Eating Out: Social Differentiation, Consumption and Pleasure* (2000, with Alan Warde) and *Gender and Consumption: Domestic Cultures and the Commercialisation of Everyday Life* (2007, with Emma Casey).

Claudia Mitchell is a James McGill Professor in the Faculty of Education of McGill University, Montreal, Canada, and an Honorary Professor at the University of KwaZulu-Natal in Durban, South Africa. Her research looks at youth and sexuality in the age of AIDS, children's popular culture, with a particular focus on girlhood, teacher identity, and participatory visual and other textual methodologies. She is the co-editor of *Girl Culture: An Encyclopedia* (2 vols), and is also the co-editor of *Girlhood Studies: An Interdisciplinary Journal*.

Agnes Nairn is a Professor of Marketing at EM-Lyon Business School in France and at RSM Erasmus University in the Netherlands. Her research focuses on the interface between children and the commercial world and the ethics of marketing to children. She is co-author of *Consumer Kids* 2009).

Øivind Nakken has an MA in Health, Media, and Communication Psychology, and is associated with the project Consuming Children at NTNU Trondheim through his master thesis *Captain Sabertooth – Adventurous Brand Loyalty (2007)*. He is now the owner of the Media Company Arctic Branding Ltd.

Johanne Ormrod is a licensed psychologist practising in Aarhus, Denmark. She is a chartered fellow of the Danish Psychological Society, working in private practice as well as in a specialist division of the Aarhus County Council. Johanne specializes in psychopathology, and is a consultant and supervisor. A visiting scholar at the University of Bath, England 2005, Johanne was involved in a research project regarding the links between materialism and wellbeing of children. Since then she has coauthored a policy report and contributed to articles on the broader subject of consumer culture and mental health.

Mari Rysst is a Senior Researcher at The National Institute for Consumer Research, Oslo, Norway. Her research focuses on children, gender, body, class and ethnicity. The title of her PhD thesis is '*I Want To Be Me. I Want To Be Kul. An Anthropological Study of Norwegian Pre-teen Girls in the Light of a Presumed "Disappearance" of Childhood* '(2008).

Håvard Skaar is an Assistant Professor of Norwegian language and literature at Oslo University College, and a project collaborator at the Norwegian Centre for Child Research, NTNU, Trondheim, Norway. He has published articles about learning and commercial aspects of children's use of digital media in national and international books and journals. The title of his thesis is *Digital media literacy: Children in and out of school* (2009). Skaar has also written a textbook and a number of articles about Norwegian literature.

Jacob Smith is an Assistant Professor in the Department of Radio–Television–Film at Northwestern University. His book, *Vocal Tracks: Performance and Sound Media* (2008) is an examination of the styles of vocal performance that developed in tandem with sound media technologies. He has also published articles on media history and performance in journals such as *Film Quarterly, Screen, Film Criticism, Television and New Media, Velvet Light Trap, Early Popular Visual Culture* and *Journal of Popular Music Studies*.

Vebjørg Tingstad is an Associate Professor and Deputy Director at the Norwegian Centre for Child Research, NTNU, Trondheim, Norway. Her current research interests involve children's online networking, consumption, food culture and childhood in contemporary societies. Among her publications are *Children's Chat on the Net. A Study of Children's Social Encounters in Two Norwegian Chat Rooms, Barndom under lupen* (Exploring Childhood-Growing up in a Changing Media Culture, 2006) and *Discourses on child obesity and TV advertising in the context of the Norwegian welfare state* (Palgrave). She is co-editor of the Nordic journal *Barn*.

Janet Wasko is the Knight Chair in Communication Research at the University of Oregon. She is author, co-author or editor of 18 books on media, including *Understanding Disney: The Manufacture of Fantasy, How Hollywood Works,* and *Dazzled by Disney: The Global Disney Audience Project.* Her research and teaching focuses on the political economy of communications.

Randi Wærdahl is a post-doctoral researcher at the Department of Sociology and Human Geography, University of Oslo, Norway. After finishing her doctoral thesis "Learning by Consuming. Consumer Culture as a Condition for Socialization and Every Day Life at the Age of 12" (2003), she has worked in the areas of childhood, families, consumer culture and new methodologies for comparative studies of childhood. Her most resent research has focused on changing conditions for childhood in times of rapid economic change. Her latest international engagement was at the China Youth and Children Research Center (CYCRC) in Beijing, China, in 2006. Other publications in English from the present project are *Consumer Socialisation and Value Orientations among Estonian and Chinese Young People,* (with Veronika Kalmus and Margit Keller in Children and Society (2009) and *Teddy Diaries: A Method for Studying the Display of Family Life* (with Marit Haldar 2009).

Introduction

David Buckingham and Vebjørg Tingstad

Commercial marketing to children is by no means a new phenomenon. Indeed, historical studies show that children have been a key focus of interest at least since the inception of modern mass marketing (e.g. Cook, 2004; Cross, 1997; Seiter, 1993). Nevertheless, in recent years children have become more and more important both as a market in their own right and as a means to reach adult markets. Marketers are seeking to target children more directly and at an ever-younger age; and they are using a much wider range of techniques that go well beyond conventional advertising. Marketers often claim that children are becoming 'empowered' in this new commercial environment: the market is seen to be responding to needs and desires on the part of children that have hitherto been largely ignored or marginalised, not least because of the social dominance of adults.

However, these developments have also led to growing public concern about the apparent 'commercialisation' of childhood. Popular publications, press reports and campaigns have addressed the damaging impact of commercial forces on children's physical and mental health. These concerns are often part of a broader lament about the decline or corruption of childhood itself. Such arguments typically presume that children used to live in an essentially non-commercial world; and that their entry into the marketplace over the past several decades has had a wide range of negative consequences for their well-being, which range from concerns about obesity and eating disorders to issues such as 'sexualisation' and materialism. Far from being 'empowered', children are typically seen here as victims of a powerful, highly manipulative form of consumer culture that is almost impossible for them to escape or resist.

Before we introduce the studies contained in this book, it is important to sketch these debates in a little more detail, since they largely

1

frame the topic we are addressing. Like other debates about childhood, and particularly about children and media, debates about children's consumption are often highly polarised. Children are either powerful agents or passive victims; either sophisticated and 'media literate' or innocent and naïve; either competent or incompetent. One of the aims of this book as a whole is to look beyond these opposing positions, and to develop a more nuanced and more complex account of how the commercial market operates, and how children relate to it.

Constructing the child consumer: critics and marketers

In the wake of Naomi Klein's influential *No Logo* (2001), there has been a flurry of popular critical publications about children and consumer culture: prominent examples include Juliet Schor's *Born to Buy* (2004), Susan Linn's *Consuming Children* (2004) and Ed Mayo and Agnes Nairn's *Consumer Kids* (2009). Other such books include discussions of children's consumption alongside broader arguments about the apparent demise of traditional notions of childhood – as in the case of Sue Palmer's *Toxic Childhood* (2006) or Richard Layard and Judy Dunn's *A Good Childhood* (2009). The arguments in these publications are, by and large, far from new. One can look back to similar arguments being made in the 1970s, for example by groups like Action for Children's Television in the US (Hendershot, 1998); or to announcements of the 'death of childhood' that have regularly recurred throughout the past two centuries (e.g. Postman, 1983). Even so, there now seems to be a renewed sense of urgency about these arguments.

Many of these books link the issue of consumerism with other well-known concerns about media and childhood: as well as turning children into premature consumers, the media are accused of promoting sex and violence, junk food, drugs and alcohol, gender stereotypes and false values, and taking children away from other activities that are deemed to be more worthwhile. Of course, this is a familiar litany, which tends to confuse very different kinds of effects and influences. It constructs the child as innocent, helpless, and unable to resist the power of the media. These texts describe children as being bombarded, assaulted, barraged, even subjected to 'saturation bombing' by the media: they are being seduced, manipulated, exploited, brainwashed, programmed and branded. And the predictable solution here is for parents to engage in counter-propaganda, to censor their children's use of media, or simply keep them locked away from corrupting commercial influences. These books rarely include the voices of children, or try to take account of their perspectives: this is essentially a discourse generated by parents *on behalf of* children.

Meanwhile, there has been a growth in marketing discourse specifically focused on children. Again, there is a long history of this kind of material. Dan Cook (2004) has shown how the children's clothing industry has historically attempted to articulate the child's perspective, to construct the child as a kind of authority, not least by means of market research. More recent examples of such marketing discourse would include Gene del Vecchio's *Creating Ever Cool* (1997) and Anne Sutherland and Beth Thompson's *Kidfluence* (2003). Perhaps the most influential account, however, is Martin Lindstrom and Patricia Seybold's *Brandchild* (2003). *Brandchild* focuses on the relatively new category of the 'tween' – which is itself a good example of how the market purports to have identified a new category of consumer, whose needs it then claims to identify and meet (cf. Cook, 2004). According to Lindstrom and Seybold, tweens are a digital generation, 'born with a mouse in their hands'; and they speak a new language, called Tweenspeak. Yet they also have anxieties – and the stress of growing up, the fear of global conflict and so on, mean that brands are all the more important for them, in helping them to enjoy life despite their difficulties. Indeed, tweens are seen to have a 'spiritual hunger' that brands and marketers alone can satisfy. The strategies these authors recommend to reach tweens are a long way from conventional advertising, and include peer-to-peer marketing, viral marketing and virtual brands. These are tactics that rely on the active participation of the peer group – and they are precisely those that alarm the critics mentioned above. For the marketers, however, these practices are all about empowerment – about children registering their needs, finding their voices, building their self-esteem, defining their own values, and developing independence and autonomy.

The most striking contrast between these accounts and those of the critics of consumer culture is the very different construction of the child consumer. The child is seen here as sophisticated, demanding and hard-to-please. Tweens, we are told, are not easily manipulated: they are an elusive, even fickle market, sceptical about the claims of advertisers, and discerning when it comes to getting value for money – and they need considerable effort to understand and to capture. This idea of the child as sovereign consumer often slips into the idea of the child as citizen, as autonomous social actor; and it is often accompanied by a kind of 'anti-adultism'. This approach is very apparent, for example, in the marketing of the global children's television channel Nickelodeon (Banet-Weiser, 2007; Hendershot, 2004). Significantly, children are defined here primarily in terms of being *not adults*. Adults are boring; kids are fun. Adults are conservative; kids are fresh and innovative. Adults will never understand; kids intuitively *know*. In the new world of children's consumer culture, kids *rule*.

Polarization and paradox

These two perspectives thus provide quite contrasting constructions of the child consumer. On the one hand, the campaigners present children as powerless victims of consumer culture. From this point of view, the pleasure of consumption is something to be suspected, a matter of inauthentic, short-term gratification – unlike the apparently authentic pleasures of human interaction, true culture, or spontaneous play. This argument stands in a long tradition of critical theory, from Adorno and Marcuse (and indeed more conservative critics like F.R. Leavis and Ortega y Gasset) through to contemporary authors such as Stephen Kline (1993). One of the most evident problems with this perspective is that it is always *other people's* consumption that is regarded as problematic: the argument is informed by a kind of elitism, whereby largely white, male, middle-class critics have stigmatised the consumption practices of others – women, the working classes and now children (Seiter, 1993).

By contrast – and perhaps ironically – it is the marketers who emphasise the competence and autonomy of children, and who pay tribute to their sophistication. To be sure, there are definite limits to this: the power that is being celebrated here is ultimately no more than the power to consume. And of course, given the political pressure that currently surrounds the issue of marketing to children (most notably around so-called 'junk food'), marketers are bound to argue that advertising has very little effect, and that children are 'wise consumers'. Even so, this kind of argument aligns quite well with the emphasis on children's autonomy and competence that characterises contemporary research in the sociology of childhood. For some researchers at least, there is an alarming coincidence in this respect between their own views and those of marketers. Indeed, there are some surprising political alliances – or potential alliances – here. On the one hand, child welfare campaigners seem to share a common cause with the moral majority; while on the other, some childhood researchers are making arguments that are very close to those of the marketers.

One of the recurring problems with this debate – as in other debates about media effects – is its tendency to displace attention away from other possible causes of the phenomena that are at stake. For example, there is a growing tendency in many countries to blame marketers and advertisers for the rise in childhood obesity; and this is an issue that is also becoming an increasing preoccupation for researchers (see Buckingham, 2009a, b; Tingstad, 2010). Yet there may be many other complex reasons for this phenomenon. In fact, poor people are most at risk of obesity – and this clearly has something to do with the availability and price of fresh food, and the time that is available to people to shop and prepare their own meals. The rise of obesity might also be related to the rise of 'car culture', and the fact that children (at least in some countries) are now much less independently mobile. As with violence, blaming the media allows politicians to displace attention away from other potential causes, while also being seen to be 'doing something' about the problem. The key point here, however, is that it makes little sense to abstract the question of children's relationship with advertising, or with consumer culture, from the broader social and historical context. The growth of consumer society is a complex, multifaceted, long-term social development; and displacing broader and more complex problems onto the issue of advertising inevitably results in a neglect of the real difficulties at stake.

Ultimately, the limitations of this debate derive from the broader assumptions about childhood on which it is based. It seems to be assumed that there is a natural state of childhood that has been destroyed or corrupted by marketers – or alternatively that children's 'real' innate needs are somehow being acknowledged and addressed, even for the first time. It is believed that there is something particular to the condition of childhood that makes children necessarily more vulnerable – or indeed spontaneously more wise and sophisticated, for example in their dealings with technology; and that adults are somehow exempted from these arguments.

Aside from the sentimentality of these assumptions, this kind of polarization fails to acknowledge some of the paradoxes here. For example, it is entirely possible that children (or indeed adults) might be active and sophisticated readers of media, but might nevertheless still be influenced – or indeed that an *illusion* of autonomy might be one of the pre-requisites of contemporary consumer culture. On the other hand, the campaigners often fail to acknowledge the difficulty that marketers have in reaching children – the fact that the market in children's products rises and falls in unpredictable ways, and that the failure rate for new products is much higher in the children's market than in the adult market (McNeal, 1999).

Theoretically, the question here is how we understand the relationship between structure and agency (Buckingham and Sefton-Green, 2003). On the one hand, the market clearly does attempt to construct and define the child consumer: it offers children powerful definitions of their own wants and needs, while purporting to satisfy them. Yet children also construct and define their own needs and identities – not least by how they appropriate and use consumer goods. The paradox of contemporary marketing is that it is bound to construct children as active, desiring and autonomous, and in some respects as resisting the imperatives of adults, while simultaneously seeking to make them behave in particular ways. Structure requires agency, but agency only works through structure.

Moving beyond these simple dichotomies also requires us to understand consumer culture – and indeed its historical evolution – in relation to other social factors. The children's market works through and with the family, the peer group and – increasingly – the school. We need to address how consumption practices are carried out in these different settings, and how they are implicated in the management of power, time and space. Anthropological and sociological studies of childhood have begun to address these dynamics in other areas of children's lives (see Qvortrup *et al.*, 2009); and much of the work presented in this book seeks to extend this into the analysis of consumer culture.

Contents of the book

The 'explosion of discourses' about the child consumer in recent years has also been accompanied by a significant expansion in academic research. This work derives from a range of disciplines, including the sociology of childhood, history, social psychology, media and cultural studies, and marketing and business studies. This book emerges from the third in a series of international, multidisciplinary conferences on 'Child and Teen Consumption', which have been held every two years since 2004 (previous volumes drawn from earlier conferences may be found in de la Ville, 2005; and Ekstrom and Tufte, 2007). The conference, which we organised, was held at the Norwegian Centre for Child Research in Trondheim in April 2008. This volume brings together a carefully selected collection of the best papers from the conference, written both by well-known scholars in the field and by emerging researchers. Our selection reflects a certain Nordic emphasis, but it includes contributions from the UK, the United States, Canada, China and Israel, as well as Norway and Sweden.

The book contains five parts organised around broad themes, each with three chapters. Part I about *History*, begins with a contribution by Gary Cross, which offers a broad analysis of the changing relationships between adults and children in US consumer culture over the past century. Cross argues that the communicative relationship between the advertiser and the child is more problematic than recent marketing research models suggest. Based on his analysis of US print and television advertising and specific historical episodes of parental reactions to new youth-oriented products, Cross shows how adults have repeatedly projected onto children their own contradictions and desires. On the one hand, adults repeatedly seek to regulate advertising and children's consumption; yet on the other, they spend money on children in their efforts to restore their lost wonder and their memory of childhood. This contradictory behaviour has produced tension between children and parents, as well as confusion between marketers and care-givers. It has also led to the modern extension of childhood and teenage tastes and products into adulthood. Cross suggests that the culture of teenage 'cool' (marked both by a rejection of parental restrictions and an embrace of parents' indulgence) has become a lifestyle shared by adults and children instead of a life stage abandoned at maturity.

In Chapter 2, 'Proper Toys for Proper Children', Tora Korsvold offers a detailed historical case study of the Norwegian company *Riktige Leker* (Proper Toys). In contrast with previous historical studies of the US toy market, this analysis draws attention to the very different context of the post-war Norwegian welfare state. The toys marketed by this company appear to be very pedagogical and appeal to particular notions of 'good parenting': there are no war games or 'sexualised' toys here. However, the process of selecting toys has become more complicated over time, as contemporary toy manufacturers and marketers seek to define childhood as a time for children's exploration of play and fun. The Proper Toys company builds on a tradition that defines play as progress, and on an old adult hegemony that claims to know children's 'own good'; but it has also had to accommodate to market forces, not least by presenting itself as a niche company, appealing to adult nostalgia. Korsvold's analysis focuses on how the distinction between 'proper' and 'improper' toys is defined and sustained, and how it has changed over time; and interprets this in terms of broader shifts in social values and in the ideologies and practices that characterise contemporary parenting.

The final chapter in Part I, by Jacob Smith, provides another historical case study, of the marketing of children's phonograph records in the early decades of the twentieth century. In 1924, the Victor Phonograph

Company proclaimed the possibilities of the 'boundless and almost untouched children's market' in embarking on a marketing campaign for 'Bubble Books', a very early example of a hybrid 'trans-media' product combining print texts with recorded sound and music. Examining advertisements for these products in trade journals and in the popular press, Smith explores how the child audience was constructed and addressed, and how parents were implicated in this process. It considers how the products sought to combine appeals based on education and on entertainment, and to repackage an oral tradition of children's nursery rhymes and songs. The direct marketing strategies adopted here in many ways presage those of Disney and other companies that followed; and in this respect, the analysis offers an important addition to previous accounts of the historical development of consumer culture and of contemporary constructions of childhood.

Part II moves on to address broader questions of theory and method in research on children's consumption. In Chapter 4, Daniel Thomas Cook offers a theoretical critique of the widely-used concept of consumer socialisation. This concept, and the research that has followed from it, tends to posit the child as moving in a linear fashion from unknowing to knowing and from a simple to a complex being. It is a paradigm that carries the embedded assumption that there is some point where the human organism 'enters' consumer life from a place or time 'outside' of it; and that there is a known (or knowable) end-point to the development of the consumer — usually that of the 'competent' adult. By contrast, the concept of 'commercial enculturation' developed in this chapter places attention on the multiple, layered and overlapping webs of cultural meaning that precede any individual child. Children, in this view, are not so much socialised into becoming specific kinds of consumers as they are seen as entering into social relationships with and through goods and their associations. This is a variable process that is not necessarily linear or temporally determined, but which has the general shape of an ontological trajectory.

Chapter 5, 'Subjectivities of the Child Consumer: Beings and Becomings', discusses the forms of consumer subjectivity available to contemporary Nordic children, and relates these to notions of 'being and becoming' as they are used in childhood research. Barbro Johansson draws on interviews with children aged 8–12, but also seeks to develop a broader theoretical analysis of the role of consumption in the construction of a 'generational order', in which people in different life stages are organised in relation to each other, and power and responsibility are allocated between them. Drawing on recent debates within childhood studies, on actor-network theory and the work of Deleuze, the chapter seeks to move beyond the polarisation between 'being' and 'becoming'. It argues that these concepts carry different meanings, and are defined situationally; and as such, they need to be seen more as events than as properties of the individual. These ideas are explored through an analysis of six distinct consumer subjectivities – that is, six ways in which children perform or construct themselves as consumers. This approach shifts attention away from individuals and entities to the flows and connections between events, and to the role of non-human actors such as objects, techniques and structures.

The final chapter in Part II, by Claudia Mitchell, makes a case for studying the *material culture* of childhood as a means of empirically grounding the emerging body of sociological and cultural research on children's consumption. Drawing on a range of perspectives from different disciplines and traditions, as well as on her own and her colleagues' extensive empirical research, Mitchell shows how the analysis of material objects can help to theorise abstract concepts in a very grounded manner. The objects of childhood offer a particular significance for further study, both because of their connections to memory and autobiography and particularly because of how they illuminate the gendered nature of children's consumption. Mitchell illustrates her argument with examples drawn from studies of toy packaging, dolls and doll-play, photographs and drawings, and displays in children's bedrooms. This chapter seeks to position the study of children's material culture within visual studies and cultural studies more broadly, effectively arguing for a 'new materialism' in childhood studies, while also providing promising hints and suggestions for further empirical research.

In Part III, the focus shifts to the practices of contemporary marketers. In Chapter 7, Janet Wasko explores the phenomenon of children's online social worlds, drawing particularly on forms of critical analysis developed within the 'political economy' approach to media and communications. Wasko argues that this perspective is especially important in a context where there has been a proliferation of new products and media forms, and a range of new marketing and advertising strategies targeted at children. Her brief overview of these general developments is followed by detailed case studies of two leading children's sites, Neopets and Webkinz. The analysis looks at the economic models on which the sites operate, and the ways in which they are connected with other forms of marketing and commercial activity targeting children. Wasko also focuses on the appeals of these sites to children – as is apparent in their form and content, and their mode of address – as well as the ways in which they define and produce children as consumers, and the forms of 'consumer ideology' they promote.

In Chapter 8, Ingunn Hagen and Øivind Nakken explore the phenomenon of children's consumer 'crazes' – situations where highly marketed media products and their spin-offs suddenly 'catch on' and become very popular with children. By contrast with well-known global examples such as Pokemon, Teenage Mutant Ninja Turtles, and Harry Potter, this chapter focuses on a nationally specific example, in the form of the Norwegian character Captain Sabertooth. This pirate figure, who features in books, cartoons, toys, a theme park and an animated film, has been popular among Norwegian children for the last 18 years, and is principally targeted at 2–8-year-olds, especially boys. Hagen and Nakken focus on the strategies used by the producers to achieve long-lasting brand loyalty and thereby move beyond the ephemeral nature of the 'craze'. These include strategies such as synergy, inclusion and brand control, which have all contributed to the lasting success of the brand, and its relative longevity as a 'child classic'.

Chapter 9, by Lydia Martens, analyses the UK consumer exhibition The Baby Show, which is targeted at new and prospective parents. Martens focuses on two dimensions of the Show, which she refers to as the spectacular and the practical. On the one hand, the Show has been set up to entertain, displaying the aesthetics of 'cuteness' and radiating a sense of (dis-)organised fun. On the other hand, it speaks to a variety of more practical and utilitarian concerns that cohere with the specific life course experiences of its visitors. The chapter discusses these apparently opposing features in some detail, and then goes on to outline how they are related. In doing so, it explores how 'what it means to become a parent' in contemporary society is culturally constructed alongside and in relation to 'what it means to be a baby' – constructions that are essentially created by adults working discursively on the cultural distinction between adulthood and childhood. In this latter respect, the chapter makes useful connections with some of the main themes of debate in the literature on children's consumer culture, such as child agency and oppositional marketing.

Part IV contains three chapters exploring the diverse *Social Contexts* of children's consumption. In 'The Stuff at Mom's House and the Stuff at Dad's House', Caitlyn Collins and Michelle Janning consider the implications of parents' divorce for children's use of consumer goods. Drawing on in-depth interviews with adolescents and young adults in the Pacific Northwest of the United States, they analyse how the children of divorced parents use artefacts of material culture to construct the meanings of domestic spaces and to form identity. The decoration and display of consumer goods in bedrooms, and the use of media technologies, are analysed in terms of how adolescents assert their tastes, opinions and beliefs, and establish their place within the family. Where there are disparities between two locations in terms of the availability, use or access to desirable objects (such as computers, video games and musical equipment), the young people are often very aware of their own agency. This chapter thus provides an engaging case study of the significance of children's material culture, and the ways in which its meaning varies according to social settings and relationships.

In Chapter 11, Randi Wærdahl considers a very different cultural context, namely that of children and parents living in the midst of China's so-called 'consumer revolution'. In this context, children have become increasingly significant as consumers, and yet there have also been concerns about the dangers of them developing materialistic attitudes, and about their vulnerability to commercial persuasion. Chinese scholars point to diverging trends in parents' attitudes towards their children's consumption: on the one hand, parents are keen for their children to enjoy the things of which they themselves were deprived; and yet there is also concern that excessive spending on children is a result of parents' lack of 'quality time' to spend with the family. This chapter draws on questionnaires completed by sixth-grade children and their parents in urban one-child families in Beijing; and on in-depth interviews and home visits. The analysis explores changing and contested ideas about the difference between 'good' (or appropriate) and 'bad' (or excessive) consumption, and relates these to broader philosophical traditions in Chinese thought.

Finally, in Chapter 12, Agnes Nairn, Paul Bottomley and Johanne Ormrod explore the complex relationships between deprivation, materialism and wellbeing among families in the UK. Drawing on two large-scale quantitative surveys, the authors analyse the associations between measures of economic deprivation and levels of materialism, and the popular assumption that things become more desirable precisely when they are less easy to obtain. The findings suggest that deprivation is indeed positively related to levels of materialism, as defined by standardised scales; and that materialism and wellbeing are inversely related. However, more deprived children did not have lower levels of self-esteem and depression than less deprived children. Further analysis suggested that the correlation between materialism and wellbeing was more sensitive for the less deprived children; whereas for the more deprived children, greater materialism did not result in lower self-esteem or wellbeing.

Taken together, the two studies suggest that the potentially negative influence of consumer culture may be greater for those who are more affluent – thus disturbing the commonsense assumption that 'those who have less want more'.

Part V addresses the theme of *Identities*. In his chapter 'Branded selves', Håvard Skaar explores the use and significance of branding and marketing materials in children's presentation of self on a popular social networking site. Drawing on a broader ethnographic study of a group of Norwegian classmates aged 11–12, Skaar analyses how the children made use of branded resources and tools in creating their individual profiles, and how this related to the existing social dynamics and hierarchies within the peer group. He distinguishes between those he calls 'collectors' and 'elaborators': the simple collection of branded resources appears to need less work and be more convincing and more unassailable than elaborating them into more complex and creative self-presentations. Social competition tends to reinforce a uniform use of brands and branded resources, thus proving an obstacle to the development of individual creativity. Skaar's analysis offers a valuable challenge to more optimistic, and more superficial, accounts of children's participation in such online environments.

In Chapter 14, Mari Rysst discusses the ambiguities and ethical dilemmas at stake in young girls' views about the aesthetics and design of clothing. As she suggests, the fashion industry typically assumes that 'tweenage' girls want to dress 'older than their age'; while media debates often express concern at the apparent 'sexualisation' of girls' clothing. Rysst contrasts these accounts with data drawn from ethnographic fieldwork in two contrasting socio-economic settings in Oslo, Norway. The analysis suggests that girls operate norms and controlling mechanisms within the peer group that are predicated on not acting significantly 'older than their age'. They have clear views about not exposing too much of their bodies, and such behaviour often meets with sanctions and ridicule. Yet they also have to strike a balance between not being interpreted as too childish, and not acting too old. In practice, it seems that sexuality is not the key issue in their selection of clothing: rather, their interest is in being seen as fashionable and 'cool'. These findings are related to broader arguments about the construction of gender identity: the chapter argues that gender distinctions should not be 'theorised away', but that research should continue to take account of the material, bodily dimensions of identity formation.

In the final chapter, Dafna Lemish and Nelly Elias explore the role of fashion in the lives of immigrant children and adolescents from the former Soviet Union living in Israel. Drawing on in-depth interviews, they focus particularly on the complex personal and social challenges resulting from immigration and the need to solidify a new identity, and the role of consumption in that process. Clothing and fashion appeared to have significant implications for constructing new hybrid identities as well as re-confirming old ones in the realms of gender, adolescence, Rusianness and Israeliness. As the 'social skin' of both immigrants and local youth, clothing served variously as an identity card, a declaration of cultural war, or a means of exhibiting personal and social transformation. Here again, young people's consumption is located within a specific social and cultural setting; and while young people are implicitly presumed to be making active choices in terms of what they buy and how they appear, they are also doing so in circumstances that are not of their own choosing, and which they cannot always control.

Conclusion

We began this introduction by identifying some of the binary oppositions that typically characterise the debate about children and consumer culture. On the one hand, we have the view of children as competent, sophisticated, empowered consumers, frequently espoused by the marketers; and on the other, the view of them as innocent, naïve and vulnerable, adopted by many concerned campaigners. The contributions presented here take us beyond the comforting simplifications of this debate; and in doing so, they sketch out new issues for research. Taken together, they suggest that we need to analyse children's activities as consumers in their broader social and historical context; that we need to understand the complex interactions between the power of the marketers (structure) and the power of consumers (agency); and that we need to see contemporary childhood as inevitably and inextricably embedded within the broader operations of our consumer culture.

References

Banet-Weiser, S. (2007) *Kids Rule! Nickelodeon and Consumer-Citizenship*. Durham, NC: Duke University Press.

Buckingham, D. (2009a) 'The appliance of science: the role of research in the making of regulatory policy on children and food advertising in the UK', *International Journal of Cultural Policy* 15(2): 201–15.

Buckingham, D. (2009b) 'Beyond the competent consumer: the role of media literacy in the making of regulatory policy on children and food advertising in the UK', *International Journal of Cultural Policy*, 15(2): 217–30.

Buckingham, D. and J. Sefton-Green (2003) 'Gotta catch 'em all: structure, agency and pedagogy in children's media culture', *Media, Culture and Society*, 25(3): 379–99.

Cook, D. (2004) *The Commodification of Childhood: The Children's Clothing Industry and the Rise of the Child Consumer*. Durham, NC: Duke University Press.

Cross, G. (1997) *Kids' Stuff: Toys and the Changing World of American Childhood*. Cambridge MA: Harvard University Press.

Del Vecchio, G. (1997) *Creating Ever-Cool*. Louisiana: Pelican.

Ekstrom, K. and B. Tufte (eds) (2007) *Children, Media and Consumption: On the Front Edge*. Goteborg, Sweden: Nordicom

Hendershot, H. (1998) *Saturday Morning Censors: Television Regulation Before the V-Chip*. Durham, NC: Duke University Press.

Hendershot, H. (ed.) (2004) *Nickelodeon Nation: The History, Politics, and Economics of America's Only TV Channel for Kids*. New York: New York University Press.

Klein, N. (2001) *No Logo*. London: Flamingo.

Kline, S. (1993) *Out of the Garden: Toys, TV and Children's Culture in the Age of Marketing*. London: Verso.

Layard, R. and J. Dunn (2009) *A Good Childhood: Searching for Values in a Competitive Age*. London: Penguin

Linn, S. (2004) *Consuming Kids: The Hostile Takeover of Childhood*. New York: New Press.

Lindstrom, M. and P. Seybold (2003) *Brandchild*. London: Kogan Page.

Mayo, E. and A. Nairn (2009) *Consumer Kids: How Big Business Is Grooming Our Children for Profit* London: Constable

McNeal, J.U. (1999) *The Kids' Market: Myths and Realities*. New York: Paramount.

Palmer, S. (2006) *Toxic Childhood: How the Modern World is Damaging Our Children and What We Can Do About It*. London: Orion

Postman, N. (1983) *The Disappearance of Childhood*. London: W.H. Allen.

Qvortrup, J., Corsaro, W. and M. S. Honig (eds) (2009) *The Palgrave Handbook of Childhood Studies*. London: Palgrave Macmillan.

Schor, J. (2004) *Born to Buy: The Commercialized Child and the New Consumer Culture*. New York: Scribner.

Seiter, E. (1993) *Sold Separately: Parents and Children in Consumer Culture*. New Brunswick, NJ: Rutgers University Press.

Sutherland, A. and B. Thompson (2003) *Kidfluence: The Marketer's Guide to Understanding and Reaching Generation Y*. New York: McGraw-Hill.

Tingstad, V. (2009)' Discourses on child obesity and TV advertising in the context of the Norwegian welfare state', In James, A., A. T. Kjørholt and V. Tingstad (eds), *Childhood, Food and Identity in Everyday Life*. Basingstoke: Palgrave, pp. 172–91.

de la Ville, V. I. (ed.) (2005) *L'Enfant Consommateur*. Paris: Vuibert.

Part I

History of Children's Consumption

1

Valves of Adult Desire: The Regulation and Incitement of Children's Consumption

Gary Cross

A few years ago I was asked by the editor of a marketing journal to read and comment on a stack of articles by leading authorities in children's consumer research. I was struck by how these papers focused on one basic issue: how children are socialized to become competent agents, capable of rationally evaluating advertising claims and purposes. Of course, many factors were explored, including the gender, racial, and social differences among child consumers. The authors suggested that knowledge about the child's capacities could address simultaneously the interests of child protection advocates and of merchandisers (e.g. Goldberg, 1982; John 1999; Goldberg & Baumgartner, 2001).

This is laudable, to be sure, but to a modern historian of consumption and children's material culture this approach seems curious. For the first half of the twentieth century, advertising to children was very limited. It was viewed either as an interference in the parent's right to control their offspring's desires or a waste of money and time because children had little to spend and presumably little influence over the purchase decisions of their elders. By contrast, marketing literature today tends to regard parents' claims and concerns as supplemental influences in shaping the child's response to advertising (Carlson *et al.*, 2001). The focus is on the child as a potential free agent in the market and seldom is the moral or social priority of the parent/child relationship addressed.

Belief in the child's free agency is perhaps natural in contemporary America and increasingly elsewhere, where individual and increasingly children's rights dominate other social or cultural goals. But not only is the age of reason and thus of agency more difficult to discern, but its value to parents is more ambiguous than is suggested by the highly rationalist approach taken by many consumer researchers. In many ways, adults prize the child's *lack* of free agency and attempt to shelter its innocence, even when they find themselves utterly confused about who has innocence and when it ends. All this may say more about the cultures, attitudes and political configurations of adults than the capacities of children.

The age of agency may be arbitrary, but in the matter of advertising today there is generally no legal age limit below which advertising to children is deemed unacceptable. Advertisers have gradually broken with an old code of childhood innocence and have rationalized it with the assumption that children are by nature autonomous, have inbred, presocial needs, and have the free speech right to learn about products through advertising (Cook, 2000; Schor, 2004). Still, many parents continue to reject this modern idea and insist on the moral imperative of prolonging childhood and parental authority, even as pressures both within the family and from television and other media push the child into the market.

Underlying all this confusion is the fact that over the last hundred years, adults have constructed a curiously ambivalent notion of childhood that, in turn, has shaped both parents' and children's responses to consumption. Modern adults view children at once as 'innocents' who must be protected from the consumer market and, at the same time, as recipients of parental love through consumer spending. While efforts to shelter the child have extended the age of 'innocence', the identification of the child with spending has gradually undermined traditional bourgeois paths to maturity and created an ageless land of the cool. This is a product of the historically extraordinary parental (and adult) ambiguity about commercial culture and about modernity itself.

Modern childhood may be understood as a construct of adult longings and frustrations emerging with the 20th-century market society. In the early years of the last century, parents increasingly came to regard children not as a source of labour or as heirs of property but as guarantors of private life and even as the refuge of simplicity. Thus, they tried to isolate children from the market and all of its implications (Zelizer, 1985). At the same time, childrearing also gave expression to material longings (both of adults and their offspring). Put another way, children became valves of adult desire not just or even primarily sexual desire (as noted by Anne Higonnet (1998) and others), but of consumer desire. This view explains a lot of modern consumer behaviour. Adults use children to restrict spending (their own and others', as well as children's) especially when other ways of controlling the market prove impossible. Efforts to control desire through protecting the innocence of childhood have had limited success, but in individualistic and market-dominated countries like the US, such efforts may be inevitable. At the same time, adults spend in order to evoke delight in children. This meets parental needs, but it also has the effect of awakening desire in children and in general rationalizes pleasure-seeking consumption. Moreover, as children grow up in a culture that defines the young as sheltered from desire and yet as depositories of desire, they rebel against limits, seeing constraint as childish and parent-driven. At the same time, children extend parental indulgence into their own world of fantastic desire (sometimes expressed as sexuality in girls and action/violence in boys). This provokes anger among adults/parents, even as merchandisers learn to exploit the push and pull of youthful desire. More subtly still, it produces a culture of the cool, a form of rebellion against adulthood (as well as against the constraints and delights of childhood) and against traditional paths to maturity.

Closing the valve of consumption: the struggle over regulation

In US history especially, the goal of protecting the child has served as a key rationale for controlling consumption. Americans have long equated freedom with the right to buy and sell, but they have also a rich religious tradition of self-control and protecting communities from the perceived vice and corruption that inevitably emerges from a free consumer market. The same country that has experienced waves of alcohol, tobacco, and other drug addictions has also been the home of prohibition and stringent smoking regulations. This contradiction may be explained by the fact that the traditional and informal controls of family and community have seldom been effective in moderating consumption. In contrast to most historical European societies, for example, the mobility and vastness of the US allowed Americans to escape (or lose the moral support of) those families and communities by migrating, often westward (Findlay, 1986).

The possibility of regulating childhood consumption remains because people support it across ideological lines, even if the free market remains sacred in most circles. First, parents can claim private rights to shape and control the child, free from the outside pressures of Hollywood or tobacco companies. This is a position perfectly consistent with Victorian family values as well as with modern leftwing criticisms of manipulative advertising. Second, both the left and the cultural (though not economic) right assert that the child lacks the information and even ability to make rational consumer choices and, thus, advertising can be seen as inherently unfair, especially in markets for compulsive and self-destructive goods like tobacco, alcohol, gambling, and violent, sexual, or morally unacceptable entertainment. Third, the religious doctrine that desire begets obsession (concupiscence) may no longer be accepted in modern secular society, but it survives when applied to children. Many Americans and Europeans still believe that desire awakened through marketing destroys the child's innate simplicity and even interferes with the growing child's ability to become a creative, rational adult able to defer gratification. Attempts to protect childhood from aggressive marketers have not been particularly successful. Still, the very difficulty, especially in the US, of imposing any restriction on markets has made these arguments about the innocent child central to containing consumption.

Throughout the 20th century, much anti-consumption rhetoric was buried in the cult of the child. Not only had the child become 'priceless', and therefore adults could no longer send their children to work for money, but a new model of scientific child-rearing stood in opposition to the indulgent and promiscuous world of consumerism (Zelizer, 1985). Educational toys and the teaching methods of preschool and kindergarten were supposed to isolate the child from the crowd's fads and indulgences. When moralists tried to control the content of movies, as they did repeatedly, they claimed that they were guarding children's interests. Despite the potential commercial advantage of selling directly to children, merchandisers were very careful not to offend the sentiments of parents by advertising directly to the young. Until the 1950s, toy makers appealed to parents, not children; and toy and candy companies did not advertise on children's radio programmes in the 1930s or 1940s. Instead, children's radio programmes sold commercials to makers of breakfast cereal (which was not presweetened until after 1945), coffee, and other adult products. These ads lured children into pressuring their parents into purchases with the promise of toys and other children's trinkets when the child mailed in sufficient coupons or box tops from their products. Also from the 1910s onwards, manufacturers of electric trains and air rifles offered tips on how to get parents to buy these relatively expensive (and in the case of the BB gun, potentially dangerous) toys. But encouragement of children's 'pester power' was limited. The merchandisers' self-constraint (moral or economic) meant that legislation to protect the child was unnecessary and parental complaints were limited.

However, this voluntary restraint by merchandisers and the advertising media collapsed within a decade after World War II. The growth of new kinds of goods designed for children and the spread of new means of disseminating them provoked new concerns from parents and consumer cultural critics who called for new regulation of the market's access to children. These changes included the production of new sugared breakfast cereals and drinks, the more aggressive marketing of toys based on licensed images from children's film and TV fantasy, and the growing use of children's entertainment programming to advertise directly to the young. A trend toward aggressive direct advertising to children began with the *Mickey Mouse Club* (1955). The year-long promotion of toy lines replaced the older seasonal approach to advertising that was limited largely to Christmas, and was accompanied by heavy advertising of sugared cereal and sweets to children during Saturday morning and late afternoon cartoons.

Together, these developments led to increased parental concerns about children's consumption, which culminated in the late 1960s and 1970s (Cross, 1997: chs 6–7). In the late 1960s, the New England-based organization Action for Children's Television petitioned regulatory agencies to protect children from excessive and manipulative advertising. In 1971, this and similar groups called for the elimination of commercials on children's TV, claiming that advertisements were an interference with parents' rights to educate their own children and that youngsters under 12 were incapable of making consumer choices. Finally in 1978, the Federal Trade Commission (FTC, the agency responsible for regulating unfair marketing) expanded its traditional work against 'deceptive' advertising by claiming that all commercials directed toward children too young to understand their intent were 'unfair' and thus could be banned (Pertschuk, 1982: 11, 69, 70). This prohibition would not be a violation of free speech, officials claimed, because the 'state has a legitimate interest in curtailing speech that interferes with the paramount parental interest in the child rearing process' (FTC, 1978: 267; Goldberg, 1982: 13).

In response, advertisers attacked any interference in the so-called right of children to have information about the products they bought, and lobbied heavily against the FTC proposal. In the spring of 1980, Congress suspended the FTC's proposal to ban 'unfair' ads (rather than openly deceptive ones), thus ending an extraordinary period of consumer rights activism (Perschuk, 1982: 69). The consequences of this defeat became apparent in the 1980s during the Reagan administration with further deregulation that allowed the programme-length commercial, cartoons produced by toy companies to feature and essentially advertise new toy lines.

A generation of parents concerned that the desires created by direct advertising to children subverted the rights of parents (and educators) to shape their offspring was thus effectively defeated by free market orthodoxy. However, another opportunity to close the valve of children's desire emerged in a new regulatory surge relating to tobacco use. And here these efforts were also a substitute for direct forms of restricting adult desire. Despite libertarian trends, public disapproval of smoking increased in the 1980s, leading to widespread bans on public smoking. Soon the focus shifted to the impact of smoking on the innocent young. Urging parents to quit, the Surgeon General warned against the effects of passive smoking on fetuses and young children. Meanwhile, health officials became increasingly frustrated by the continued success of cigarette makers in inducing new generations to adopt the smoking habit, despite the 1971 ban on electronic tobacco advertisements. Because up to 90 per cent of adult smokers adopted the habit when they were teenagers, the tobacco companies had an obvious interest in promoting their products to the under-aged (below sixteen years old). By protecting the young from tobacco advertising, the government also could further restrict tobacco use without violating adult choice and thus meet Supreme Court standards. The argument was simple: when under-aged children were lured into smoking, they could not fully understand the health risks. This argument undermined the standard defense of the tobacco industry since 1965 (when warnings were placed on cigarette packs) that consumers freely chose to smoke despite the possible consequences. The Federal Drug Administration (FDA) introduced a series of proposals to ban cigarette vending machines where minors had access, outlaw tobacco billboards within 1000 feet of a playground or school, and ban cigarette logos displaying tobacco sponsorship of sporting or other cultural events. The FDA even argued for a two-dollar tax per pack to create a substantial economic barrier to underage smoking. The tobacco companies objected that all this denied adult access to information about tobacco products. The FDA responded that their proposals did not deny information, only the emotional appeals of the ads. In effect, by protecting children from their own pre-rational responses to tobacco ads, the FDA tried to impose rationality upon adults by making it a bit more difficult to smoke (FDA, 1995).

The FDA's program was only a partial success. The United States Supreme Court ruled in June 2000 that the FDA could not regulate tobacco without legislative authority (which Congress refused), causing all the FDA regulations to be dropped. Still, the tobacco companies agreed in a Master Settlement Agreement with the states in 1998 to voluntarily refrain from advertising to children through the use of cartoon characters (like Joe Camel) or sponsoring sporting or music events with significant youth audiences. The Agreement also banned most outdoor and bus and train advertising and sale of merchandise with tobacco logos in hopes of reducing children's exposure to tobacco ads. Many states imposed further restrictions on outdoor advertising and age requirements to purchase cigarettes. Whatever the ultimate fate of this strategy of regulating tobacco through child protection, it remains a powerful tool in limiting the American worship of free markets and consumer desire (Cross, 2000: ch. 7; Nelson, 2006; American Heart Association, 2008).

Opening the valve of desire

This said, why has the innocence strategy not had greater success? Of course, the political power of commercial interests and the broad influence of libertarian ideas (as in the rejection of the 'nanny state' and the belief that parents can and should filter their children's access to the market) have had much to do with it. But another way that adults have understood childhood also helps explain this failure. Adults' expression of love for children has also justified and encouraged *more* consumption, bringing us back to the idea of children as valves of desire. Restricting children's access to sex and drugs has been relatively successful, but damping down consumer desire has not. This is not entirely the responsibility of advertising and other commercial attempts to awaken children's desire. Especially since the beginning of the 20th century, children have been drawn into a fantastic world of new goods and entertainment. Ranging from the illustrated adventures of the Brownies to the teddy bear craze, whimsically disrespectful comic strips, and the indulgences of ice cream cones and candy bars, these products allowed adults as well as children to indulge in playful, even anarchic, moments. An escape from the rational world of the market and technology, these invitations into dream worlds and fresh longings of children also opened up that valve of adult desire (Cross, 2004, ch. 3).

First, adults desired what I have called 'wondrous innocence', seen in the child's look of surprised delight. While this might be evoked by taking the child to the sea or the mountains, after 1900 it was increasingly sparked by adults offering commercialized gifts. One of the greatest pleasures of modern parenting became the act of giving fresh and unexpected pleasures – a donkey ride on the beach in 1900 or a ride on Peter Pan's Flight at Disneyland in the 1950s. This joy became the centrepiece of Christmas, birthday, and even Halloween giving, all of which became both commercialized and infantilized in the decades around 1900. Annual vacations also shifted dramatically towards becoming rituals of childhood.

There is much behind this adult pleasure, but one subtle goal was to recapture a feeling of wonder lost in the parent over years of consumption, but still fresh and reflected in the child's delighted response to gifts. While consumer culture constantly produces the new and exciting, it also generates boredom and disappointment (Campbell, 1987). The consuming child came to represent desire in its most 'original' and innocent form, a delight in things that was marred neither by disappointment nor by obsession. By giving to children, parents restored their own long-lost pleasure in things. Increasingly adults identified wonder with the child-like (rather than say the cultivated religious or aesthetic experience). The child's pleasure in an unexpected toy trumped the graduation gift of a car for the teenager. Yet ultimately, the wide-eyed innocent became the bored and unappreciative brat when repeatedly exposed to the wonders of modern consumption. This led to a ratcheting up of gift-giving in an attempt to evoke the old wonder in the child, with inevitable further erosion of wondrous innocence.

Second, parents opened the young to a fantasy world that met adult needs for coping with accelerating change by identifying children both with a timeless past and a fun-filled future. The amateur camera (after the snapshot introduced in 1888 by Kodak) promised to freeze time in the child's photo album (West, 2000: ch. 5). Although the teddy bear began as a fad on the New Jersey Shore in the summer of 1906, it very soon came to suggest a natural unchanging realm of childhood, as subsequent generations of toddlers received and embraced toy animals in plush. At the same time, adults offered youngsters gifts of novelty – the latest toy or media fad, from the pogo stick (1919), Hula Hoop (1958), and Beanie Babies (ca. 1994) to Mickey Mouse (1928–), Star Wars (1977–), and Pokemon (1996). Because childhood implied ever-changing futures, adults learned to become comfortable with the new by giving it to their children (Cross 1997: ch. 4).

Third, adults expressed a new tolerance for the naughty and desiring child. The Kewpie and other dolls that parents gave their children in the early 20th century featured eyes turned askance to suggest a slight impishness, but also showed dimples and rosy cheeks that affirmed their basic decency (Formanek-Brunell, 1993). This image reflected a 20th century trend – more tolerant, indeed permissive, views of children, propagated through new developmentally-based child-rearing manuals, but also family comic strips and Norman Rockwell illustrations. It reflected a new acceptance of the psychological complexity of children and a realization that the 'terrible twos' is merely a stage. Parents also began to accept, sometimes encourage, their children to breach boundaries in naive and exuberant play, allowing adults to participate vicariously in these moments of disorder. The mischievous Peter Pan in Never Land was embraced as much by adults as children (Wullschlaeger 1995). The secret power of the naughty-but-nice youngster so often portrayed in comic strips from 'The Yellow Kid' (1896) to 'Dennis the Menace' (1951) was that it gave pleasure to adults while giving children freedom from adult control. Despite intentions of sheltering the young from work, physical danger, and other people's 'bad children', parents introduced children to a fantasy world of desire, unbounded freedom, and even rebellion (Jenkins, 1998: ch. 1).

By the beginning of the 20th century, the desiring child became a trademark image on new products and in advertising. Grace Drayton's Campbell Soup Kids (1905), those rosy-cheeked 'Dutch' youngsters in overalls, suggested that canned soup made for the health and vitality of children in a time when memories of high rates of infant mortality were still fresh. The Campbell Kids also expressed a spunky willfulness in children that was soon associated with many new products. Magazine ads for Kellogg's Corn Flakes featured children displaying an insatiable need for this new breakfast cereal soon after its introduction in 1906. Typical was the image of a sweet little girl in glowing light cradling a box of cereal in her arms. The caption reads: 'You'd be selfish too.' A possessive desire for corn flakes and much else was no longer something to control and discourage in children; rather, advertising taught that such desires were natural and good in the young. In fact, ads for new products promised that such desires were no longer a threat to family order. Wesson Oil boldly asserted: 'We hope you have a fussy family' because this vegetable oil could help mothers cope with demanding offspring and, even more, because those desires should be accommodated (*Ladies Home Journal*, Aug. 1913, back cover; *Ladies Home Journal* Jan 1934, back cover).

How can we account for this new willingness of parents to open the valve of children's desire? Sharp decreases in child morality produced more optimistic attitudes toward the survivability of the young. In 1900, American parents faced a 62 per cent probability that one of their children would die before adulthood. By 1940, that rate had dropped to 16 per cent; and by 1976, it was 4 per cent. This improvement in children's health and survival contributed to a shift in the image of the child, from a frail innocent to a vital and all-desiring being. Equally important was the decrease in family size: there were 40 per cent fewer children per American family in 1940 than in 1900. Smaller families allowed parents to lavish more attention on the delight of the child and to be more tolerant of naughty (if nice or innocent) behaviour (Preston and Haines, 1991: 3–5, 51).

Of course, other factors are in play. As Allison Pugh notes in her book, *Longing and Belonging: Parents, Children, and Consumer Culture*, children's desires are awakened by their need to participate in peer groups whose boundaries are often identified by commercial markers of belonging and exclusion – and parents are eager to reduce the chance of their children being isolated socially. This also drives the child/parent relationship and makes parents more agreeable to spending than they might otherwise be. But, especially in the young child, the needs of the parent for 'wonder' have driven the giving of gifts to children.

However, the images, goods, and rituals of a commercialized childhood soon led to a fantasy culture from which parents were excluded and which appeared to be anything but innocent. Desire, fantasy, and the challenging of cultural boundaries combined to transform children's culture. What had been the cute, ultimately controlled by parents, became the cool, expressing freedom from adults' possessive needs. The first clear signs of this appeared among older boys in the 1930s and 1940s with the mechanical and even bleak visions of science fiction fantasy on radio and in comic books (for example, Buck Rogers and Superman). The rebellious cool in girls (too closely associated with the sexual) had to wait until 1959 with advent of the Barbie doll. Parental opposition slowed down its appearance in younger children until monster and action-figure toys replaced baby dolls and Tinkertoys, beginning in the mid-1960s. Much of this shift was facilitated by the creation of new media outlets for children beginning with Saturday movie matinees and after-school radio programmes and culminating with Saturday morning TV cartoons and video games, all available for advertising or character merchandising (Harris, 2000; 1–21).

Adults responded by attempting to draw a line between acceptable and dangerous play and pleasure. In a long series of moral panics, defenders of parental rights over the media exposure of their offspring attacked those movies, pinball machines, comic books and video games that they deemed too violent or sexually explicit. In subtle ways, these attacks associated these expressions of the cool with minority or working-class culture (from which they often originated) and thus as threats to middle class white youth (Cross, 2004: ch. 5). The great irony of this was that the very adults who opposed the cool were in many ways its cause: by abandoning Victorian ideals of sheltering and nurturing the child to assume confined sex roles and sober notions of maturity, and by seeking to recover wonder in and through their children, they had effectively pulled their offspring into the very heart of a new consumer market built on fantasy.

The result of all this was and is much confusion. Coinciding with the birth of modern consumer society at the beginning of the twentieth century was a new definition of the child–parent relationship, wherein the young became both a reason for parental spending and a bulwark against an over-commercialized society. Children became a kind of valve for adult desires, both opening and restricting consumption.

Implications for teenagers and adults

This adult construction of the child as a wondrous consumer resulted in more than confusion in child-rearing. It also shaped the later teenage journey to adulthood and subverted traditional scripts for reaching maturity. In effect, it led to a wider reluctance to accept traditional markers of adulthood and the perpetuation of the cool as a blend of the child and adult. This is a very big topic, but a few general links can be sketched in here. An important corollary of the adult cultivation of wondrous innocence and the consequent emerging cult of the cool is that they undermined the older image of the sheltered child who was trained to become an adult. As Philippe Aries and Neil Postman have shown, the aim of isolating the child from adults was ultimately to raise children to become more 'adult-like' adults – capable of controlling emotions, pursuing goals and responsibilities rationally (Ariès, 1962; Postman, 1982). Cultures of the past displayed adults who were more childlike and children who were less innocent than today, because they did not rigidly separate the child from the adult. It was only in the 17th century that the church and state made a deliberate effort to isolate the child from the chaos and vulgarity of the street and thus foster the self-discipline and refinement that would make for more sober adults. Techniques included schools (with age-based classes), middle-class withdrawal from patronage of festivals, and more recently 'educational toys,' youth groups like the scouts, summer camps, and adult-organized sport. This was a long process and affected more the children of the elite than the poor.

The twentieth century cultivation of wondrous innocence in consumer culture challenged the Victorian ideal of sheltered childhood not only by opening up the valve of desire but also by rejecting this traditional model of maturation through isolating and training the child. The end result (at least in leisure if not working life) has been a cult of the cool that has short-circuited older passages to growing up and has become a goal not only of the 'tween' child but a state of consciousness and behaviour that young (and not so young) adults resist abandoning (Cross, 2008: ch. 2, 8).

This complex trend has had many manifestations, but one has been the blending of ages in the appeals of a growing number of consumer goods. An example is the shift in the US toward PG-13 rated films. Instituted in 1983 as a buffer between 'adult' R-rated films and the family themes of PG-films, the number of PG-13 films rose 50 per cent between 1995 and 2001 (while PG movies dropped by 45 per cent). Deemed to be acceptable to 13-year-olds and older (even though the rating is only advisory and thus younger children frequently attend), these films not only expose children to adult vulgarity and violence, but adults (who also watch them) to the bathroom humour of children. The result has been a general 'return' to a less restrained, more childlike media culture, apparent in films like *Big Daddy, Austin Powers, Idiocracy*, or *Borat*. The thrill of these films comes from breaking a taboo on vulgarity, which is now brought out in the open and even shared in 'mixed company'. In the past, women were supposed to be guarantors of propriety, keeping the taboo away and in its place (the locker room or men's poker party, for example). However, with the decline of Victorian notions of women, protecting the innocence of the young played this role. The gross-out humour of the Austin Powers movies breaks this final taboo: rated PG-13, they are deemed acceptable for both children and young adults.

In recent years, the meaning of maturity especially in males seems to have changed: the contemporary definition of being older often entails freedom from parental control and the right to more violent video games (encouraged by the rating system that marks Teen and Mature ratings by their digital violence). In subtle ways, this has been part of a trend toward erasing the distinction between childish and adult pleasures. Thus, we see adult men playing with the video games that also attract 12-year old boys. According to the Entertainment Software Association, which represents the video game industry, in 1997 more than half of all video game players were younger than 18. By 2001, the trade group estimated that 57 per cent of players were adults, with an average age of 28. In 2005, the average age rose to 33 (with 40 being the age of the most frequent purchasers of games): 25 per cent of gamers are over 50 and 44 per cent aged between 18 and 49 (Entertainment Software Association, 2006).

Likewise, appeals in ads to young (and not so young) adult males since the late 1980s have increasingly taken on a distinctly childish quality. They often celebrate compulsive, even selfish behaviour – an appeal to the naughty boy, be he 10 or 40 years old (Cross, 2008: ch. 5). In the past, the quest to protect the child from the market was partially based on a model of maturation that stressed deferred (and repressed) gratification and social responsibility. That rationale has certainly lost much of its cultural power today.

This phenomenon may well be the result of new media (that, as Postman (1982) argues, no longer separate adults from children). Certainly, advertisers and Hollywood have encouraged these trends by their desire to extend their markets both up and down the age range. However, I would argue that this trend has more subtle roots. Its ultimate source is the cult of the cool that was born from the idea of wondrous innocence, emerging in the bosom of the modern family. The culture of teenage cool (marked by both a rejection of parental restrictions and an embrace of parents' indulgence) has becomes a lifestyle shared by adults and children alike, instead of a life stage abandoned at maturity (Kimmel, 2008).

As valves of desire that adults try to turn on and off, children are at the heart of the ongoing ambiguity that many adults today feel toward consumer culture. And, no doubt, this causes confusion to the young. When is the valve opened, when is it closed? Is 'growing up' mostly about children learning to control their own valve or about freedom from adults shutting it off? As this implies, understanding children's consumption requires us to look beyond the dyadic relationship between the child and the merchandiser. The issue may be less when and whether children understand the intent of advertising, but rather how the desires of parents shape the desires of the young.

References

American Heart Association, 'Tobacco, Federal Regulation of', http://www.americanheart.org/presenter.jhtml?identifier=11223, accessed 19 December 2008.

Ariès, P. (1962) *Centuries of Childhood: A Social History of Family Life*. New York: Vintage.

Campbell, C. (1987) *The Romantic Ethic and the Spirit of Modern Consumerism*. Oxford: Blackwell.

Carlson, L., L. Russell and A. Walsh (2001) 'Socializing children about television: an intergenerational study', *Journal of the Academy of Marketing Science*, 29, 276–88.

Cook, D. (2000) 'The other child study: figuring children as consumers in market research', 1910s–1990s, *Sociological Quarterly*, 14 (3), 487–507.

Cross, G. (1997) *Kids' Stuff: Toys and the Changing World of American Childhood.* Cambridge: Harvard University Press.

Cross, G. (2000) *All-Consuming Century: Why Commercialism Won in Modern America.* New York: Columbia University Press.

Cross, G. (2004) *The Cute and the Cool: Wondrous Innocence and Modern American Children's Culture.* New York: Oxford.

Cross, G. (2008) *Men to Boys: The Making of Modern Immaturity.* New York: Columbia University Press. Entertainment Software Association, http://www.theesa.com/archives/files/Essential%20Facts%202006.pdf (accessed 2 August 2006).

Federal Drug Administration (1995) 'Regulations restricting the sale and distribution of cigarettes and smokeless tobacco products to protect children and adolescents', *Federal Register* (11 August 11), 41314–41351.

Federal Trade Commission (1978) FTC Staff report on television advertising to children, Washington: US Government Printing Office.

Findlay, J. (1986) *People of Chance: Gambling in American Society from Jamestown to Las Vegas.* New York: Oxford.

Formanek-Brunell, M. (1993) *Made to Play House: Dolls and the Commercialization of American Girlhood, 1830–1930.* New Haven: Yale University Press.

Goldberg, M. (1982) 'TV Advertising Directed at Children: Inherently Unfair or Simply in Need of Regulation?', in Shapiro, S. and L. Heslop (eds) *Marketplace Canada: Some Controversial Dimensions*, pp. 1–31. Toronto: McGraw-Hill.

Goldberg, M. and H. Baumgartner (2001) 'Cross-country attraction as a motivation for product consumption', *Journal of Business Research* 55 (1): 1–6

Higonnet, A. (1998) *Pictures of Innocence: The History and Crisis of Ideal Childhood.* London, Thames and Hudson.

Harris, D. (2000) *Cute, Quaint, Hungry and Romantic.* New York: Basic.

Jenkins, H. (1998) *Children's Culture Reader.* New York: New York University Press.

John, D. R. (1999) 'Consumer socialization of children: a retrospective look at twenty-five years of research', *Journal of Consumer Research,* 26 (December): 83–213.

Kimmel, M. (2008) *Guyland: The Perilous World Where Boys become Men.* New York, Harper.

Nelson, J. P. (2006) 'Cigarette advertising regulation: a meta-analysis', *International Review of Law and Economics,* 26 (2, June): 195–226.

Perschuk, M. (1982) *Revolt against Regulation.* Berkeley: University of California Press.

Postman, N. (1982) *The Disappearance of Childhood.* New York: Dell.

Preston, S. and M. Haines (1991) *Fatal Years: Child Mortality in Late Nineteenth-Century America.* Princeton: Princeton University Press

Schor, J. (2004) *Born to Buy: The Commercialized Child and the New Consumer Culture.* New York: Scribner.

West, N. (2000) *Kodak and the Lens of Nostalgia.* Charlottesville: University Press of Virginia.

Wullschlaeger, J. (1995) *Inventing Wonderland.* London: Methuen.

Zelizer, V. (1985) *Pricing the Priceless Child,* New York: Basic.

2
Proper Toys for Proper Children: A Case Study of the Norwegian Company A/S Riktige Leker (Proper Toys)

Tora Korsvold[1]

Over the last century, the consumption of commercial goods has become an increasingly significant aspect of children's experience. The range of products on the market has increased significantly, and children have become one of the most targeted groups of consumers. This chapter examines those products that are perhaps most strongly associated with the consuming child: toys. In describing and analysing the market for children's toys, and focusing specifically on the Norwegian company Proper Toys (*A/S Riktige Leker*), I address the following questions: What characterizes 'proper toys' according to the definition of this company, and what is the basis for such a definition? By looking at how 'proper' toys are defined and differentiated from other ('improper') products, we also acquire an insight into how adults define childhood, how children's play is valued, and how children are regarded as modern consumers. The aim here is not to investigate a 'typical' toy store. Rather, Proper Toys was chosen because of its significant historical background, combined with the assertion implied in its very name: that it sells 'proper' toys. The analysis here builds on relevant research in the field of childhood and consumer culture (Buckingham 2000, Buckingham and Tingstad 2007 among others) and particularly studies of the history of marketing to children (Cook 2004, Cross 2004).

Children and consumer culture

As Daniel Cook has written in his book *The Commodification of Childhood*, children today are born, live and grow up in tandem with consumer culture. The twentieth century was not only 'the century of the child', as it was christened by the Swedish pedagogue and novelist Ellen Key in 1909 – it must also be seen as the century of the child consumer (Cook 2004). Yet although markets and consumer culture play a key role in the shaping of individual identities, it should be emphasised that the specific forms of consumer culture and notions of childhood itself are embedded in differing national contexts. For example, the company Proper Toys is situated within a welfare state with rather powerful restrictions on consumption, although it also stresses children's rights in the society in a manner that is historically quite specific to the Norwegian, or Nordic, context.

As Cook describes, in the United States in the 1920 and 1930s the perspective of marketers gradually shifted from a focus on the mother to beginning to see the world through children's eyes (Cook 2004). This change can be observed in Norway too, but only some decades later. It is a change that encodes and enacts the beginning of a larger-scale transformation in the cultural construction of the child within a consumer society, from seeing children as a means to reach adult markets, to seeking to target children directly. This process can be interpreted as a process of extending to children the status of more or less full persons, or at least of seeing them as individualized, self-contained consumers (Cook 2007). Again, this has been a development over time, which has taken longer and assumed a different form in Norway and the Scandinavian countries compared with the United States. Perhaps more importantly, in the case of Norway, consumption has been more strongly framed both by state restrictions introduced to protect consumers and reduce consumption, and by a Nordic 'child-centredness', with the aim to protect children and to ensure their welfare. Notions of childhood, therefore, are of particular interest when we consider the following historical study of the Norwegian company Proper Toys.

The case study

Proper Toys was founded in 1946 in Oslo, and is today one of the leading national toy stores. Its reputation is based on selling high quality, pedagogical toys to both private and corporate customers. Proper Toys started out with a strongly ideological mission. In the 1950s and 1960s it was mostly a special shop for kindergarten equipment and material for child therapy. Over the last two decades there has been a steady growth in the company's market share, especially among private customers. Proper Toys continues to specialize in selling toys to child care institutions, although the proportion of corporate customers has declined.

Our empirical case study draws on a range of material, historical as well as contemporary, including a limited number of important historical sources, both retrospective interviews and some in written form, and observations from visiting the company and its web-site.[2] We have also studied advertisements from the formative years of the company in the professional periodicals *Småbarnspedagogen* (The Pre-school Pedagogue) and *Oss i mellom* (Us Between), and from more recent years, in the company's virtual online catalogues.

Above all, we have gathered information by conducting qualitative interviews with important people connected to the company in various ways: the current managing director, who has worked for the company for more than twenty years, and the chairman of the board, who has been with the company for an even longer period. In line with the 'Statues of the Company Proper Toys 1946, § 6', the document which founded the company, the chairman of the board and the managing director are still both trained pre-school teachers. Our third informant was Norway's first Ombudsman for children and a former customer of Proper Toys. As the leader of a psychological institute for children in need of therapeutic help (the Nic Waal Institute, founded after World War II), she was involved with the company in the 1960s. In addition, we interviewed a pre-school educator who has been a shareholder since the founding of the company in 1946, and a customer on behalf of several kindergartens which she helped to found. All these informants had a great deal of knowledge of the company's history. It was also clear to us that all the informants were speaking from a certain position of power, a rather elite position, at least as regards pedagogical and psychological knowledge of children and childhood.

The company has been handed down from generation to generation; and this, along with the fact that the running of the company has been continuous and that it has never been sold to 'outsiders' or gone out of business due to bankruptcy or other conditions, was helpful to us in obtaining valuable information. Our qualitative approach is based on gathering and analyzing various sources in an effort to reconstruct the history of Proper Toys and especially to understand this company's 'properness'. By arguing that some toys are 'proper' for children while some are not, at some level this company is reflecting and promoting certain notions of what childhood is and how adults should relate to children. Bringing these notions of childhood to the surface is the 'hidden agenda' of this chapter.

The foundation of Proper Toys

In the founding of the company in 1946, the active figures were pre-school teachers, psychologists and others with a great interest in the welfare and upbringing of children. The idea was to open a toy store offering toys that were '*riktige*' in the Norwegian sense of the word. One of the founders of Proper Toys had, in Sweden, come across a toy store named '*Riktiga Leksaker*'. The Swedish word '*leksaker*' is equivalent to the Norwegian word '*leker*', both meaning toys. Both the Swedish and Norwegian words '*riktiga*' or '*riktige*' can be translated into 'real', meaning that the store offers 'real toys' to children. In the Norwegian case, however, the word '*riktig*' would more accurately be translated as 'proper': the meaning changed into toys which were 'proper for children', 'right for children' or 'correct to play with'. The idea, therefore, was to open a toy store offering toys that were 'proper' to play with, an idea that was developed further by pre-school teachers who played an important role in the founding and development of the company (Bomann 2007).

Learning about the importance of providing children with toys, which toys were proper for different age groups and how to make such toys available, were all part of the education of Norwegian pre-school teachers in the 1950s (Korsvold 1997). According to 'The Statutes of the Company Proper Toys 1946, § 3' the aim was to raise the level of toy production, both pedagogically and in terms of quality. The potential of the 'proper toy' for developing the child pedagogically, ergonomically and psychologically was an important aspect of this endeavour. It had to match the child's individual level of competence, being neither too easy nor impossible to master. A typical indicator of this level was the child's age. Help in the selection of 'proper toys' came from the 'recommended list of toys' which was agreed upon in 1959 by the organization *International Council for Children's Play* (ICCP). This list was 'conceived as an aid to all those responsible for the care and upbringing of the child in their effort to raise the general standard of play material so important to his development'. It was divided into three columns: the first shows the toy's category, the second shows the types of toys within the category, and the third the age that indicates the earliest point of time when the toy may contribute to the development of the child. In the 1950s, the list served as a guide for Proper Toys, providing evidence of the place of the company within a larger professional environment with international connections and associates. Developmental psychology thus had a strong impact on what were regarded as 'proper' toys, and the rhetoric of 'play as progress' (Sutton-Smith 1997) became very much the dominant position.

From the very beginning the company had an idealistic profile, seeking to provide both kindergartens and parents with the ability to acquire affordable and 'pedagogically correct' quality toys, not only by making such products available in their store, but also by spreading information about which toys were good, that is, suitable and correct to play with. In its formative years the company can be regarded more as an aid to kindergartens and other institutions in their task of bringing up children than as a company aiming at economic success by profiting from this need. Toy announcements from the company show toys for outdoor activities such as 'buckets and spades, skipping ropes, climbing ropes with wooden steps, seesaws'; toys like 'trolleys, prams (in wood), cars (in wood), rocking horses (in wood), wooden boxes'; as well as 'screw and hammer peg toys, lotto, dominoes, bricks, modelling materials, cutting materials (paper), song books, picture books and other books' (*Pre-school Pedagogue* 1949–52).

In the Nordic countries children traditionally played with objects from nature, such as stones, pieces of wood, seashells, pine cones and the like. Drawing on this tradition, wood in particular was regarded as a proper material from which to make good quality toys. As the former stockholder said to us in the interview: 'We were influenced by the idea that toys should be made of wood.' In the 1950s and 1960s, wood came to be regarded as a particularly suitable material from which to make good quality pedagogical toys, as long as it was appropriately handled so that it was safe for the children to play with.

In accordance with its founding statutes, Proper Toys had a trained pre-school teacher attached to its office and appointed a 'pedagogical council' consisting of three individuals to ensure that the toys offered in the store were 'proper' for children. The members of the council shared the same professional or academic background as the initial founders and stockholders. This shared background also led to a shared view of what were 'proper toys' for children. A new interest in the selection of 'child-friendly' toys, stimulating children's development and putting the 'children's point of view' at the forefront, were central elements from the beginning.

Vision, ideology and morality

Although in fact it was structured as a commercial enterprise, the idealistic pedagogical aims of Proper Toys contributed to the Norwegian Ministry of Social Affairs supporting the company financially with a subsidy from the very beginning. This was mainly because of the company's information work. Norway, which had experienced war and occupation, was in a build-up phase. More important, the social-democratic government did not consider the toys available in other stores at the time to be either especially stimulating nor proper for children to play with. A government report of the time claimed that these toys were 'non-durable, expensive and not satisfying children's fantasy and creativity'. Examples of the latter were 'mechanical toys that you could wind up, electrical trains' and so on, while the former included 'poorly made wooden toys that would splinter and fall apart, and maybe hurt children' (St. pr. nr. 48, 1948, p. 3). As a control, a member of staff from the Ministry of Social Affairs also participated within the board of the company.

The range of toys produced and sold by Proper Toys was therefore very selective. In many instances, it would have been possible for parents and pre-school teachers to recognize the same toys from their own childhoods: tradition and nostalgia were important elements informing the selection. However, those criteria were far from the only ones. The founders also wanted to protect children from war toys, guns or the like, which were being widely produced in the global market. There was a clear pacifist ethos on the board of Proper Toys in the late 1940s and 1950s, which could be seen both as a response to the Norwegian experiences of the years of (German) occupation during World War II as well as to the emerging Cold War between east and west. This led to particular concerns about the marketing of certain toys to pre-school children, as the following letter addressed to all 'toy merchants' suggests:

> We think it is sad to see toy store windows filled with war toys. These shiny canons, rifles, bomber planes and soldiers give the children an adventurous image of war. We do not mean that playing war games should be banned. The children will play war games as long as they experience, hear of and read about war. But we should let the children decide for themselves when they feel the urge to play war games. We must not lead them to such games unnaturally by providing them with tin soldiers and play tanks. If the children need material for their war games, they should make it themselves. War toys should not lie around to tempt and inspire them to play war games. We ask you to consider this thoroughly, and help us in our work to raise Norwegian toy production to a higher pedagogical and quality level (*Pre-school Pedagogue* nr. 2 1949: 45).

The battle against war toys was therefore one of the most important causes the company took on; but, as we shall see, this was part of a broader process that entailed the exclusion of some 'mass market' products. This process of selection reflects the imposition of a certain kind of cultural capital, as described by Pierre Bourdieu in his book *Distinction* (1995). According to Bourdieu, cultural capital consists of knowledge, tastes and preferences: it is the totality of an individual's learning, both formal and informal, and is a key mechanism in the maintenance of social status. As Bourdieu succinctly puts it, taste classifies, and it classifies the classifier: it serves as a marker of individual distinction, but also as a manifestation of wider processes of social reproduction. In his detailed study of the lifestyles of the Parisian middle class of the 1960s, Bourdieu outlines how the social practice of consumption reflects existing forms of class stratification. Significantly, he links the emphasis on what he calls the strictly 'invertible' educational value of toys with the supportive role of teachers and psychologists who often present their own lifestyle as an example to others (Bourdieu 1995: 224). Proper Toys might be seen as a similarly 'middle class' project: its founders belonged to the pre-school profession, which, at least in the 1950s and 1960s, was influenced by middle-class values (Korsvold 1997). In the case of Proper Toys, adults claimed to know what was 'proper' for children: they defined what was 'out' as well as what was 'in' through a process of exclusion, and thereby sought to sustain adult hegemony. At the same time, the company's approach to consumption and toys can also be interpreted as a kind of resistance towards modernity. The idea was that parents could no longer care for their children without help from experts or professionals. The notion of 'properness' thus reflects judgments of taste, value and morality that in turn embody and sustain relationships of power, both between adults and children and between different social groups.

Protecting children's rights and the legacy of social democracy

In its first formative decades, the protection of children's rights – which can be seen as part of a historical form of Nordic 'child-centredness' – was an important motivation for Proper Toys. As we have seen, Ellen Key had urged the governments of Nordic countries to make the twentieth century the 'century of the child'. In this respect, the Nordic countries have in many ways been regarded as ahead of the field as far as children's services, children's interests and rights are concerned (Satka and Eydal 2005, Kristjansson 2006). This is reflected in the high level of political commitment to establishing and supporting welfare services, combined with a general concern about children's health and well being, and the long history of laws to protect children. The Swedish sociologist Göran Therborn suggests that Nordic children were in a special position in Europe in the early twentieth century in this respect and that the public authorities played a prominent role in this development (Therborn 1993). The child-oriented legislation enacted in the decades following the war was a further manifestation of an active welfare state with a focus on public measures for children, who were seen to have a right to be protected. As we have seen, the founding concept of Proper Toys had some of the same features or characteristics.

Likewise, the state's attitude towards consumption in the formative period after World War II must also be understood as having been formed and influenced by social-democratic policy. This inheritance also includes strong state regulation of the market (Sejersted 2005). After World War II, a strongly regulated market policy in Norway resulted in modest consumption compared to other Nordic or European countries. With the Marshall Plan in the 1950s, it became more evident that Norwegian society was changing rapidly, although rations and other restrictions lasting from wartime continued to reduce consumption. Some products, such as those popular with children, like chocolate, were only distributed on a limited scale until 1950 (Lange 1998). During 'the golden years' of social democracy, we therefore find a strong state with regulations and restrictions aimed at creating a rational, conscious consumer. However, the lack of consumer goods available for children was also obvious, despite clear differences between social groups: in a sense, there was little consumption to actually regulate.

The balance between proper and improper toys today

To what extent, and in what ways, has Proper Toys managed to sustain its 'properness' into the present era? From a social constructionist perspective, every society has particular concepts of children and childhood which require and encourage the younger generation to learn certain ways of behaving, thinking, speaking and interacting in time and space. Collective definitions of the group we call children are thus the outcome of social and discursive processes, where particular assumptions about what kind of social beings children are and should be are historically reinforced and 'naturalized' (Buckingham 2000). As such, we would probably expect to find a different form of 'properness' in the company today.

The 'properness' of Proper Toys has indeed become more subtle, at least compared with the formative years of the Norwegian welfare state.

This may partly reflect broader structural changes. In the 1980s, new safety regulations for toys were introduced by the government, requiring certain forms of testing and documentation which could not be provided by the local toy manufacturers. This, along with the economic and cultural globalization of society in general, led to Proper Toys having to look internationally for new suppliers who could provide toys that would stand up to their new definitions of 'properness'. After struggling through the changes and economic challenges of the 1980s, on the threshold of the next decade, a new phase began for Proper Toys: it started making money (Bomann 2007).

Today, Proper Toys markets a broad selection of toys to its customers. Material quality is still of major importance. The chairman stresses in the interview: '...the toy should be solid, not only for economic purposes, but also it has to be solid so you can preserve the child's affection for it'. However, the definition of 'properness' has changed, or at least is growing more complex. The company is still selective concerning the range of products that is offered in the store. Proper Toys distinguishes itself from other toy stores by not focusing on heavily marketed, popular toys, nor on the even more short-lived toy 'crazes', spin-offs from media texts, and toys that 'every' child 'has to have' for a relatively short period of time (although in fact some such toys also reappear with new generations of children: Schor 2004).

However, there are further principles that guide the company's selection of toys. Individual differences between children are given as an important reason. The company stresses the notion of diversity, that is, the ability to offer toys for every child, at least in the age group 0–6, whether a boy, a girl or a child with special needs. However, this emphasis might also be seen to reflect the principle of freedom of choice that is closely related to modern consumerism, with its characteristic emphasis on individuality (Cook 2007).

Thirdly, nostalgia is an underlying element that should not be overlooked when studying the selection of 'proper' toys. 'Even Batman and Superman have a nostalgic appeal' the manager points out. Parents want 'the best' for their own children, and their reference point for this often seems to be certain positive memories of their own childhood. They associate certain products with their own youth and nostalgically pass certain genres of toys on to their own children. The following quotation from Proper Toys' webpage illustrates this: 'In our [web-] page you will find a selection of exciting, fun, not to mention developmental toys, often toys you cannot find elsewhere. [...] including toys you might remember from your own childhood. [...].'[3] Symbols of a past childhood, such as toys with a nostalgic appeal (at least in terms of outward appearance), are important within the toy industry more broadly (Cross 2004). Proper Toys particularly capitalises on this, as it offers a broad selection of toys which have a nostalgic appeal to both parents and grandparents, even though which toys have this appeal is constantly changing (Bomann 2007).

Defining 'properness' through 'improperness'?

However, treating some toys today as 'improper' toys has created a new complexity. As we have seen, Proper Toys appears to have made an effort to preserve its legacy of idealism concerning what is 'best for the child'. The company still does not sell toy weapons of any kind or 'aggression-promoting toys',[4] for example action figures such as *Teenage Mutant Ninja Turtles* or *Transformers* or any modern figures that use 'high-tech' weapons. It does sell superheroes like *Superman* or *Batman*, but not their 'violent' accessories. On the other hand, it also sells certain historical figures like Norsemen, pirates, knights or cowboys, even though these figures also often tend to be holding weapons. The company's argument for selling historical figures with weapons is that they create possibilities for play with certain narrative qualities, including characters and story-lines. Here we find fictional portrayals of childlike figures, created in agreement with an adult image of children, and often exposed to challenges which they must handle in order for the story to take the 'right' turn and for the characters to develop in the 'right' direction. This behaviour involves agreeing with, and taking lessons from, the values that are regarded as 'proper' by adults. Meanwhile, as Gary Cross (2004) suggests, this adult hegemony increasingly seems to produce the reaction of children rebelling against it.

The company clearly faces a dual dilemma here: on one level, this is a moral or ideological dilemma, but it is also a commercial one that relates to its unique market 'niche'. The legacy and history of Proper Toys commits it to not selling war toys; and the company still filters out the kinds of toys which are thought to send wrong or morally incorrect messages to children, exemplified by 'violent' and 'sexualized' toys. It wants to retain adult customers who expect to find carefully selected 'proper' toys in its store, something different from what is being sold in other toy stores. And yet the company has to modernize and select continually in order to stay in business. One of the strategies it has adopted has been to include a few of the new spin-offs from multimedia phenomena. Popular toys, even some of the 'crazes' such as *Pokèmon* from the Nintendo Company, have been included for a while. In such situations the spin-off products are often justified by being given the status of 'educational' toys (Bomann 2007).

Although the company still prefers toys which are useful for children's development or pedagogically correct above those which are generally popular and heavily marketed as entertainment, they have loosened their selection criteria. Fun for children seems to have become more important than 'the right progress of the child'; or at least there does not necessarily have to be an opposition between them. There is a greater appreciation of the entertaining function of toys here. The manager admits: 'I have turned this around a bit (...) in the way that: Is this toy OK? Does it give pleasure to any child, is it funny?' And he states: 'We have always had our focus on children; we have never focussed on jumping from one 'craze' to another (...). Our basis, call it developmental toys, pedagogical toys – they will always be there.' The changing nature of the selection shows that Proper Toys has opened its doors to toys which are popular. Although this popularity is mainly commercially produced, the focus on spin-off products rather than the 'main attraction' means that the company still does not appear like other toy stores. If it were to do so, it would probably lose a key segment of the market: its core business depends upon continuing to present itself as a niche company, appealing to adult nostalgia through carefully selected 'proper toys'.

Like the Lego company (Hjarvard 2004), Proper Toys is thus in some way a rather restrictive enterprise. Its development and power (or at least its symbolic power) seems to be based on certain ideas and values relating to childhood, and to the protection of children, that are perhaps distinctive to Nordic culture. An example of this protectiveness can be found in the attitudes of both companies towards the *Barbie* doll, an example of an item that Proper Toys chose not to sell. Its decision to exclude *Barbie* dates back to the early 1960s, and was based on a view of the doll as an 'improper' toy, just as much as the war toys. *Barbie*'s youthful soap-universe, in which exclusive leisure activities, above all fashion, make up the dominant play activity, was considered 'improper'. The *Barbie* doll and its mass marketing also caught the attention of feminist researchers, who were critical of the unrealistic body image *Barbie* conveys and the way in which it normalizes whiteness (McDonough 1999). Although the current managing director acknowledges that *Barbie* is different today than she was in 1960s, and that the general attitude towards her has changed, he still has reservations. As was also the case for the Lego company, some fictional genres and narrative components are still seen to be missing. Not only is 'violence' strongly deprecated, but some 'sexual' themes are also completely absent. For example, the *Bratz* dolls were considered acceptable for a while, until the new collection for the summer season came along. There were fewer and fewer clothes on the dolls, the manager explained to us in the interview, 'so I said "This is getting more and more "porno"; get rid of it!". As an alternative, Proper Toys sell dolls from the lesser known brand *Only Hearts Club* where the dolls are more 'normal' looking, with various faces resembling children (rather than teenagers or young women) in real life.

A fragmented landscape

While it has to maintain an appeal to children, Proper Toys primarily seeks to address adult consumers by appealing to their taste. The forms of cultural capital that are at stake here involve various types of knowledge and expertise, and extend from moral values to issues of access and control across a wide range of toys; and as we have seen, they function by including some toys ('proper' toys) and excluding others. In this way, consumption is governed by a form of moral and cultural gatekeeping.

Gary Cross has shown how toy companies and the new media in the United States have increasingly realized that they have to appeal to the wishes – and the spending power – of children if they want to stay in business. Different companies learned at different times how to create a special world of children's own consumption; and in doing so, they also pulled young children much further away from their parents' culture and experiences (Cross 2004). Still, toys are more than tools for children's play, as Cross declares. They are also significant in the relationship between children and parents, where they serve as messages telling children what their parents expect of them, while also telling parents that their children seek recognition and freedom from them. Here, as Cross implies, adults have created their own 'monsters'. 'Cute' toys, reflecting adults' romanticized fantasies and idealized notions of 'the good childhood' have increasingly been challenged by 'cool' toys – improperly sexual, violent, grotesque objects threatening the 'innocent landscape of childhood'.

In the case of Proper Toys, we find a different rhetoric. We still do not find war games or 'sexualized' toys, but the process of selection has become more complicated. Today toy-makers base new toy designs on children's *own* fantasies and desires, which are seen as separate from those of adults. Many companies invite children to help them in

designing new products (Seiter 1993); and they claim to positively identify with children by adopting their point of view and perspective on
the world. Proper Toys' navigation of this fragmented landscape, with
respect to global consumption, involves several challenges and dilemmas. Its identity as a 'niche' store depends upon it filtering out toys
that are perceived as 'improper' by adults, mostly on both ideological
and moral grounds; and its selection of toys still appeals to adults' nostalgia and cultural capital. Nevertheless, it has been bound to shift and
renegotiate its position in a market and a society which have changed
fundamentally since it was founded more than sixty years ago.

Conclusion

By exploring how toys are defined and selected, we also acquire an
insight into the ways in which adults define childhood, how children's
play is valued, and how children are considered as modern consumers
amid an ever-increasing level of marketing. Markets produce and reproduce wider social meanings, as well as generating particular meanings to
do with the place of childhood within consumer culture.

By largely refusing or failing to address children directly as customers,
Proper Toys ideologically supports the notion that children should be
protected due to their vulnerability – a stance that is in line with certain
attitudes of the Norwegian welfare state, which created guidelines to
protect children from consumer culture. As the Danish scholar Jesper
Olesen puts it in the conclusion of his book, the 'right' or 'good' child
consumer is seen here as a *non-acting* consumer (Olesen 2003).

For Proper Toys, both children and childhood are value-laden notions
as well. The rhetoric of 'play as progress' – as a vehicle for development
and learning – has a strong tradition within Proper Toys. Yet this tradition has weakened over time: individuality and diversity are now more
important, and Proper Toys takes a pride in offering something for every
taste. Even so, while it seeks to strike a balance between pedagogical
discourses of progress on the one hand and market forces on the other,
it clearly aims to stimulate some kinds of play while excluding others.
According to Sutton-Smith, the rhetoric of play as progress is pursued
in order to maintain adult hegemony. He finds it paradoxical that children, who are supposed to be the players among us, are allowed much
less freedom for irrational, wild, dark or deep play in Western culture
than adults, who are thought not to play at all (Sutton-Smith 1997).

The company's changing definitions of 'proper' and the 'improper'
toys are therefore part of a wider discourse produced by adults about

children. The selection of toys is made by adults and promoted to adults, who provide them for their children. Toys given in such a way also serve as a message from parents in telling children what is expected of them. The company markets itself primarily towards adults who prioritize providing 'the best', or at least something special, for their children. By filtering out 'violent' and 'sexualized' toys it supports adults who want to protect children, or to keep them away from what are seen as negative manifestations of consumer culture. The store's name carries a legacy which seems to legitimize its right to define 'properness', although it draws a fine line between an ideological commitment to the past and the position of a commercial company in a contemporary society defined in part by consumption.

Notes

1. Tora Korsvold's 'Selling childhoods and the history of marketing to children' is a subproject within the interdisciplinary project led by David Buckingham and Vebjørg Tingstad, Consuming children: commercialization and the changing construction of childhood (Buckingham and Tingstad 2007), funded by the Norwegian Research Council. The present chapter is based on and further developed from Linda Bomann's master's thesis, 'Proper Toys of Norway. On the track of Norwegian childhood and the consuming child: a case study of the Norwegian company A/S Riktige Leker (1946–2007)', which was part of the subproject.
2. http://www.riktigeleker.no/ (Visited 14.10. 2008).
3. http://www.riktigeleker.no/default.asp?page=3 (Visited 14.10. 2008).
4. http://www.riktigeleker.no/default.asp?page=3 (Visited 14.10. 2008).

Sources

Interviews: Four interviews with central individuals within the company of 'A/S Riktige leker', Oslo, spring 2007.
Professional periodicals: Småbarnspedagogen (Pre-school Pedagogue) 1949–1952 Oss imellom (Us Between) 1953–1963 Småbarnspedagogen 1964–1965.
Vedtekter for a/s riktige leker, 7. mai 1946 (Stautes of the company).
International Council for Children's Play 1956 (Guidelines).
Royal Proposition: St. prp. Nr. 48 (1947/48): Om bruk av overskottet av barnetilskuddsordningen fra okkupasjonstiden (On the use of the surplus generated from an income supplement during the years of (German) occupation).

References

Bomann, L. (2007) *Proper Toys of Norway. On the Track of Norwegian Childhood and the Consuming Child: A Case Study of the Norwegian Company A/S Riktige Leker (1946–2007)*. Trondheim NTNU.

Bourdieu, P. (1995) *Distinction*. Cambridge: Harvard University Press.

Buckingham, D. (2000) *After the Death of Childhood*. Cambridge: Polity Press.

Buckingham, D. and V. Tingstad (2007) Consuming Children: Commercialisation and the Changing Construction of Childhood. A Project Description, *Barn* 2: 49–71.

Cook, D. T. (2004) *The Commodification of Childhood*. Durham: NC Duke University Press.

Cook, D. T. (2007) 'The Disempowering Empowerment of Children's Consumer 'Choice': Cultural Discourses of the Child Consumer in North America', *Society and Business Review*.

Cross, G. (2004) *Cute and the Cool: Wondrous Innocence and Modern American Children's Culture*. Oxford: University Press.

Hjarvard, S. (2004) 'From Bricks to Bytes': The Mediatization of a Global Toy Industry', *European Culture and the Media*. Bristol: Intellect Books.

Korsvold, T. (1997): *Profesjonalisert barndom: statlige intensjoner og kvinnelig praksis på barnehagens arena 1945–1990*. *(Professionalized childhood: State intentions and women's praxis in the day-care arena 1945–1990)* (Diss.). NTNU, Trondheim.

Kristjansson, B. (2006) 'The Making of Nordic Childhoods,' in J. Einarsdottir and J. T. Wagner (eds) *Nordic Childhoods and Early Education: Philosophy, Research, Policy, and Practice in Denmark, Finland, Iceland, Norway, and Sweden*. Greenwich: Information Age Publishing.

Lange, E. (1998) *Samling om felles mål 1935–70*. *(Unification for a common goal 1935–70)* Aschehougs Norgeshistorie Vol. 12. Oslo: Aschehoug.

McDonough, Y. Z. 1999 (ed.) *The Barbie Chronicles*. New York: Touchstone.

Olesen, J. (2003) *Det forbrugende barn*. *(The Consuming Child)*. København: Hans Reitzels Forlag.

Satka, M., and G. B. Eydal (2005) 'The History of Nordic Welfare Policies for Children', in H. Brembeck *et al.* (eds) *Beyond the Competent Child: Exploring Contemporary Childhoods in the Nordic Welfare Societies*. Roskilde University Press, Roskilde.

Sejersted, F. (2005) *Sosialdemokratiets tidsalder*. *(The social-democratic periode)*. Oslo: Pax.

Seiter, E. (1993) *Sold Separately: Parents and Children in Consumer Culture*. Brunswick, NJ: Rutgers University Press.

Schor, J. B. (2004) *Born To Buy: The Commercialied Child and the New Consumer Culture*. New York: Scribner.

Sutton-Smith, B. (1997) *Ambiguity of Play*. Havard: Harvard University Press.

Therborn, G. (1993) Politics of Childhood: 'The Rights of Children since the Constitution of the Modern Childhood. A Comparative Study of Western Nations', in F. G. Castles *et al.* (eds) *Families of Nations. Patterns of Public Policy in Western Democracies*. Dartmouth: Aldershot.

3
The Books That Sing: The Marketing of Children's Phonograph Records, 1890–1930

Jacob Smith

Juliet B. Schor has argued that in contemporary American consumer culture, children form the link between advertisers and the "family purse," and children's tastes and opinions shape corporate strategies. Schor states that the centrality of children to the consumer marketplace is a relatively recent phenomenon, and that not long ago children were merely "bit players" who were approached by marketers primarily through their mothers (Schor, 2005, p. 9). Schor, like many other scholars, refers to the widespread introduction of television as an important turning point in the development of marketing to children because of the way in which it allowed advertisers a more direct link to young audiences (see Schor, 2005, p. 17, and Kline, 1993, p. 165). However, the work of scholars such as Daniel Cook, Ellen Gruber Garvey, Lisa Jacobson and William Leach has indicated that children were seen as more than "bit players" in home consumption decades before television and even radio. Jacobson argues that middle-class children became targets of advertising more than half a century before television, and warns that identifying the 1950s as "the pivotal historical moment" in marketing to children risks falling into a "technological and economic determinism" that can obscure "a host of earlier efforts to inculcate brand consciousness" (Jacobson, 2004, p. 17).

One such "earlier effort" at marketing to children has been overlooked in examinations of early twentieth century children's media culture. In 1924, a major American media corporation eagerly referred to the novel opportunities provided by reaching the "boundless and almost untouched children's market." That corporation was the Victor Phonograph Company, which was embarking on a marketing campaign for one of the earliest lines of mass media products targeted specifically at young children: "Bubble Books"; the first book and record hybrid for children.[1]

The phonograph industry provides an important missing chapter in the history of the design and marketing of media products for children. Phonograph records have been largely absent from the scholarly history of children's media entertainment. Overviews of children's media typically move from discussions of dime novels to the nickelodeon film theatre, and from there to radio and television, without any mention of the phonograph industry (see for example, Bruce, 2008, Pecora, 1998: 118). As I will demonstrate, records for children were actively marketed to parents and children decades before Disney and television. Advertising materials for Bubble Books reveal a lost phase in the development of marketing media products to children, and index the anxieties that surrounded the arrival of such products into the home.

Notably, children's records such as the Bubble Books did not provoke the kind of public controversy inspired by dime novels, early cinema, radio, or television, despite aggressive marketing by the record industry in popular magazines, department stores, and even in schools. The fact that children's phonograph records sparked such little public debate is certainly one of the reasons that children's records have been off the scholarly radar, but also poses some significant questions concerning the study of children and the media: why did children's records not inspire the same controversy as other forms of children's media? Why do some forms of new media for children provoke more cultural concern than others? The following analysis then, is concerned not only with adding the phonograph industry to historical accounts of children's media, and with documenting early strategies for marketing children's media products, but also with identifying aspects of that marketing which allowed these pioneering instances of home media products for children to be woven into the fabric of everyday American family life.

Juvenile records

It can be argued that the history of the children's phonograph record begins with the history of recorded sound itself, since the oft-repeated "creation story" of the phonograph has Thomas Edison reciting the nursery rhyme "Mary Had a Little Lamb" into his tinfoil recording device. Phonograph historian Patrick Feaster has pointed out that this heart-warming anecdote is quite probably a re-write of history: given Edison's penchant for salty humor, the first test was likely to have been quite different. Nonetheless, from the very beginning, the phonograph was cast as a device with a certain affinity for children's entertainment. In fact, one of Edison's earliest intended uses for recorded sound was to make children's dolls that could speak. In 1890, Edison outfitted his laboratory in West Orange, New Jersey as a production line for dolls containing tiny phonograph players. The dolls did not sell well, and the company folded in 1891, by which time the market for entertainment phonograph cylinders had begun to take off (Wood, 2002: 161). Though the phonograph would not speak to American children through dolls, the major phonograph companies actively sought to develop a child market for phonograph players and records as early as the 1890s and 1900s.

The first "Victor Talking Machine" product to be nationally advertised was the "Toy Gram-o-phone," which is shown in a December 1900 ad in *Munsey's Magazine*, with copy that reads, "The most wonderful Christmas gift ever offered for children."[2] In a November 1907 advertisement in *McClure's Magazine*, we see the image of two little girls amazed by the phonograph horn, while the copy proclaims "The Edison Phonograph as a Christmas Present": "No single thing furnishes so much entertainment, amusement and enjoyment to a family, especially where there are children and young folks, as an Edison Phonograph" (p. 39). The phonograph industry continued actively to pursue the child market both indirectly through parents and through direct appeals to children, as is illustrated by the use of a Victor promotional brochure entitled "The Victor: For Every Day in the Week" (1907), which promoted the phonograph as a multi-purpose form of children's entertainment. In the Victor trade journal *The Voice of Victor*, the company advised retailers on how to use the brochure: "This booklet can be used in conjunction with your window display... in some localities it may be better to distribute them upon dismissal of school" ("New Victor Booklet," 1907: 9). In the brochure, we see the image of a phonograph player being delivered to a home, as copy proclaims, "There certainly is pleasure for us every day in the week with the Victor." A series of illustrations follows, depicting the various ways in which the phonograph could entertain children: on Monday, a group of youngsters wear military uniforms and march around the nursery to the sounds of John Philip Sousa; and on Tuesday, the children listen to Mother Goose stories on the phonograph player and put on a Punch and Judy show.

Such "Mother Goose stories" or "juvenile records" were made by performers such as William F. Hooley, who identified himself as "Uncle Will," and began recitations of material such as "The Death of Cock Robin" by telling listeners: "Now, children, draw your little chairs nearer so that you can see the pretty pictures." Gilbert Girard was the premiere vocal mimic of the early phonograph industry, and frequently applied his talents to making records for children. On titles such as "A Trip to the Circus" (Victor 1901) and "Auction Sale of a Bird and Animal Store" (Edison 1902), Girard and Len Spencer presented animal mimicry, auctioneer performance, and broad jokes: a range of offerings that could appeal to both children and adults. "A Trip to the Circus" (Victor 1901) is introduced as a "descriptive selection for the little folks," and then we hear Spencer announce, "Now children, hold tight to my hand, and don't get too near to the animals." "Oh, see the elephants," Spencer declares, and Girard provides a loud trumpeting sound.

"Juvenile records" from the early decades of the twentieth century demonstrate that the phonograph industry was quick to recognize the importance of the child audience for home media entertainment. In fact, a major campaign to market children's records began in 1917, when Columbia Records formed a partnership with Harper & Brothers Books to manufacture 5½-inch diameter records and market them to children.[3] The Bubble Books were the brainchild of Ralph Mayhew who, in 1914, was working for Harper & Brothers on a children's book of verse in which he planned to have "a child sitting blowing bubbles which ascended and burst into the little pictures and nursery rhymes" (Rhodes, 1921, p. 23). Mayhew conceived of combining children's books with phonograph records, and was eventually able to convince Harper & Brothers and Columbia to back his idea. The first edition of the Bubble Books – which contained three single-sided 5½-inch records featuring musical versions of traditional children's verses sung by Henry Burr, and an accompanying package with illustrations by Rhoda Chase – was pressed in 1917 and met with immediate success: "hardly had the salesmen gone out when the orders began to pour in," *Printer's Ink* noted, adding that nine thousand copies were sold in the month after it was released (p. 25). These initial strong sales figures continued over the next several years: according to one 1920 advertisement, more than one and a half million Bubble Books were sold between January and May of that year.[4] Indeed, the Bubble Books sold well enough to inspire subsequent editions through the early 1930s, with the copyright and patents controlled by the Victor Company after 1924.[5]

The Bubble Books were the first book and record hybrids marketed to children, and so represent a pioneering instance of cross-media synergy between book publishing and the record industry. An examination of the ad campaign designed to sell Bubble Books reveals early strategies for developing a child audience for home media products, and the kinds of media texts that were considered to be beneficial to children.

Into the heart of the family

At a time when American toy manufacturers were entering the mass market, Columbia and Harper & Brothers began advertising Bubble Books in both the popular and trade press. In regards to the latter, Daniel Cook warns that the use of trade journals as evidence "demands circumspection," since the "bald, forthright approach to markets" found in such discourse was intended for a very particular audience. Cook suggests that trade material should be considered as "providing an entrée into a historically situated semantic domain," and can provide insights into the process by which commercial portrayals of children and childhood are constructed (Cook, 2004, pp. 18–19). Trade advertisements for Bubble Books in *Talking Machine World* were targeted to record store owners and reveal some of the motivations and assumptions behind the marketing of children's media entertainment.

For example, retailers were encouraged to use children to reach adult consumers indirectly. "The easiest way to win the good-will of customers is through their children," stated a 1923 *Talking Machine World* ad targeted to phonograph dealers: "You know how freely the most reticent mother will talk, if you get her started on the subject of her little boy or girl."[6] A 1924 Victor company publication noted that nothing ingratiated a merchant with the public as much as "being of service to children." "Parents," Victor therefore advised its retailers, "will feel more than ever well disposed toward you... for bringing a desirable thing to their children's hands" ("Victor Bubble Books Open New Market," 1924: 13). Children were also thought to be able to influence their parents through what marketers have subsequently described as the "nag factor" or "pester power," in which children are encouraged to make purchase requests of their parents (Schor, 2005: 61–2). A 1921 *Talking Machine World* ad asked, "How many children are working for you? No, we don't mean in the store but outside, in your customers' homes. The dealer that sells Bubble Books has one or more persistent salesmen in every home in his town."[7]

Not only were children a means of reaching parents, but trade press ads also asserted that they were potentially "serial purchasers." That is, the importance of the child market lay in the fact that children were eager to purchase multiple items in a particular line, or as the Bubble Book ads bluntly stated, "when you sell one – you sell a habit!" Ralph Mayhew was not the first person to recognize the "serial" potential of the children's market. Ellen Gruber Garvey has described how children in the 1880s and 1890s had collected advertising trade cards, which they arranged in scrapbooks: "no single trade card," Garvey writes, "was enough" (Garvey, 1996: 49). Nonetheless, the idea of exploiting children's seemingly limitless appetites struck *Printer's Ink* as a novel aspect of Bubble Book marketing: it was Mayhew's "keen marketing imagination" that had perceived that a second Bubble Book could be sold to the same people "who had bought the first one. And they were right" (Rhodes, 1921: 25). "With most kinds of merchandise the sale is the end of the transaction," stated the copy in a 1922 *Talking Machine World* ad, "but with Bubble Books it is another story. When you sell your first Bubble Book you have only just begun. For there is one sure thing about Bubble Book buyers – they always come back for more."[8] A Victor company trade journal described how one of the most "satisfying features" of selling records to children was the fact that "every sale sows the seeds" for an "endless chain" of future sales ("There's a School in Every Town," 1924: 6). A 1919 ad visualizes both the child as serial purchaser and as a link between the marketplace and the home: an illustration depicts a pied piper holding a portable gramophone, leading a line of dancing children from the city to "Ye Talking Machine Shoppe," while the copy beneath reads, "lure the children to your store with these enchanting little volumes, and they will take you right into the heart of the family. When the youngster has bought one he always comes for more."[9] Bubble Books could thus create a "serial" market for records in a manner similar to film serials in the 1910s, which Terry Staples argues were designed to stimulate regular cinema-going in children (Staples, 1997, p. 8).

Trade press advertisements for Bubble Books demonstrate strategies for marketing children's media products that have since become commonplace. However, the trade press ads I have been describing were only one aspect of what was considered to be an unprecedented advertising campaign for children's products. In fact, the use of a large-scale print advertising campaign was itself a notable aspect of the marketing of Bubble Books. A 1920 ad in *Talking Machine World* announced a "great national Bubble Book campaign" at a cost of $75,000.[10] The trade journal *The Bookseller, Newsdealer and Stationer* stated that this would be "the largest advertising campaign ever devoted to books...the sum to be expended in the advertising campaign for them exceeds anything ever before spent on a single juvenile line" ("Books for Children," 1920: 477). Advertisements in that campaign appeared in mass-circulation magazines such as *Ladies' Home Journal* and *Woman's Home Companion*, and provide a commercial discourse that ran parallel to the trade journals described above.

Magic wonder books

It will not come as a surprise that popular press ads for Bubble Books targeted women, since it was thought that they did the bulk of the family's consumer spending and of the child-rearing. The growth of a market for both mass-produced toys and children's records was tied to the emergence of new family roles that were in turn shaped by campaigns against child labour, the decreasing size of the middle-class family, and the introduction of scientific discourses of childrearing.[11] Ellen Seiter stresses that children's consumption should be placed in the context of the increasing demands placed on women's time; demands that made "children's goods appealing, even necessary for mothers" (Seiter, 1995, p. 20). Daniel Cook also points to the importance of mothers for the marketing of children's goods, and describes the emerging belief among marketers in the 1920s and 1930s that "mothers are like no other class of trade because they will forego their own happiness to provide for their children, a circumstance favorable to selling better grades of merchandise" (Cook, 2004: 53). During this same period, advertisers were fashioning contemporary theories of child guidance into a "cogent merchandising strategy," and advertisements often encouraged middle-class women both to "invest more emotional energy in their role as mothers," and to "recognize that they would be judged more heavily than ever by their successes or failures in this role" (Marchand, 1985: 229). Bubble Book ads targeted to retailers sometimes made explicit reference to new regimes of parenting. A 1924 *Talking Machine World* ad noted that parents were making a "study of their children these days": "They have learned from child psychologists that the first six years of life are the most important. Impressions gathered during these – the formative years – are lasting. That's why they want the best of everything for their children."[12] The rhetoric found in this ad corroborates Nicholas Sammand's claim that an increasingly important part of a mother's parental responsibilities at this time came to be the regulation of her child's consumption of branded goods (Sammond, 2005: 111).

In their appeal to mothers, marketers downplayed the Bubble Books' status as a sound recording, and described them instead as a unique hybrid of toy and book. Popular press advertisements suggested that children would be captivated by Bubble Books as though by a toy: "When they're tired of balls and tops and blocks and marbles and dolls, here's something new."[13] Bubble Books' quasi-toy status was also encouraged by innovative packaging, with one edition featuring cut-out toys to accompany listening: "Make the little people in the Bubble

Books dance to the music of their own songs," an ad urged. Children could place cut-out figures in the center of their Bubble Book records as they played, so that the "little Bubble Book friends go round and round – just as though they were dancing," the ad copy suggested. "Then you can work out little plays and have the Bubble Book people do the things that the records sing about."[14] We might see these cut-outs as an early example of what Schor calls "trans-toying," whereby everyday objects such as toothbrushes are turned into playthings (Schor, 2005: 63). Here the spinning phonograph record itself becomes a toy, further blurring the line between plaything, record and book.

Though ads suggested that children would enjoy Bubble Books as they would a toy, parents were also urged to see their book-like qualities. As their name and slogan ("the books that sing") indicated, they were to be regarded as a type of book. Parents were urged, for example, to start a Bubble Book "library." A 1919 ad in *Ladies' Home Journal* stated that "the Bubble Books are not play things for the moment only. They are books of permanent value that will train your children's taste for poetry and rhythm and beauty of color."[15] The Bubble Books' hybrid status was offered to mothers as the vehicle for guilt-free relaxation, since children would be educated by their book-like qualities at the same time that they would be captivated as though by a toy. In a section entitled "Long Hours of Peace and Quiet," ad copy stated that "mother can sit quietly by sewing or reading, for she knows the children will be entertained for hours together, and at the same time they are learning."[16] In an ad entitled "It Keeps them Happy on Rainy Days," a mother explained that "Rainy days used to be the bane of my life... The children used to drive me to distraction asking me for something to do... But now, since I got them some Bubble Books, they just wish for the rainy days because it means real joy for them. They are busy and happy the live-long day... and the best part of it is that while they are playing with these magic wonder books they are learning something worth while."[17]

It is safe to assume that the success of the Bubble Books owed much to the powerful appeal of ads such as these, wherein a female voice addressed mothers busy with new kinds of housework and parental expectations. Phonograph records, it was suggested, could benefit mothers and children as a hybrid of book and toy that offered mothers time for relaxation and educated children at the same time. We find here an approach to selling children's records that is similar to Ellen Seiter's discussion of the "Toys That Teach" articles that appeared in *Parents* magazine in the 1920s and 1930s (Seiter, 1995: 67). Seiter argues that this rhetorical strategy was meant in part to balance "conflicting feelings toward consumption and its hedonistic and emulative aspects," and adds that such educational claims were "usually limited to desks, toy typewriters, or chalkboards and to specialized educational toy manufacturers such as Playskool" (Seiter, 1995: 68). Bubble Book ads reveal a similar educational discourse being used for media products beginning in the 1910s.

Let me sing to your child

The "education" that Bubble Books provided consisted of a repackaged oral tradition of children's nursery rhymes and songs. Short forms of children's entertainment like nursery rhymes were well-suited to the time limitations of early records: with only approximately four minutes of recording time per side, it was difficult to develop longer narrative forms. But nursery rhymes also helped to associate these mass-produced records with oral traditions of parenting. This is apparent in the following ad from a 1920 issue of *St. Nicholas Magazine*:

> When your grandmother was a child, she loved those songs, and she, in turn, rocked your mother's wooden cradle gently to the same quaint, old nursery rhymes. And your mother loved them and sang them, just as you love them. Only you don't have to sing them to your children. They can listen to them to their hearts' content as they are sung by the BUBBLE BOOKS. For the pictures in the BUBBLE BOOKS are new and charming – lovelier than any you could get when you were a little girl... the songs themselves... are not only the songs your grandmother sang – not only the ones your mother knew and you loved – but *all* the dear, familiar rhymes and melodies that all children have loved from time immemorial and will go on loving to the end of time.[18]

The rhetoric of this ad connects Bubble Books to a timeless matrilineal oral tradition, and at the same time attempts to upstage that tradition by arguing for the supremacy of the modern media: records could stockpile and reproduce *all* the dear, familiar rhymes, and with accompanying pictures lovelier than anything available in the past. Further, while the ad portrays the mother as the vehicle of a beloved tradition, it imagines a future in which her role was replaced by the phonograph. Thus, a 1918 ad in *Ladies' Home Journal* presents "Tom the piper's son," who asked mothers, "Let me sing to your child ... I've always wanted to tell those children of yours my story, and to sing them a song – and now at last I can do it."[19]

A further example can be found in a fictional sales scenario in *The Voice of Victor* trade journal, in which "a little mother drops into the store on her way home from the sewing club to buy a few records for her three small daughters." The Mother explains that she is looking for records of songs that would help her little girls in learning to sing, since her own voice "is not good any more, and not at all the sort I should want them to imitate." The salesman replies, "Yes, indeed, we have many beautiful little songs recorded especially for children; and they have been made, too, with just such a situation as yours in mind. Very careful attention has been given to enunciation, voice quality, thought-content, rhythm, melody, and instrumentation." At one point, the salesman asks whether the girls were familiar with "old Mother Goose." "Surely," replies the mother, "she is a much-loved member of our household!" "Then, let me play for you these 'Mother Goose Songs'" returns the salesman. The mother is impressed: "These are wonderful! I know I shall enjoy them quite as much as the children. And what a delight for them to meet their dear little story friends in these songs" ("Children's Records For Home and School," 1920: 49).

We might identify this sales pitch as an example of what Cook calls the "storybook strategy" in 1920s discourse on marketing to children: the attempt to "associate products with children's characters and imagery" in order to make commercial appeals "invisible or at least innocuous to parents" (Cook, 2004: 73). However, we also find here a vivid drama-tization of some of the same themes found in the *St. Nicholas* ad cited above: the substitution of the phonograph for the mother's voice and a tradition of oral nursery rhymes. In his examination of the trade press for children's clothing in the first decades of the twentieth century, Cook found that the mother came to stand as "a gatekeeper at the interface between home and market, between the sacred and profane, who must arbitrate between these spheres": "As the middle term between market and child, the mother as consumer in a sense purifies economic exchange by imbuing commodities with sentiment" (Cook, 2004: 64). Bubble Book ads like the one described above were similarly aimed at mothers as the "middle term" in the chain of family consumption, but implied that the phonograph could "cut out the middleman" between oral tradition and the child; the middleman being the mother, who was reminded of her parental responsibilities even as her role was threatened. Bubble Book ads thus took part in a larger tendency of advertising copy of this era to address feelings of regret at the loss of earlier traditions, and to offer consumer goods as a means of assuaging anxieties about the passage to a culture of mass consumption. Such ads suggested that the modern consumer could simultaneously enjoy both the modern and the traditional via the product, and so, in Roland Marchand's words, civilization could be "redeemed" (Marchand, 1985: 223–4).

Bubble Book ads claiming that traditional characters like "Tom the piper's son" wanted to speak directly to children may have made their media products more "innocuous to parents," but that rhetoric also reveals some of the underlying anxieties that parents were feeling concerning their children's consumption of mass produced media. It was of course, the record companies and Harper & Brothers, not "Tom the piper's son," who were looking for new ways to speak directly to children. Bubble Book marketers explored several avenues for such a direct link to the child audience, one of which was through the use of radio.

Bubble Book broadcasting

Phonograph retailers were urged to start a Bubble Book Hour both on local radio stations and in their stores. A 1923 *Talking Machine World* ad declared that "children love to hear their favorite nursery rhymes and games. And the radio 'powers that be' know that the best way to interest parents in their radio is to please children. That's why the songs and stories of the Bubble Books are broadcast from every radio station."[20] In another ad, Harper & Brothers wrote that "more than 1,000 letters are being received every week by us as a result of the broadcasting by radio of the Bubble Books."[21] Retailers were also urged to play the records in their stores at a regularly scheduled time: "Announce the fact that one afternoon a week... you will give a recital of the 'books that sing.' Such a weekly event will draw to your store the parents as well as the children. You can see how a Bubble Book Hour will stimulate sales in all other departments of your store."[22] It is hard to know how many retailers engaged in either form of "broadcasting," but the *New York Times* radio programming schedule indicates that station WJZ in Newark, New Jersey regularly featured "The Bubble Book That Sings" at 6:30 p.m. in 1922 ("Today's Radio Program," 1922: 32); while the *Christian Science Monitor* listed "Bubble Book Stories" at 6 p.m. on New York station WJY in 1923 ("Events Tonight," 1923: 2).

Another form of Bubble Book "broadcasting" involved promotional parties held in department stores across America. *Printer's Ink* noted that, "so remarkably have the Bubble Books fitted into the life of the children of America that Bubble Book parties have now become quite the rage in the tiny tots' social world" (Rhodes, 1921, p. 25). I have found evidence of such events taking place in 1921 and 1922 in Wisconsin, Iowa, Indiana, New York, New Hampshire, Texas, Massachusetts, California and Connecticut. The *Appleton [Wisconsin] Post-Crescent* reported in 1921 on a "Tippy Toe Bubble Book" party at the Appleton Theatre that featured games, pantomime, elaborate scenery and costumes, and appearances on stage by Mother Goose, characters from the Bubble Books, and "many little girls from Appleton."[23] Bubble Book parties were well-suited to a contemporary marketing scene in which department stores in major American cities were establishing year-round toy departments that were "not simply selling spaces but fantasy places, juvenile dream worlds" (Leach, 1993: 87). William Leach notes that strategies for enticing children to such spaces included parades and "little fairy-tale playlets for children in makeshift theaters in toy departments or in store auditoriums" (Leach, 1993: 330). Similarly, Miriam Formanek-Brunell describes how doll retailers and manufacturers sponsored dolls' tea parties, doll carriage contests, and parades in department stores during the 1910s and 1920s (Formanek-Brunell, 1993: 161, 178).

Bubble Book parties should be added to historical accounts of toy departments as spaces of both marketing and spectacle, but they also stand as precursors to marketing techniques later made famous by Walt Disney. Disney connected his animated creations to the spaces and experiences of shopping. Mickey Mouse became a "fixture in department stores across the country" after Disney sold the licensing rights for "Mickey" merchandise in 1929 (deCordova, 1994: 204–5). The Mickey Mouse Club, whose members numbered one million by 1932, also took part in "collective rituals" with child peer-groups in addition to cinemagoing: children saluted the American flag, joined in community singing, and took part in activities such as "picnics, competitions, prizes and fund-raising" (Staples, 1997: 51). Bubble Book marketing explored similar kinds of collective rituals in department stores across the country.

Conclusion

The comparison with Disney can allow us to return to the question posed at the beginning of this chapter: why is it that some children's media become more controversial than others? In the case of the Bubble Book marketing campaign, we find that common triggers of adult anxiety about children's media were avoided or defused.[24] The Bubble Books' "authentic" nursery rhymes were clearly age-appropriate and represented a traditional form of middle-class children's culture;

phonograph records were safely consumed in the home, under the aegis of parental supervision; the small-scale 5½-inch format of the Bubble Books and children's toy phonograph players would not be confused with larger adult records and Victrolas; unlike the radio, parents had control over media content brought into the home; and finally, fears about children's passive media consumption were averted since children arguably took an active role in the playing of records on their own phonograph players, as well as in activities associated with the Bubble Books such as play with cut-out dolls, records made to accompany dances and games, and local Bubble Book parties.

The fact that Bubble Books managed to sidestep many familiar criticisms of children's media allowed them to be marketed across various platforms and without significant controversy. Jacobson claims that early-twentieth-century children's advertisers were able to avoid organized opposition by aligning themselves with the "very institutions of early-twentieth-century childhood that sought to sequester childhood as a wholesome, play-centered stage of life": they secured the cooperation of the public schools; romanced the "companionate family"; and associated their products with "children's developmental needs and mothers' quests for more leisure" (Jacobson 2004: 55). The marketing strategies used by the record industry followed a similar pattern with similar results, enabling records such as the Bubble Books to proliferate in middle-class homes, schools, on the radio, and in department stores without major opposition.

Though they certainly did not match Mickey Mouse in terms of cultural impact, the Bubble Books were a significant part of pre-World War II children's media culture. The phonograph has a unique position in the history of the cultural industries, as the first form of pre-recorded media entertainment consumed in the home. The phonograph industry has, until recently however, received scant attention from scholars in the fields of Media and Cultural Studies. Nonetheless, the market in children's records trail-blazed by the Bubble Books exploded in the 1940s, and helped to fuel a postwar resurgence in the phonograph industry. The market for children's phonograph records – pioneered by the Bubble Books – has thus had a significant and enduring impact on American cultural life. Though the "books that sing" came to be overshadowed on the American children's market by film and later television, they still have much to tell us about the emergence of children's media, and techniques of marketing to parents and children at a pivotal time in the history of consumer culture. The Bubble Books and their surrounding commercial discourse provide an early example of media texts offered to mother and child, and the complex and multiple appeals, desires, and anxieties that such an enterprise entailed.

Notes

1. The Bubble Books were inducted into the Library of Congress' National Recording Registry in 2003 on the grounds of being the first book and record hybrid. See http://www.loc.gov/exhibits/treasures/trr150.html
2. This advertisement is part of the RCA-Victor holdings at the Camden County Historical Society library, Camden, New Jersey.
3. An earlier series of 5 ½-inch records called "Little Wonder" records were an important part of the industrial back-story to the Bubble Books, but since they did not feature material expressly intended for children, I have not included them in the discussion here. For more information, the best source is: http://www.littlewonderrecords.com/little-wonder-history.html
4. This ad can be seen here: http://www.littlewonderrecords.com/Advertisement%20BB%20Harpers%20Mag%20Adv%206-20.jpg
5. For a complete discography of the Bubble Books, see http://www.littlewonderrecords.com/bubble-book-discography.html. Another wonderful resource for children's records, primarily from the period between the 1930s and 1950s, is Peter Muldavin's http://www.kiddierekordking.com/index.html
6. *Talking Machine World*, August 15, 1923, p. 57.
7. *Talking Machine World*, May 15, 1921, p. 63. Similarly, the Victor Company's journal, *The Voice of the Victor*, wrote in October 1924 that children were "valuable missionaries for the Victrola in thousands of homes, where the needs and desires of the children take precedence over all else" ("There's a School in Every Town," 1924, p. 6).
8. *Talking Machine World*, May 15, 1922, p. 134.
9. *Talking Machine World*, June 15, 1919, p. 153.
10. *Talking Machine World*, September 15, 1920, p. 14.
11. For an insightful comprehensive overview, see Jacobson 2008.
12. *Talking Machine World*, April 15, 1924, p. 19.
13. *Ladies' Home Journal*, November 1919, p. 105.
14. Advertisements found online at http://www.littlewonderrecords.com/cutout-bubble-book.html.
15. *Ladies' Home Journal*, November 1919, p. 105.
16. *Ladies' Home Journal*, November 1919, p. 105.
17. *Atlantic Monthly*, October 1920, p. 24.
18. *St. Nicholas*, December 1920, viewed at http://www.littlewonderrecords.com/advertisements.html
19. *Ladies' Home Journal*, November 1918, p. 48.
20. *Talking Machine World*, viewed at http://www.littlewonderrecords.com/advertisements.html
21. *Talking Machine World*, April 15, 1923, viewed at http://www.littlewonderrecords.com/advertisements.html
22. *Talking Machine World*, May 15, 1923, p. 157.
23. *Appleton [Wisconsin] Post-Crescent* (1921), November 7, p. 12.
24. For a useful overview of concerns about children's media, see Bruce, 2008.

References

Books for Children (1920) *The Bookseller, Newsdealer and Stationer*, November 15, p. 477.

Children's Records For Home and School" (1920) *The Voice of the Victor*, vol. 15, no. 3, March, p. 49.

Events Tonight (1923) *Christian Science Monitor*, July 28, p. 2.

New Victor Booklet (1907) *The Voice of the Victor*, vol. 2, no. 1, January, p. 9.

The Bubble Books (1920) *Sound Box*, June, p. 127.

The Edison Phonograph as a Christmas Present (1907) *McClure's Magazine*, November, p. 39.

There's a School in Every Town (1924) *The Voice of the Victor*, vol, 19, no. 10, October, p. 6.

Today's Radio Program (1922) *New York Times*, April 2, p. 32.

Victor Bubble Books Open New Market (1924) *The Voice of Victor*, September, p. 13.

Bruce, A. (2008) 'Children's Media Consumption and Struggles for Cultural Authority in the Nineteenth and Twentieth Centuries,' in Jacobson, Lisa ed. *Children and Consumer Culture in American Society*. Westport, Connecticut: Praeger.

Cook, D. (2004) *The Commodification of Childhood*. Durham and London: Duke University Press.

deCordova, R. (1994) 'The Mickey in Macy's Window,' in Smoodin, Eric ed. *Disney Discourse*. New York: Routledge.

Formanek-Brunell, M. (1993) *Made to Play House*. Baltimore and London: John Hopkins University Press.

Garvey, E. Gruber (1996) *The Adman in the Parlor*. New York: Oxford University Press.

Jacobson, L. (2004) *Raising Consumers*. New York: Columbia University Press.

Kline, S. (1993) *Out of the Garden*. London: Verso.

Leach, W. (1993) *Land of Desire*. New York: Vintage Books.

Marchand, R. (1985) *Advertising the American Dream*. Berkeley: University of California Press.

Pecora, N. O. (1998) *The Business of Children's Entertainment*. New York: The Guilford Press.

Rhodes, R.M. (1921) 'New Fields Opened By Appealing to Children,' in *Printers' Ink Monthly*. Vol. III, No. 1, June, pp. 23–25.

Sammond, N. (2005) *Babes in Tomorrowland*. Durham: Duke University Press.

Schor, J. B. (2005) *Born to Buy*. New York: Scribner.

Seiter, E. (1995) *Sold Separately*. New Brunswick: Rutgers University Press.

Staples, T. (1997) *All Pals Together*. Edinburgh: Edinburgh University Press.

Wood, G. (2002) *Edison's Eve*. New York: Alfred A. Knopf.

Part II

Theory and Method in Research on Children's Consumption

4
Commercial Enculturation: Moving Beyond Consumer Socialization[1]

Daniel Thomas Cook

The scholarly attention paid to children's commercial lives and the consumer culture of childhood in recent years belies some of the slippages and disjunctions that remain between the fields of childhood studies and consumer studies. On the one hand, as I have argued elsewhere (Cook 2004b, 2008), those writing in and for a specifically "childhood studies" audience tend to ignore or marginalize the material and commercial aspects of children's existence, with some notable exceptions (e.g. Zelizer 2002; Marsh 2005). This indifference occurs perhaps because the hallmark of childhood studies – the active, agentive child – is also central to marketers', advertisers' and retailers' constructions of the child consumer. This coincidence of similarly imagined children does not fit well with the liberatory posture and agenda of many in childhood studies: the knowing, meaning-making child resembles rather too closely the marketer's dream. On the other hand, a good deal of mainstream social–cultural "consumption theory" and studies of consumer society either ignore children and childhood completely or see children as appendages or adjuncts to the central claims, preoccupations and problems of this field of study (Cook 2008).

The research and writing coming out in the last fifteen years or so that takes children's consumer lives and culture as its central focus has in many ways taken up the challenge of childhood studies. Many researchers recognize children as meaning-making beings in the here and now, account for children's active participation in the world of goods and are vigilant about conceptualizing children in non-derivative terms (Seiter 1993, 1999; Buckingham 2000; Chin 2001; Zelizer 2002; Pugh 2009). Yet there remains at least one key area of children's consumer studies that continues to draw upon conceptions of children and childhood which are out of sync with the understandings and challenges posed by childhood studies theory. The notion of consumer socialization, as it has arisen and is often used, fits awkwardly with the emerging formulation of an active, knowing child consumer.

In this chapter, I offer an alternative notion to commonly held understandings of children's consumer socialization (Ward 1974; John 1999; see Ekström 2006), which I call "commercial enculturation".[2] It is a notion that dovetails not only with the worldview advocated by childhood studies proponents, but also with the contemporary and emerging experiences and contexts of parents and children living in the consumer cultures of wealthy nations. The discussion in this chapter offers a critique of the concept of consumer socialization by addressing its assumptions and use in consumer behaviour research and literature, concentrating on how it posits a view of "the child" that conflicts with that developed in childhood studies. I argue that consumer socialization, as it is understood and used in research, presents not only a particular and particularly narrow view of "the child" and "development" as they pertain to consumption activities, but also a similarly narrow and specific view of what constitutes "market" or "economic" behaviour and action, and thus what constitutes "consumption".

Consumer socialization

Scott Ward first named and defined the phenomenon of consumer socialization in 1974 as "[the] processes by which young people acquire skills, knowledge, and attitudes relevant to their functioning as consumers in the marketplace" (p. 2). The usefulness of studying consumer socialization is manifold for Ward. He suggests that such study may help marketers be more efficient in targeting young people, assist in understanding which attitudes and behaviour are transmitted across generations, shed light on how early childhood learning affects later consumption and extend stage theories of cognitive development (pp. 1–2).

Implicit in general psychology's concept of socialization is the assumption of "the child" as moving from an unknowing to a knowing being, whose abilities demonstrate a concomitant change from simple to high-level information processing. Psychologists attached to this Piagetian view understand development as occurring along an essentially unidirectional, linear trajectory (Greene 2006; Hogan 2005). At each level or stage of development there are thought to be abilities and competencies that the child should demonstrate in a more or less defined sequence and timing in order to be thought to be developing in an "appropriate" manner.

Cognitive psychology has endured many critiques over recent decades, many of which have stemmed from those seeking to build the study of children and childhood from a different foundation than developmental stages. In essence, the critique centres on how general psychology understands the "child" as a passive being, subject in large part to natural growth, who is brought along through the developmental process with little effort of its own. This "child" is conceived of as a pre-social being who acquires cognitive capacities which are then enacted in social worlds (Jenks 1996; Christensen and Prout 2005). The endpoint of this development is adulthood, conceptualized as a static, universalized version of rationality (James and Prout 1991); childhood is thus seen as an apprenticeship phase, and children as the apprentices to the expert adults and their world. The child, in this view, does not have an ontology in its own right and has no volition that matters. As Chris Jenks aptly puts the matter: "[childhood] is conceptualized as a structured becoming, not a social practice nor as a location for the Self" (1996, p. 12). There is evidence that, in some quarters of psychology, movement is afoot to find rapprochement between psychological insights and sociological and anthropological perspectives (Hogan 2005; Greene 2006).

However, work conducted under the rubric of consumer socialization remains virtually untouched by the understandings put forth by childhood studies scholars – that is, that children need to be understood as actors in their own right who make meaning and encounter the world on their own terms, rather than as derivative of and incomplete in comparison to adults. It is the underlying conception of the incomplete child which has set the parameters for the bulk of the work in consumer socialization. Research and writing in this vein, consequently, evinces this very same tendency toward normative understandings as cognitive psychology concerning how children come to know about and behave toward market transactions, commercial settings and consumer objects. In addition, consumer socialization theory and research rests on normative assumptions about social practices which are beyond the scope of cognitive psychology proper.

Deborah Roedder John's (1999) substantial twenty-five year retrospective review of consumer socialization research can be seen as representative of the central worldview presumed in consumer socialization thinking, and provides an opportunity to examine its claims in some depth and detail. John states her purpose as creating a *"unified story* of the way consumer socialization proceeds as children mature throughout childhood and adolescence" (p. 183, emphasis added). It is clear at the outset that John feels that the various studies from the previous quarter century sufficiently address the same phenomenon in comparable ways such that they can be pulled together into a singular narrative.

The narrative of cognitive development serves to cohere different studies of consumer socialization into something of a singular statement, whereby the focus is placed on ascertaining age-related "improvements" in cognitive ability and social development (p. 183). John presents her own organization of the research in an effort to form a kind of über-theory that marries developmentalism and consumer behaviour: "We propose that consumer socialization... be viewed as a developmental process that proceeds through a series of stages as children mature into adult consumers. Integrating the stage theories of cognitive and social development... a clear picture emerges of the changes that take place as children become socialized into their roles as consumers" (p. 186). In the process, John reinforces and reinscribes the epistemology of linear human development whereby the child initially exists in some presocial space, separated from the social world – including the world of consumption – and is subsequently brought into "the consumer role". The occupation of this role is not complete until adulthood, when it is posited that one "matures" into it.

John proposes three stages of consumer socialization tied to age, which admittedly overlap with Piaget's. There is the perceptual stage, ages 3–7, where there is a surface-level focus on a single dimension or attribute (p. 187). In the analytic stage, ages 7–11, the child shifts from perceptual to symbolic thought and is "more flexible" and "more adaptive" in making decisions (p. 187). Children in this stage demonstrate a more sophisticated understanding by focusing on underlying dimensions of a product or commercial. In the reflective stage, ages 11–16, "knowledge about marketplace concepts such as branding and pricing becomes even more nuanced and more complex as children develop more sophisticated information processing and social skill" (p. 187). This stage is characterized by a shift in the degree, rather than the kind, of knowledge processing.

Throughout John's discussion of past research and her organization of it into her own stages, the spectre of the normative "good" or "mature" consumer casts its shadow, as will be discussed below. In addition, working assumptions, either by John or the researchers she reviews, come to the fore. For instance, she posits that it is not until the analytical stage that children can comprehend the "true differences" between advertising, selling intent and programming (p. 188). Here, the received understanding resides in the unexamined idea that commercials intend to "persuade" while programmes seek to "entertain", a view which rests on top of the developmental assumption. The view of what constitutes correct, "true differences" between commercials and programming arises from the researcher and from the adult world. In a child's world, many television programmes can and indeed do function to capture audiences and sell associated merchandise (Banet-Weiser 2007; CSPI 2003). However, the child's view is not considered because the child is not seen as an active, meaning-making being.

John interlaces normative statements about the form, content and direction of consumer knowledge throughout her review. She writes of the attributes of "mature" decision makers (p. 197) and discusses the "best", "most adaptive" and "most important" skills and strategies against which the younger, immature or less mature child is measured (p. 199). A chart that summarizes her findings (p. 204) contains phrasing which indicates the teleology of the paradigm she adopts and adapts: for instance, a *limited* vs. *increasing* brand awareness from the perceptual to the analytic stage; an *emerging* vs. *fully developed* understanding of value from the analytic to the reflective stage; a *full repertoire* of strategies characterizes those in the analytic stage; and older children exhibit a *sophisticated* understanding of consumption symbolism (emphasis added).

Researchers who continue to write about consumer socialization tend to remain in the epistemological tradition and nomenclature of cognitive, developmental psychology (see Lunt and Furnham 1996). The role of parents, media exposure, peers and consumer experiences generally (such as shopping) are now being acknowledged as factors which modify, in some measure, the essentially hard-wired cognitive processes (Dotson and Hyatt 2005; see Ekström 2006). Furthermore, some are examining how culture – often conceptualized as national or ethnic culture – plays into the timing of acquisition and content of consumer knowledge (see McNeal *et al.* 1993; Lunt and Furnham 1996). It must be noted, however, that despite these attempts to offer social and cultural context to the developmental process, normative and teleological assumptions continue to dominate the overall conceptualization of the phenomenon.

The 'good' consumer

There is no doubt that changes take place in children's knowledge of and understanding about consumer goods, meanings and processes over the early life course. It would make no experiential or analytical sense to think otherwise. The issue here is how scholars imagine and characterize these changes and their mutability or immutability.

Critiques of socialization theory (Jenks 1996, James and Prout 1991, James, Jenks and Prout 1998) make clear that it offers no serious consideration of the child's ontology, experience and volition, which are summarily dismissed as epiphenomenal to the onward march of development. Social processes such as a child's experience (Dotson and Hyatt 2005) or parental involvement and "communication" (Mochis *et al.* 1984; Carlson and Grossbart 1988; Carlson *et al.* 1992; see also Ekström 2006: 76–7) are sequestered to a subordinate, minimally influential role regarding what and how children learn about consumption and consumer life. The guiding presumption remains that of an asocial process; the impact of cultural or social factors lies outside the basic conceptual structure.

These concerns and critiques apply to socialization theory generally. When attention turns specifically to consumer socialization, another set of issues arises. The assumption of a competent, mature consumer – often explicit in consumer socialization research – serves as a model not only for the antithesis of childhood (that is, adulthood), but also for what it means to be a "good consumer", and thus speaks to assumptions about the nature, boundaries and exigencies of consumer culture itself. That is, consumer socialization theory posits right and wrong, good and bad consumption practices as part of its construction of the endpoint of the development process.

A "fully socialized" adult is a savvy consumer, who seems, according to John (1999: 196), to have the acumen of a trained economist:

> Perhaps the reason children pay little attention to pricing is that they have relatively undeveloped notions about how prices reflect the valuation of goods and services. Adults, for example, see prices as a reflection of the utility or function of the item to the consumer, the costs of inputs incurred by the manufacturer to make the item, and the relative scarcity of the item in the marketplace.

In this line of thinking, there are better ways to consume and to think about consuming, which are determined by logical, rational consideration rather than, say, local understandings, practices, relationships and meanings. Consumer socialization theory, in the main, thus enjoins neoclassical economic theory by assuming and positioning an economically rational adult as the ideal actor and the desirable endpoint of the maturation process (Cook 2008). When scholars write of children becoming "better shoppers" as they get older (Reece and Kinnear 1986), acquiring consumption "skills" and "knowledge" (Ward 1974; John 1999) or gaining the ability to "function effectively" as consumers (Pliner *et al.*1996), they are wittingly or unwittingly accepting and deploying particular understandings of human motivation and nature based on a belief in economic rationality – a view critiqued and contested by many (England 1993; Carrier 1997; Slater and Tonkiss 2001; Zelizer 2005).

Commercial enculturation

Consumer socialization scholarship arises mainly from those interested in "consumer behaviour", rather than consumer culture, hence the alliance with developmental, cognitive psychology as opposed to sociology or perhaps anthropology. Nevertheless, the term is often used by socially and culturally oriented researchers, apparently often without consideration of the ensuing conceptual and ideological ramifications of the concept. It is often simply deployed as a substitute for consumer "learning".

The concept – and the normative, teleological and behavioural assumptions upon which it relies – does not speak to the multiplicity of childhoods, economic circumstances or ways of behaving as a consumer. It reflects a modernist view of childhood, placing growth and development on a single, inevitable trajectory whereby the child moves from an unknowing to a knowing and from a simple to a complex being. No space is made for the child's various understandings of her place in the social-commercial world. Parental involvement, peer relations or the activities of marketers become relegated as "externalities" to the essentialized child and the inexorable developmental process.

Karin Ekström's (2006) recent discussion of consumer socialization strikes some similar chords as she argues that consumer behaviour scholars should widen the scope of inquiry beyond developmentalism by adopting social-cultural, interpretive approaches to studying consumption. Her calls for pluralism in method and approach strike me as astute and useful interventions into the remaining vestiges of a dominant paradigm. However, Ekström takes the matter to the brink but not into the place I think required in order to break from the multiply intertwined assumptions that form the basis of the concept of *socialization*. It is a concept I see as beyond rehabilitation in large part because its foundational assumptions cannot be divorced from its construction of the "child" as a secondary, derivative manifestation of overarching, inexorable processes. Analytically, I find it necessary not to revisit consumer socialization, but to move beyond it.

I propose the concept of "commercial enculturation" as a means to capture and emphasize the variety of ways in which children come to "know" and participate in commercial life. The term demands no *de facto* static endpoint where a child becomes a "complete" consumer (adult) and it does not require an *a priori* definition of the boundaries and behavioural dimensions of "consumption" and market activity. Commercial enculturation, rather, places attention on the *culture* in "consumer culture" as multiple, layered and overlapping webs of meaning which precede any individual child. It assumes that consumption and meaning, and thus culture, cannot be separated from each other but arise together through social contexts and processes of parenting and socializing with others. Children, in this view, are not so much socialized into becoming one specific kind of consumer as they are seen as entering into social relationships with and through goods and their associations. This is a variable process that is not necessarily linear or temporally determined, but socially and culturally embedded in under-standings of childhood, adulthood and market relations.

The concept has the advantage of breaking from the assumptions of consumer socialization while at the same time acknowledging and accounting for changes that occur over the early life course in children's relationship to the world of goods. The term "enculturation" highlights the notion that engaging with goods, advertisements, brands and packaging – as well as with parents, peers, siblings and others – entails encountering and dealing with a variety of meanings which do not live in abstract space, but which are found in and experienced through social relations. It does not imply that every child comes to know and relate to consumer life in the same way or along the same path.

The term differs from Lisa Penaloza's idea of "consumer accultura-tion" (1994) which speaks to the varied experiences and practices of consumers who are ethnically different from the mainstream society in which they are living. Acculturation works transitively between "host" and "newcomers", in this case Mexican immigrants, rather than simply assuming a one-way assimilation of immigrants. Penaloza and Gilly (1999) take the concept further to examine how marketers serve as influential agents between immigrants and commercial institutions and practices, whereby a variety of adaptation strategies and outcomes are possible, depending on a range of factors (p. 93).

The notion of commercial enculturation addresses "culture" more broadly, as the practices and relations which form and transact meaning in social life. These can and do include ethnic and national cultures as well as those encountered in specific localities and regions, in specific social classes and through gender and its expressions. The larger "culture" at issue here is "consumer culture" – itself not monolithic in content, scope or effect (Slater 1997). I concur with the line of scholarship that recognizes consumer culture as something socially and historically identifiable and distinct and which is variable and is experienced in different ways (Campbell 1987; Miller 1987; Slater 1997;). Commercial enculturation calls attention to the way in which market-consumer life involves the handling and negotiation of meanings arising from different quarters; it also brings into relief the idea that people's encounters with and learning of these meanings and this consumer culture are themselves culturally variable and informed.

Rethinking the boundaries and contexts of 'consumption'

The concept of commercial enculturation therefore recognizes the varied ways in which children and adults encounter the goods, meanings and social relations associated with what is known as "consumption". From the perspective advocated here, the beginnings of a child's involvement in consumer culture can extend from the moment of birth and indeed prior to this. Marketers as well as mothers and loved ones imagine children into being in part by imagining the kinds of consumer goods she or he will have and will want (Layne 2000; Clarke 2004;). Children born into the contemporary consumer cultures of wealthy nations of the Global North often enter into somewhat ready-made identities awaiting them in the form of clothing, room decorations, food and media-educational devices. "Consumption" – as in purchasing – may not be carried out by the neonate of course, but these acts and goods form part of the context through which a child enters social worlds. In the context of family, siblings and, later, peers, children form and re-form meanings about the material-commercial world in ways that emplace products in social relations and social relations in products (Clarke 2004).

Attending to the variable processes of enculturation, as opposed to the single process of socialization, helps problematize the boundaries, contexts and exigencies of "consumer behaviour" as well as the ways in which children come to know and understand the commercial-consumer world. In consumer socialization theory, consumption and the consumer role have fairly limited domains of action often tied to knowledge of specifically "market" actions and transactions, brands and products (see Ekström 2006: 73–6). Positing "the market" as a distinctive sphere in social life defines anything that is not technically a purchase as outside the realm of consideration. For those ensconced in the cognitive psychology-consumer socialization paradigm, a television commercial is considered part of the market but not the watching of the cartoon show and the television network on which it is shown; in this view, buying or requesting to have purchased a breakfast cereal is a form of market behaviour, but desiring it in the first place is not; and receiving an electronic game for one's birthday clearly ties in with commercial life, but playing with it and fighting over it with friends and siblings does not.

The perspective put forward here understands "consumption" more broadly, beyond the acts of purchasing things. Consumption, as I have written elsewhere (Cook 2006), involves the knowing of and desiring of goods, as well as their purchase; the viewing and touching of things as much as their ownership. One often consumes something visually without ever taking physical possession of it; indeed a key element of branding is to effect such consumption so as forge positive, affective relationships between a person and a symbol.

Consumer socialization research brings its own categories – not only "adult" categories, but historically embedded, class- and race-based categories (see below) – to bear upon the study of children. Asking, for instance, about the extent to which children understand the difference between a commercial and program or the "true" intent of advertising, as is standard practice (see John 1999: 187–9), inscribes these differences as given, stable, true and relevant. Yet programming on television and feature content in print may not be as distinct from "advertising" in children's experiences or in marketing intent, as when for instance a good deal of programming made for children serves as a vehicle for generating merchandise sales and cross-promotions.

The cross-promotion of goods in various media and sites and web platforms renders almost moot the typical concerns of consumer socialization about the extent and timing to which children come to know "the persuasive intent" of an advertisement. The question itself arises out of the multiple presumptions upon which consumer socialization relies; namely that "persuasive intent" lies in the content of identifiable advertisements. When one takes a larger, cultural view not only of the means by which children engage in and with the world, but also of how that "world" is now constituted, one comes away with different sorts of questions not anticipated by consumer socialization. For instance, one may rightfully ask: What is the persuasive intent of a website? or of a video game? or of a toy or t-shirt or greeting card? What is the persuasive intent of a film? a hamburger? a "kid-ified" container for milk? the colour of a drink? Each product mentioned here might be seen to "advertise" but is not itself an advertisement. Such questions can only be asked, addressed and engaged with when one sheds the language of socialization, and the associated views of "the consumer" as a model of an integrated, adult person (Qvortrup 1987), and of "consumption" as a superficially economic act.

Diverse forms of enculturation

The concept of commercial enculturation thus accounts for the contexts, lives and perspectives of children, eschewing not only the linear trajectory posited by consumer socialization but also its cultural, racial, class and ethnic biases and presumptions. John (1999: 189), for instance, unfortunately and uncritically repeats the language and underlying assumptions from research that finds children from lower income and black families "exhibit lower levels of understanding of advertising's persuasive intent" and are found to be "less discerning" about the truthfulness of television commercials. The incomplete comparisons (lower than who? less than who?) here highlight the extent to which the normative standard of "correct" growth and socialization is based not simply on the psychological development of "children," in the generic, but on a conceptual model of the white, middle-class child who stands as an ideal.

Adopting the stance of commercial enculturation turns attention away from inquiring whether or not children acquire the correct or proper skills and knowledge in the correct or proper order and toward investigating the *kinds* of knowledge, skill and dispositions children adopt by virtue of their social memberships. Elizabeth Chin's (2001) work with poor, African-American children demonstrates how their appropriation of consumer goods and their understandings articulate both with the specificity of their economic, spatial and familial circumstances, as well as with larger, shared meanings concerning the status of certain goods, the colour of their skin, their position as children, and the relations between these things. *What* these children learned about consumption arose through their experiences in their worlds and cannot be divorced from *how* they learned about goods, consuming and social relations.

With a posture and perspective open to plural childhoods and multiple understandings of consumption, the lived, socially embedded experiences of consumption and material life come to the fore, allowing for varied understandings about how children encounter the "commercial world". Allison Pugh (2009) offers insightful, detailed description and analysis of how gender, age, class and race/ethnicity infuse the social exchange of goods and meanings among children in a diverse, Oakland, California area. The knowledge or ignorance about products and their possession or non-possession figured in children's, and sometimes parents', understandings about and ability to negotiate social membership and feelings of social belonging. The "knowledge" of the children, for both Chin and Pugh, is not to be measured by an *a priori* normative standard supposedly applicable to all children; rather, the focus is on how forms of knowledge enact and inform social practice.

Commercial enculturation draws attention to the dialogic character of consumption and consumer culture, as Ekström (2006) points out, and moves away from assumptions of a simple, one-way movement of influence from knowing adults to unknowing children. As Prout and James (1991: 16) put it: "if children are competent interpreters of the social work they do and if they, in fact, possess a separate culture, then the study of adult–child interaction is no longer a process of socialization but of cultural assimilation and of meaningful social interaction, not simply passive reaction or receipt". Children do not unproblematically become assimilated to the consumer culture they experience. Rather, they sift through and handle the various meanings and associations of commerce and media in the contexts of their lives and circumstances (see in addition to the above, Marsh 2005; Seiter 1993, 1999; Dyson 1997; Buckingham 2000; Willett 2008;) and regularly introduce goods and media to their parents and households (McNeal 1999; Sutherland and Thompson 2001; Coffey *et al.* 2006;).

Acknowledging and attending to the active, knowing child enhances rather than diminishes the place and role of other actors like parents, teachers, peers and marketers. The enculturation perspective does not presume a pre-given, virtually immutable direction, content and sequence of learning about and engaging with consumer culture. Nor does it pretend that the world is a blank slate on which children simply write their own consumer destinies. Born into and required to engage with ongoing social, economic and cultural practices and institutions, children forge understandings and meanings with the materials they have at hand, and they do so in concert with, in opposition to or in the presence of others. It makes little analytic or practical sense to begin from a position of positing an individuated, encapsulated child if only because parents, mothers especially, remain inextricably bound up in their children's material lives (Clarke 2004; Martens *et al.* 2004; Coffey *et al.* Siegel and Livingston 2006; Cook 2008)

Learning to consume, as Lydia Martens (2005) argues, takes place as much outside of specifically "market" sites as it does in the store or in front of the television. Parental networks, child peer associations, the geography of the local neighbourhood, among other things, all contribute to how children come to know about and negotiate their ways through various commercial worlds. These must be accounted for in terms of the variable and multiple kinds of consumer knowledge that become active and useful in their lived experiences.

Indeed, commercial agents and interests often work in tandem with parents and children, blending sometimes seamlessly into the practices of everyday life. Research I conducted with mothers about how they think about and prepare birthday parties for their young children offers a case in point. It reveals a wide context of knowledge and involvement of the child and mother, as well as the assistance of store workers. In one interview, a thirty-two year old mother of two, Leeann, related how she engaged her three-year-old in the preparations for her fourth birthday:

> The birthday was at the very end of July. And so in June we sort of starting prepping her for her birthday, if you will, what did she want, what kind of cake did she want, what kinds of things did she want.
>
> She came with me to the bakery and the lady sat with her at the table and said "What kind of cake do you want?" Of course, the chocolate. "What kind of filling do you want?" "Chocolate." She wanted to be very involved in the whole process. She filled the piñata, they picked out the candy they wanted...

Here, Leeann encourages her daughter to take social ownership of aspects of her birthday party. The girl's desires and choices are affirmed and given space for expression in what Annette Lareau (2003) has identified as a strongly middle-class form of parenting. Through active, practical engagement with the child, the lady at the bakery helps complete an arc of a circuit which connects mother, child and commercial culture together with a ritual that will involve family and peers.

Concluding remarks

When researchers start from children's subject and object positions in the world and attempt to see and understand the world from their perspectives, they are situated in a way that does not presuppose the world merely as it is given to children but that attends to how children take and make parts of that world. The consumer socialization perspective,

I have argued, should be left aside along with its strong presumptions of linear development and immutable sequential learning. This is not to say that all insights arising from this research tradition are wrong or not useful; indeed, much can be mined from studies conducted over the last three decades. It is to say, however, that theory and research focusing on children and consumer life needs to integrate the view of the active, knowing, engaged child when considering how children learn about and make their way though the commercial worlds they encounter. Consumer socialization represents a paradigm tied to a view not only of the passive child, but also of the consumer as a rational (adult) actor (Cook 2008), as well as conceptualizing "consumption" as narrowly defined acts of exchange which take place at identifiable market sites.

Commercial enculturation calls our attention to the multiple trajectories of children's participation in the world of goods and meanings, acknowledges the differences among children and the connections between children and adults, and accounts for change over time without predetermining the specific pathways, timing or direction of change. The focus centres on how "consumption" and "meaning", and thus culture, arise together through social contexts and processes of parenting and socializing with others. What and how children learn about consumption occurs in contexts that are already enmeshed in the consumer world. Hence, it is difficult – in wealthy, media-saturated societies – to pinpoint a "before and after" of involvement in the world of goods and commerce. The perspective offered by commercial enculturation acknowledges the multifaceted, multifarious aspects of commercial life and the active involvement of children in it, without presupposing either the parameters of economic action or the nature and trajectory of children's participation.

Notes

1. A version of this chapter was given at the 3rd Child and Teen Consumption conference in April 2008 at the Norwegian Centre for Child Research in Trondheim.
2. See the kindred concept of "anticipatory enculturation" in Cook and Kaiser, 2004.

References

Banet-Wiser, S. (2007) *Kids Rule! Nickelodeon and Consumer Citizenship.* Durham, NC: Duke University Press.

Buckingham, D. (2000) *After the Death of Childhood: Growing Up in the Age of Electronic Media*. Malden, MA: Blackwell.

Campbell, C. (1987) *The Romantic Ethic and the Spirit of Modern Consumerism*. Oxford: Basil Blackwell.

Carlson, L. and S. Grossbart, (1988) "Parental Style and Consumer Socialization of Children", *Journal of Consumer Research*, 15: 77–94.

Carlson, L., Grossbart, S. and J. Stuenkel (1992) "The Role of Parental Socialization Types of Differential Family Communication Patterns Regarding Consumption", *Journal of Consumer Psychology*, 1(1): 31–52.

Carrier, M. (1997) *Meanings of the Market*. Oxford: Berg.

Chin, E. (2001) *Purchasing Power*. Minneapolis: University of Minnesota Press.

Christensen, P. and A. Prout, (2005) "Anthropological and Sociological Perspectives on the Study of Children", in S. Greene and D. Hogan (eds) *Researching Children's Experiences*, pp. 42–509. London: Sage.

Clarke, Alison J. (2004) "Maternity and Materiality: Becoming a Mother in Consumer Culture", in J. Taylor, L. Layne and D.. Wozniak (eds) *Consuming Motherhood*, pp. 55–71 . New Brunswick: Rutgers University Press.

Coffey, T., Siegel D. and G. Livingston. (2006) *Marketing to the New Super Consumer: Mom & Kid*. Ithaca, NY: Paramount Market Publishers.

Cook, D. T. (2004a) *The Commodification of Childhood*. Durham: Duke University Press.

Cook, D. T. (2004b) 'Beyond Either/Or', *Journal of Consumer Culture*. 4(2); 147–53.

Cook, D. T. (2006) "Leisure and Consumption", in C. Rojek, S. Shaw and J. Veal (eds) *Handbook of Leisure Studies*, pp. 304–16, Houndmills: Palgrave Macmillan.

Cook, D. T. (2008) "The Missing Child in Consumption Theory", *Journal of Consumer Culture* 8(2): 219–43.

CSPI. (2003) *Pestering Parents: How Food Companies Market Obesity to Children*. Washington DC: Center for Science in the Public Interest.

Dotson, M and E. Hyatt, (2005) "Major Influence Factors in Children's Consumer Socialization", *Journal of Consumer Marketing*. 22(1): 35–42.

Dyson, A. (1997) *Writing Superheroes: Contemporary Childhood, Popular Culture and Classroom Literacy*. NY Teachers College Press.

Ekström, K. (2006) 'Consumer Socialization Revisited', in R. Belk (ed.) *Research in Consumer Behavior*, pp. 71–98. Oxford: Elsevier.

England, P. (1993) "The separative self: andocentric bias in neoclassical assumptions", in M. A. Ferber and J. A. Nelson (eds), *Beyond Economic Man: Feminist Theory and Economics*, pp. 37–53. Cambridge, MA: Harvard University Press.

Greene, S. (2006) "Child Psychology: Taking Account of Children at Last?", *The Irish Journal of Psychology*. 27(1-2): 8–15.

Hogan, D. (2005) "Researching 'the Child' in Developmental Psychology", in S. Greene and D. Hogan (eds) *Researching Children's Experience: Approaches and Methods*, pp. 22–41. London: Sage.

James, A, Jenks, C. and A. Prout (1998) *Theorizing Childhood*. New York: Teachers College.

Jenks, C. (1996) *Childhood*. London: Sage.

John, D. (1999) "Consumer Socialization of Children: A Retrospective Look at 25 Years of Research", *Journal of Consumer Research*, 26: 183–214.

Lareau, A (2003) *Unequal Childhoods*. Berkeley, CA: University of California Press.

Layne, L. (2000) "He was a real baby with baby things": a material culture analysis of personhood, parenthood and pregnancy loss. *Journal of Material Culture*, 5(3): 321–45.

Lunt, P and A. Furnham (eds.) (1996) *Economic Socialization*. Cheltenham: Edward Elgar.

Marsh, J. (ed.) (2005) *Popular Culture, New Media and Digital Literacy in Early Childhood*. London: Routledge Falmer.

Martens, L. (2005) "Learning To Consume – Consuming To Learn; Children at the Interface Between Consumption and Education", *British Journal of Sociology and Education* 26(3): 343–57.

Martens, L., Scott, S. and D. Southerton (2004) "Bringing Children (and Parents) Into the Sociology of Consumption", *Journal of Consumer Culture*, 4(2): 155–82.

McNeal, J.U., V. Viswanathan and C. Yeh (1993) "A Cross-cultural Study of Children's Consumer Socialization in Hong King, New Zealand, Taiwan and the United States", *Asia Pacific Journal of Marketing and Logistics*, 56–69.

McNeal, J. U. (1999) *The Kids' Market: Myths and Realities*. Ithaca, NY: Paramount Market Publishing.

Miller, D. (1987) *Material Culture and Mass Consumption*. London: Blackwell.

Mochis, G, Moore, R, and R. Smith (1984) "The Impact of Family Communication on Adolescent Consumer Socialization", *Advances in Consumer Research*, 11: 314–19.

Penaloza, L. (1994) "*Atravesando Fronteras/Border* Crossings: A Critical Ethnographic Exploration of the Consumer Acculturation of Mexican Immigrants", *Journal of Consumer Research*, 21: 32–54.

Penaloza, L. and M. Gilly (1999) "Marketer Acculturation: The Changer and the Changed", *Journal of Marketing*, 63: 84–104

Pliner, P, Freedman J., Abramovitvch, R and P. Darke (1996) "Children as Consumers: In the Laboratory and Beyond", in P. Lunt and A. Furnham (eds) *Economic Socialization*, pp. 35–46. Cheltenham: Edward Elgar.

Prout, A. and A. James (1991) "A New Paradigm for the Sociology of Childhood? Provenance, Promise and Problems", in A. James and A Prout (eds) *Constructing and Reconstructing Childhood: Contemporary Issues in the Sociological Study of Children*, pp. 7–34. London: Falmer Press.

Pugh, A. (2009) *Longing and Belonging: Parents, Children and Consumer Culture*. Berkeley: University of California Press.

Qvortrup. J. (1987) "Introduction: The Sociology of Childhood", *International Journal of Sociology*, 17(3): 3–37.

Reece, B and T. Kinnear (1986) "Indices of Consumer Socialization Research", *Journal of Retailing*, 62(3): 267–80.

Seiter, E. (1993) *Sold Separately: Parents and Children in Consumer Culture*. New Brunswick, NJ: Rutgers University Press.

Seiter, E. (1999) "Power Rangers at Preschool", in M. Kinder (ed.) *Kids' Media Culture*, pp. 239–62. Durham, NC: Duke University Press

Slater, D. (1997) *Consumer Culture and Modernity*. London: Polity Press.

Slater, D., and F. Tonkiss (2001) *Market Society*. Cambridge: Polity Press.

Sutherland, A. and B. Thompson (2001) *Kidfluence*. Toronto: McGraw-Hill.

Ward, S. (1974) "Consumer Socialization", *Journal of Consumer Research*. 1(1): 1–15.

Willett, R. 2008 "Consumer Citizens Online: Structure, Agency, and Gender in Online Participation", in D. Buckingham (ed.) *Youth, Identity, and Digital Media*, pp. 49–70. Cambridge, MA: MIT Press.

Zelizer, V. (2002) Kids and Commerce', *Childhood*. 9(4): 375–96.

Zelizer, V. (2005) *The Purchase of Intimacy*. Princeton: Princeton University Press.

5
Subjectivities of the Child Consumer: Beings and Becomings

Barbro Johansson

We live in a society where age and life phases are important aspects of the production of subjectivity. The words 'child', 'youth', 'adult' and 'old' not only contain certain associations, but also assign specific positions and duties to the individual. The concept of 'generational order' refers to how people of different life phases are organized in relation to each other and how responsibility and power are distributed among them. A common perspective is to see adults as 'human beings', as responsible, rational, able members of society, while children are seen as 'human becomings', who are undergoing development and education and who are not yet full members of society (Qvortrup 1987, 2005; Alanen 1992; James and Prout 1997). On the other hand, the becoming state implies being on one's way, having potential. Children are often referred to as the future of humanity and as having a special value, since they will be taking over after those who are adults now and will hopefully succeed where the present generation has failed. The commonly used expression 'we should start with the children' reveals a conviction that we need to support children today in order to put things right tomorrow.

However, childhood is not only referred to as a becoming state. There are other discourses through which children stand out as beings. One of these is 'children as Others', according to which children are subjected to the same categorization as, for example, non-white people, the working class or women. The concept of Others relies on the image of a centre and a periphery, where certain groups have interpretative priority and their version of reality dominates. Children are sometimes regarded as Others, as a separate tribe, living their own lives, having their own exotic culture, doing other things and thinking in other ways than 'we' do. This means that children are allocated certain activities, places and identities (James 2005). The effect of this 'othering' process is that children are marginalized and sometimes also romanticized in the same way as the woman and the 'noble savage' were attributed higher moral and more sublime characteristics than the common man. Here, the child stands out as a certain kind of 'being', one representing a particular idea of Childhood. We can also detect this view in advice given to adults to take children as models and to learn to be more playful, live in the 'here and now' and 'find the child in one's heart'.

In the mid-1980s, researchers in childhood studies began to advocate another version of children as beings, claiming that both children and adults are acting subjects here and now, influencing their surroundings and their lives in multiple ways. The message was that children are worth attention and interest for their own sakes, not only for what they will become in the future, and there was an increase in ethnographic research in which children's own voices and opinions were listened to (Qvortrup 1987; Alanen 1992; Thorne 1993; James and Prout 1997). Other factors worked in the same direction. Family and school have gradually been subjected to more and more democratic influences, with children's opinions and cooperation being requested. Since 1990, the Convention on the Rights of the Child, which proclaims children's civic rights, has been ratified by most of the world's states.

However, the process did not stop there. Around the turn of the millennium, researchers started to problematize the notion of 'human beings', claiming that all people, regardless of age, are 'becomings', constantly transforming, developing and changing direction in their lives (Lee 2001; Brembeck *et al.* 2004; Johansson 2005; Prout 2005). Theoretical inspiration came from Latour (1993, 1996) and Deleuze and Guattari (1988), who displaced the interest in entities with an interest in connections and flows. This ontology implies that it is not possible to ascribe certain characteristics to an individual, a thing or an organization. Instead the focus lies on the event (Czarniawska 2004) and how different entities are connected situationally. What determines them are their relations and their possibilities to connect. Entities are engaged in constant becoming (Wenzer 2007). We are not autonomous agents, but we are always, for our agency, dependent on 'extensions' in the shape of other humans, as well as on artefacts, technology and texts (Lee 2001; Latour 1996).

The objective of this chapter is to discuss different consumer subjectivities that Nordic children are exposed to today and their association with the concepts of being and becoming as these are used in childhood research. The chapter is mainly based on a study of children in consumer society which I carried out during 2002, for which I interviewed 84 children aged 8–12 in groups of 2–4.

Being and becoming as events

In this chapter, I will discuss the concepts of being and becoming as compulsory aspects of both children's and adult's lives. I will argue that the concepts of being and becoming need to be understood in different ways, since they have different meanings and since both states might be desirable as well as undesirable, depending on the situation and the definitions which the situation generates. Becoming can be associated with dependence, irresponsibility, being taken care of and powerlessness, as well as change, development and orientation towards the future. Being can be associated with independence, responsibility and capability, but also with the capacity of living here and now. Being and becoming must both be understood as constantly flowing states, being actually or potentially present in every situation.

Children, like adults, are thus always potentially beings and becomings. In children's upbringing, parents switch between treating their children as beings and as becomings, while the latter switch between performing as beings and performing as becomings. For instance, parents can give money to their children, thus treating them as competent beings, capable of handling their own money, but at the same time the parents might expect their children to save some of the money for the future. The child, for its part, may, like the eight-year-old boy I interviewed, forcefully claim to his mother his right to play computer games for as long as he wishes, and, later in the interview, suggest that their parents should decide how long their children should be allowed to play (Johansson 2000).

When it comes to consumption, children are treated as consumers in quite different ways. When the focus is on children as becomings, they are expected either not to act in the market at all, or to do so under adult supervision and guidance (Olesen 2003; Buckingham 2000). Both of these ideals are strong in Sweden, where there is a broad consensus around the idea that children should be protected from marketing, expressed, for instance, in the prohibition against targeting children younger than twelve in TV advertising. There is also a long tradition (among others managed by the Swedish savings bank) of teaching children to save most of their money for the future.

The view of children as beings who are capable of handling money, judging advertisements and making consumer decisions is at the same time growing stronger. Even though it is companies and marketing people who pursue this view most strongly, they can find support in a more common understanding of children as active human beings, worthy of being respected and taken account of here and now. Hence a child is offered several subjectivities as a consumer, some of them relating to the becoming child, some to the being child. In the following section, I will give examples of six different consumer subjectivities available to children and discuss some of their implications.

Subjectivities of the consuming child

1 The child who does not act in the market, but saves for the future

> My money is mostly saved in the bank. Mom put it there. So, perhaps I have a little money at home, but it's not much. And mostly mom and dad buy things for me. But sometimes, when I want something and mom and dad won't buy it, they say that I should buy it with my own money. But I don't want to waste it, because I want to save it for when I'm grown up! (Girl, 9)

In this quotation, the girl defines herself primarily as an economic becoming. Not only does she save most of her money for the future, her mother is the one who takes responsibility for putting her money into the bank. When her parents suggest that she uses the small amount of money she has for her own spending, she hesitates and prefers to save it. Even if it is something she wants, she considers it wasteful to use her own money for current consumption. At the same time, the girl by no means refrains from consumption, since her parents usually buy things for her. It is true that she postpones spending her own money, but since her parents provide for her, she is seldom denied the things she wants.

Children are expected to save their money, especially when they receive greater sums. Aside from the bank, they can save their money at home, in a purse, a piggybank or, as one girl told me, in her father's weapon cabinet. They can save money for a specific item which they want, or more vaguely, as in the case above, save it until they grow up. In both cases there is a distinction between money to be saved and money to use for current consumption. One boy told me that he does not buy anything with banknotes that have a higher value than twenty Swedish crowns;[1] notes of higher values are saved. Accordingly, this implies that the physical shape determines which money it is all right to trade with.

2 The child consumer who delegates consumer choice and economic responsibility to its parents

> *Who chooses your clothes? Do you shop for yourself, or does someone else do it for you?*
>
> I just say to mom: 'Take some'. I don't care. (Boy, 10)
>
> Mom and dad bought these jeans. They are stone-washed, and mom and dad say that they're trendy. (Girl, 10)

While the young people of my own generation, born in the 1950s, often had to struggle for independence and responsibility and the right to make their own choices, children today seem more inclined to appreciate the ability to refrain from choosing and from taking responsibility. One strategy which the children in the quotations refer to is to delegate some responsibility to their parents. The advantages are obvious, since the children save time as well as avoiding responsibility in doing so. They do not need to discipline themselves, to keep up to date regarding prices and quality or to make the money last, but can leave it to their parents to take care of these obligations. Several children said that there were other things they were interested in, such as horses and riding, motorbikes or football, on which they preferred to spend their time and energy. On the other hand, there were, of course, children who had a great interest in clothes, and would not dream of leaving it to their parents to decide what they should wear.

3 The shopping child

> Boy, 10: When I have money, I usually take them to Ullared.[2] And shop.
>
> *What do you usually buy there?*
>
> Boy: Probably like a computer game every time I'm there.
>
> Girl, 12: Having monthly pocket money is so frustrating. Because it all disappears so awfully fast. I buy sweets, magazines and then I may go downtown sometimes. After that, there is not much left.

The things children buy are most often cheap: sweets, magazines, cinema tickets, accessories and small things. Gifts for birthdays and Christmas are common expenses. If they have a special interest, such as computer games, this is where they spend their money. We can also trace the delegating strategy here: many children prefer to have less pocket money, letting their parents have the main responsibility, since they find that the money is spent too quickly if they receive a larger amount once a month. Also, they have found out that they will actually have more – and more expensive things – if their parents buy them for them.

4 The collecting child

It is also possible to buy many things of the same kind:

> Mom thinks that we should stop buying more cuddly toys, 'cos we already have so many, she thinks. But I want to collect cuddly toys, so I have a little problem with that. (Girl, 10)

Even if children have their own money, which they formally decide what to do with by themselves, their parents still supervise their purchases. The children might therefore have to argue why they need certain items. It is not obvious that the parents understand why there is a need for another cuddly toy when the child already has so many, and so a problem arises. On the other hand, collecting is something that even adults could be expected to understand, which may be why the girl uses that as an argument. But the fact that discussions on these matters do take place shows that children's consumption is surrounded by moral values, presumably to a greater extent than adults' consumption. Children's purchases are expected to be motivated rationally.

5 The child who consumes rationally and moderately

> At the fair, I usually don't buy the first thing I want. I usually walk around and look. If there's something else I want, then I choose. (Boy, 9)

> I came to a sale once, and they had these long leg windings for horses. They were cotton. They usually cost 50 crowns for two. But here they cost 10 crowns for two. So I saved 80 crowns since I bought four. (Girl, 11)

Being a rational, sensible and moderate consumer is an often repeated ideal, which Swedes encounter in consumer magazines and on radio and television programmes on consumer issues. Consumer information has a long tradition in Sweden (c.f. Berggren Torell 2007), dating from the interwar period, when there was a need for knowledge of how to economize and make use of scarce resources, to today's affluent society, where there is an abundance of consumption being offered to compare and to take into consideration. Children participate more or less in their families' consumer decisions and learn from them, as well as from school, how to perform a rational consumer subjectivity.

The children above convey the ideals of not hastily rushing into a choice as consumers and of being alert and taking an opportunity when there is a good offer. They stand out as rational beings, and by showing that they are responsible consumers, they decrease the risk of anyone questioning the fact that they actually do buy things with their own money, rather than saving it for the future. In short, they stand out as competent economic beings.

6 The child who has an influence on family consumption

Do you take part in deciding what to have for dinner or what food you would buy and such things?

Boy, 12: Sure. Mom cooks, I decide.

Then, things you buy together within the family, such as a TV or sofa or fridge or car or something like that. Are you allowed to take part in deciding on such things?

Boy, 10: I usually take part in deciding the colour of the car. We usually trade in our car for a new one every other year, just 'cos dad works at a job and goes up to Norrland and goes to Italy by car and a lot of things.

Are you allowed to take part in deciding about things which you buy within the family?

Boy, 10: If it's a new computer, I guess it's me who decides, since mom hardly knows anything about computers.

In a democratic family, every member ideally has a say on family decisions, and consumer decisions are no exception. The above quotations reveal that children's participation in decision-making can involve different things, such as deciding what to have for dinner, having a minor influence on car purchases, or being regarded – or at least regarding oneself – as an expert on certain capital goods, such as computers and media equipment.

The children here appear as competent human beings, equal to the adult members of the family, in that their opinions are asked for and given importance, even though the children are not given any economic responsibility for the purchases. Children may have influence to different degrees. It could be that parents let the children decide now and then in smaller matters, to keep them happy. Or the parents might have a more articulated democratic agenda where they expect the child to have the ability to compare different alternatives, making rational decisions and seeing to the best interests of the family. In the last quotation, the knowledgeable, being child is put together with the becoming, future child, who has a certain competence in understanding a technology, which, like the child himself, is associated with the future (Johansson 2000).

Being and becoming: two sides of the same coin

In the above examples, we can see how children situationally perform as consumers in a way which can be related to the concepts of beings and becomings. We can see that these concepts have a fluid character and are not mutually exclusive. On the one hand, a child might act as a becoming, which implies taking responsibility for one's own finances and not spending one's money but saving it at the bank. On the other hand, the same child can act as a being, which implies being a consumer and spending money here and now, even though it is not one's own money. This means that children are highly interesting targets for marketing, when it comes to their family's consumption as well as their own.

Responsibility, and how it is shared between children and adults, should also be taken into consideration. From a historical perspective, it is not relevant to claim that children have either more or less responsibility than they had fifty or a hundred years ago: however, they are responsible for different things today. The child of the old rural society was given the responsibility for contributing to the support of the household, and in the 1960s children were still often free to roam the streets and find their own play spaces together with their friends. Today Nordic children go to school instead of working and they are supervised and not left alone in public environments. But they still have responsibilities and are expected to make a lot of choices: consumer choices, such as which cereals to eat for breakfast, which clothes to wear or what to put in the Saturday sweets bag, but also decisions concerning how to organize the working day in school, which activities to engage in leisure time, and, in the extreme case, which parent to stay with after the parents' divorce. Once again, states of becoming and being are intertwined in children's daily lives.

In today's consumer society, the individual is facing an increasing number of choices. We not only choose between different commodities in the shops, we also have to choose our telephone and electricity companies, in which banks and funds to place our money, and which treatment, conventional or alternative, we shall turn to when we fall ill. New areas are open for consumption. The body, which earlier could be improved only with the help of clothes, hairstyle and cosmetics, is in today's 'total makeover' era the subject of seemingly unlimited transformation and consumer projects. Our consumer roles have expanded at the expense of our professional roles; it is, to a greater degree, as consumers rather than as workers that we express our identities (Bocock 1993; Zukin 2004).

Correspondingly, children's opportunities for choice have increased. As we have seen, children not only save their money or delegate consumer choices to their parents, they also take responsibility as economic beings for buying things with their own money, and their parents also give them the responsibility for having a say in consumer decisions within the family. It is a responsibility that they have to live up to if they are not to run the risk of losing the privilege. Many children imply that they embrace the ideal of the rational, wise and moderate consumer, an ideal promoted by their parents, school and other adult authorities. Adopting this ideal is thus also a way to empower oneself, to create an individual space of consumer agency, being a human being whom one's parents can trust.

However, this strategy and the space for self-determination it creates must be related to an essential characteristic of children's life situations, namely that they are subject to their parents' authority. This means that children's activities are always more or less supervised by adults – not only their parents – who assume the right to have opinions on how children should live their lives, including how they spend their money. Children might have to account for their purchases, or there might be rules for what they are allowed to buy with their pocket money:

Are you allowed to buy what you want with your own money?

Girl, 10: No, not exactly what I want. Mom doesn't think I should buy things that I won't use. And not sweets on other days [than Saturdays]. She prefers that I buy more important things.

Boy, 10: It depends on what it is. If it's something sensible.

Boy, 10: I may buy what I want.

Boy, 9: Nothing too expensive.

When there are others who have overall responsibility for your money and your way of handling it, it is necessary to live up to their confidence, and not to run the risk of being more restricted or having one's income reduced.

From autonomous standard adult to dependent becoming

Nick Lee (2001: 11ff.) uses the concept 'standard adult' when referring to an ideal that developed in the industrialized world between 1945 and the early 1970s. '[O]nce "adult" and employed, one could expect to stay "the same" for the rest of one's life in a range of ways', including identity, geographical location, career and, by extension, family situation (ibid.: 12). Since the emergence of mass production and mass consumption, huge changes have taken place which are also of relevance for how children perform consumer subjectivities. If there was a time when everybody was expected to become a standard adult at around 20–25 years of age, and moreover was expected to appreciate and look forward to the transition from dependent, irresponsible becoming to independent, responsible adult being, today we can see a hesitation regarding *when* and even *if* this transition is going to take place. We live in a rapidly changing society, where there is a constant demand on the individual to be open to development and change, where flexibility and swiftness are more cherished values than continuity and thoughtfulness, not to mention contentment, which is almost suspect. It is a society where the individual (not the collective) is responsible for making good (consumer) choices and can only blame himself or herself if things go wrong. Did you place your pension money in a foundation which went broke? Did your children fail to get a school certificate because the private school you chose went bankrupt? Too bad for you!

Individuals might act in different ways under such circumstances, ranging from being more determined to obtain information that will help them to make wise decisions, to adopting a more playful, relaxed or even fatalistic attitude, thinking that 'I have no control, but things will probably sort themselves out in the end' (cf. Åberg 2008). In this way, 'being' and 'becoming' acquire new meanings. It is not necessarily most relevant to perform the characteristics of the standard adult. The features which have symbolically been connected to children might become attractive to people of all ages. This might even become a lifestyle: play, irresponsibility, being taken care of, delegating and living for the day. According to Yannis Gabriel and Tim Lang (2008), the trend of contemporary consumer society is obvious: today's consumers are becoming increasingly unmanageable. While industrialists dream of managing consumers, consumers themselves 'subvert, refuse, accept, interpret, surrender or embrace' (ibid.: 334). The predictable, controlled adult consumer seems more and more to be a figure of the past.

When people in general are perceived as becomings instead of beings, the focus is transferred from individuals and entities to the flows and connections of events. Agency is always dependent on supplements and extensions, which are not only humans, but also non-humans, such as things, techniques and structures. In the above examples, agency is performed in assemblages where children's bodies, age and size, taste buds and preferences are connected to other people (parents, shopkeepers, grandparents, friends), to structures (the family, the monetary system, the market economy) and to items (notes and coins, cuddly toys, jeans, food, computers, cars, horse leg windings etc.). In these processes, not only do the distinctions between being and becoming fade away, so too does the teleological interpretation of reality. 'The child' is no longer defined in relation to a developmental model with clear-cut stages, which should be coped with one by one until the child reaches adulthood. Just like 'the adult', 'the child' is a constant becoming, defined only by the actual relations in which he or she is engaged.

What if childhood does not exist?

I have described a set of subjectivities that are available to the consuming child, stressing that the child is sometimes a becoming, sometimes a being. Children have the ability to delegate consumer choices and economic responsibility to their parents, or they can take charge and make personal consumer decisions, and even influence the consumption of their parents. Their range of agency differs depending on how many other actors are included in the assemblage. The situations in which children's agency is performed are not infrequently made up of other extensions compared with the situations in which adults act. One general difference is that adults have access to more powerful extensions (higher education, stronger bodies, higher social positions, more legal rights, etc.) than children usually have. Participation is therefore a highly situational state. Accordingly, becoming and being must both be understood as constantly flowing states; in every situation, they are actually or potentially present.

Jean Baudrillard once suggested the possibility that childhood does not exist, and that the child is the only one who knows it (Gane 1993). Childhood is a category which is attributed to people by others or by the person himself or herself. This is, of course, true of every categorization (which means that a person could be characterized as, for example, a girl, Swedish, middle class, urban, Muslim, able-bodied). But there is also the possibility of talking about humans in another way, just saying that we exist, that we are all in life, and nothing more. This is a quite adequate description of a human being. Though we are inclined to categorize, and though it is sometimes necessary for practical reasons to categorize, by doing so, we at the same time draw up limitations. By saying that someone is a 'child' or 'middle class' or 'Muslim', we have also said what he or she is not. That is how we produce 'Others' – by reducing people to, in the worst case, just one characteristic, clearly marked off from all other categories. As a category, 'child' has this tendency to swallow up all other categories and to become the only category through which we perceive the other person. In this way, and often without problematizing it, we talk about children as a group and what children essentially 'are'. From a historical perspective, we can see that until quite recently the category 'woman' was treated in the same uncomplicated way, but that feminist and queer movements have problematized gender and revealed it to be contradictory, multi-faceted and ambiguous. With the growing interest in the empirical and theoretical aspects of childhood, a similar development may occur in childhood studies.

If we want to take part in any such development, we could reflect on what would happen if we took another step further and used 'an ontology of flow' (Wenzer 2007). Then we would not have to invoke all kinds of categories when we encounter another human being. Instead, we would observe what happens in the actual event and how we cooperate in producing certain kinds of agency. This means that we do not define childhood or children once and for all, but keep open the possibility of different things being important in different situations. Sometimes age is important, sometimes gender, sometimes skin colour, sometimes occupation, degree of literacy, taste in music or something else. Sometimes the body is of importance and sometimes it is not. When all of us, we who exist, we who are in life, act within a lot of different momentary assemblages, there is always something happening, but exactly what happens we never know beforehand.

Notes

1. Ten Swedish crowns is about one Euro.
2. A big shopping centre in a small town in the south of Sweden, to which people travel from long distances.

References

Alanen, L. (1992) *Modern Childhood? Exploring the 'Child Question' in Sociology.* Institute for Educational Research. Publication series A. Research report 50, University of Jyväskylä.

Berggren Torell, V. (2007) Folkhemmets barnkläder: Diskurser om det klädda barnet under 1920-50-talet. (Children's Clothes in the People's Home: Discourses on the Dressed Child in the 1920s to the 1950s in Sweden.) Gothenburg: Arkipelag, dissertation.

Bocock, R. (1993) *Consumption.* London: Routledge.

Brembeck, H., Johansson, B. and J. Kampmann (eds) (2004) *Beyond the Competent Child: Exploring Contemporary Childhoods in the Nordic Welfare Societies.* Copenhagen: Samfunnsforlaget.

Buckingham, D. (2000) After the Death of Childhood: Growing up in the Age of Electronic Media. Cambridge: Polity Press.

Czarniawska, B. (2004) *On Time, Space, and Action Nets.* GRI- report 2004:5. Göteborgs universitet. http://gup.ub.gu.se/gup/record/index.xsql?pubid=38594, date accessed 19 March 2009.

Deleuze, G. and F. Guattari (1988) *A Thousand Plateaus: Capitalism and Schizophreniza.* London: Athlone Press.

Gabriel, Y. and T. Lang (2008) New Faces and New Masks of Today's Consumer, in *Journal of Consumer Culture,* 8: 321–40.

Gane, M. (1993) *Baudrillard Live: Selected Interviews.* London: Routledge.

James, A. and A. Prout (eds) (1997) *Constructing and Reconstructing Childhood: Contemporary Issues in the Sociological Study of Childhood.* London/Bristol: The Falmer Press.

James, A. (2005) Life Times: Children's Perspectives on Age, Agency and Memory across the Life Course, in J. Qvortrup (ed.) *Studies in Modern Childhood: Society, Agency, Culture.* Basingstoke : Palgrave Macmillan, pp. 248–67.

Johansson, B. (2000) 'Kom och Ät!' 'Jag Ska Bara Dö Först...' Datorn i Barns Vardag. ('Time to eat!' 'Okay, I'll Just Die First...' The Computer in Children's Everyday Life.) Gothenburg: Etnologiska föreningen i Västsverige, dissertation.

Johansson, B. (2005) *Barn i Konsumtionssamhället (Children in Consumer Society.)* Stockholm: Norstedts Akademiska Förlag.

Latour, B. (1993) *We Have Never Been Modern.* New York/London/Toronto/Sydney/Tokyo/Singapore: Harvester Wheatsheaf.

Latour, B. (1996) *Aramis or the Love of Technology.* Cambridge, Mass.: Harvard University Press.

Lee, N. (2001) *Childhood and Society: Growing up in an Age of Uncertainty.* Buckingham/Philadelphia: Open University Press.

Olesen, J. (2003) *Alternative Modeller for Forbrugerbeskyttelse af Børn. (Alternative Models for Consumer Protection of Children.)* CFK-report 2003:1. University of Gothenburg, Center for Consumer Science. www.cfk.gu.se, date accessed 19 March 2009.

Prout, A. (2005) *The Future of Childhood,* London and New York: Routledge Falmer Press.

Qvortrup, J. (1987) *The Sociology of Childhood.* Barndomsprojektet 2/87. University Centre of South Jutland.

Qvortrup, J. (2005) Varieties of Childhood, in J. Qvortrup (ed.) *Studies in Modern Childhood: Society, Agency, Culture.* Basingstoke: Palgrave Macmillan, 1–21.

Thorne, B. (1993) *Gender Play: Girls and Boys in School.* Buckingham: Open University Press.

Wenzer, J. (2007) *Resonanser: en neomaterialistisk analys av independentscenen i Göteborg* (Resonances. A neo-materialist analysis of the indie scene in Gothenburg).University of Gothenburg: Institute of Ethnology.

Zukin, S. (2004) *Point of Purchase: How Shopping Changed American Culture.* New York and London: Routledge.

Åberg, M. (2008) Lärardrömmar: Om Makt, Mångfald och Konstruktioner av Lärarsubjektivitet. (Teacher Dreams: Power, Diversity and the Making of Teacher Subjects). Gothenburg: Mara, dissertation.

6
Researching Things, Objects and Gendered Consumption in Childhood Studies

Claudia Mitchell

Imagine a world without things. It would be not so much an empty world as a blurry, frictionless one: no sharp outlines would separate one part of the uniform plenum from another; there would be no resistance against which to stub a toe or test a theory or struggle stalwartly. Nor would there be anything to describe, or to explain, remark on, interpret, or complain about – just a kind of porridgy oneness. Without things, we would stop talking. (Daston, 2004: 9)

As Daston (2004) highlights, things and objects offer a fascinating entry point to studying "up close" the everyday world, in a way that is not blurry and diffuse, but clear, sharp and in focus. As scholars from such diverse backgrounds as media and technology (Turkle 2007), science in the case of Daston, anthropology (Miller, 1998; Brown, 1998; 2004), and most recently Joshua Glenn and Carol Hayes (2007) in Taking *Things Seriously*, have highlighted, the analysis of material objects offers the possibility of theorizing abstract concepts in a grounded manner. While the idea of childhood objects, particularly those associated with play and consumption, has found its way into the study of children's popular culture (see for example the work of Fleming, 1996), it has not figured as prominently in the study of material culture as one might expect, despite the obvious significance of children's consumption of objects and things in their play. Concomitantly, the study of children's playthings is often absent within visual studies.

This chapter seeks to position the study of children's objects of play and consumption within visual studies and the study of material culture more broadly. In drawing on a variety of approaches and tools from memory work and socio-semiotics, visual studies and archaeology, it reviews some of the research that I have been conducting with colleagues over a decade or so, and addresses some new features associated with children's consumption. In so doing, it argues for a 'new materialism' in childhood studies as a rich way to develop new theories and methodologies in the study of children's role and status as consumers.

Childhood and the Gendered Object

Just as we are collectors of things, things are collectors of meaning.
(Glenn and Hayes, 2007:1).

Edwards and Hart (2004) observe that: "Materiality can be said … to have a positivistic character, in that it is concerned with real physical objects in a world that is physically apprehendable not only through vision but through embodied relations of smell, taste, touch and hearing" (p. 3). Similarly Sarah Pink (2004) in *Home Truths* highlights the significance of sensory ethnography in understanding the meanings of gender, domestic objects and everyday life. While she does not specifically take up childhood objects, her discussion of the discrete aspects of smell, sound and touch as well as the significance of looking at the interrelatedness of these senses extends the repertoire of possibilities for analysis here. Several essays in Pat Kirkham's (1996) *The Gendered Object* offer a view on childhood objects that positions them as "marked" by such gender signifiers as colour (pastel blues and pinks for girls and solid browns, military greens, dark blues and Spiderman red for boys) and smell (albeit primarily in relation to toys marketed towards girls). In the case of *Strawberry Shortcake*, *My Little Pony* and sticker sets for example, fruit and flower scents have strong appeal; and textures are also vital (soft, puffy and fluffy versus rough and tough). These signifiers are often in evidence in the packaging, which in itself further signifies the gendered object through colour and design, including images (images of a girl or girls playing together and or of a boy or boys playing together) and even slogans, as in the case of the packaging of a construction toy directed towards boys: "Toys make the boy" (Friedman and Haddad, 1995).

Our ethnographic data on young adults looking back at toy packaging reveal vivid memories of the look of toys and related artifacts (Mitchell and Reid-Walsh, 2002). Zac, then in his early twenties, recalls:

Toy packaging was always a major part of the whole experience for me. Most of the series I played with as a kid had extensive box art and other extras incorporated into the packaging. I think GI Joe and Transformers were the big ones for that. Transformer toys always had a painting on the back of the box with the toys released in the line that year pictured together in some large "battle" scene... I also remember cutting out the pictures (paintings) on the boxes of each figure, and saving them too, so really only half of the packaging was ever thrown away. They would always be pictured in these somewhat abstract dioramic landscapes, full of little rocks and gravel, and tiny bushes. Occasionally they would include images of a happy-looking pair of kids playing with (or gazing adoringly at) whichever playsets carried the biggest price tag. These booklets became a commodity of sorts. My friends and I would save ones from each year, committing the figures to memory, owning them all in our minds, even if we couldn't in actuality. (85)

Zac also refers to the mail-order catalogues as another source of mate-riality in relation to these play objects, noting for example the sig-nificance of full-page dioramas with toys and children in evidence. Catalogue play is also a feature of the materiality of girls' play (Mitchell and Reid-Walsh, 1998; Reid-Walsh and Mitchell, in press). In memory accounts, young women in their early twenties through to women in their nineties refer to cutting out figures from the catalogue and turn-ing them into paper dolls within fictional families. Alongside the idea of narrative play, however, is the idea of the catalogue items as "texts of desire" (Christian-Smith, 1990). Joan, a cousin of mine, for example, refers in an interview a few years ago to the significance of getting the Eaton's Beauty Doll (so named after one of the first mail-order systems in Canada) as a Christmas present when she was about five. More than sixty years later, she is still amazed that her parents would have given her such a beautiful doll that she had so admired and desired based on its representation in the Eaton's Mail-order catalogue. The critical point in both Zac's and Joan's recollections is the significance of the market-ing documents themselves (the packaging or the catalogue page) as appendages to the play object. Although the same types of mail order catalogues do not occupy such a significant space in children's culture in North America today, they have been replaced by the plethora of Toys R Us-type flyers which regularly appear as inserts in newspapers or delivered door-to-door in 'publi-sacs' (plastic bags with flyers).

To add a sound-scape to the study of boy-toys and girl-toys, we might take note of the range of sounds emitted by toys, war toys, fire-fighting gear and so on, marketed principally to boys, and the range of music boxes, sing-song voices, of toys (chiefly dolls) marketed to girls. While sound is a relatively under-studied area within the literature of domestic life more generally, let alone in the area of childhood, the work of Feld and Brenneis (2004) and Rice (2003) on accoustemology and the "exploration of sonic sensibilities" provide fascinating entry points to studying sound as a feature of the materiality of child's play. Again, drawing from our ethnographic fieldwork with adults, we can see something of the richness of sound data in the account by twenty-six year old Jonah, recalling "the sound of toys":

> ...there was a period of time in my childhood when all sorts of toys were making an array of sounds, and then all of a sudden there was a new line of GI Joe figures who all came with these ridiculous oversized backpacks that housed the electronics to produce what was usually the same four or five sounds: a very synthesized sounding ratatat of a machine gun, a weird alarm noise that may have been a laser, and the ubiquitous wail of a falling bomb followed by an explosion.

Jonah then goes on to describe the sounds produced during play by the players, a further aspect of the embodiment of play. As he observes:

> I have to say that for me the sounds I most associate with toys are the ones I made myself – the assortment of gunshots, laser beams, explosions, bullet ricochets, impact wounds and so on that I rarely have occasion to make in my life now, but still remain clear in my head today.

From memory to memory work

The accounts of Zac, Jonah and Joan come from ethnographic interviews where adults look back on various aspects of objects in childhood play. *Memory work* (sometimes also called productive remembering) offers another approach to interrogating and excavating childhood memories. Ranging from studies of early memories of cowgirl play, catalogue play, playing school, and Barbie play, my colleagues and I have used a variety of approaches to memory work within childhood studies. These have included working with photographs and objects to study such phenomena as playing school (Mitchell and Weber, 1999), the use of digital images and websites (Mitchell and Reid-Walsh, 2005; Weber and Mitchell, 2007), the study of dress, including clothing from childhood

(Weber and Mitchell, 2004), and working with objects directly in our study of doll play (Mitchell and Reid-Walsh, 1995; Reid-Walsh and Mitchell, in press). As part of this work, we have also set up memory work projects which make use of what Patricia Hampl (1996) refers to as "first draft" and "second draft" memory writing. In this approach to memory, which also draws on the work on collective memory of Frigga Haug *et al.* (1987) and June Crawford *et al.* (1992), the point is to move from unselfconsciously mediated remembering (free recall or first draft memory) to working back in a systematic way that interrogates memory (second draft memory). Finally, we have been interested in the ideas around "staging" that Jo Spence and Rosy Martin developed in their research a few years ago to interrogate memory, class and childhood (Spence, 1994). For example, in one of their projects on girlhood, they dress up, as adults, in school uniforms. Each holding a cigarette, they re-examine resistance in girlhood, using both bodily representations (dressing up in schoolgirl clothing) as well as visual ones (the actual photographs taken).

In our memory work projects, the focus has been on deliberate remembering as opposed to solely accidental remembering, in line with the idea that memory can serve as a useful feminist tool for contesting (and sometimes recovering) the past. Thus, when we were studying the "afterlife" of children's popular culture for our book, *Researching Children's Popular Culture* (2002) my co-author Jacqueline Reid-Walsh and I decided to engage in deliberate remembering around cowgirl play. Drawing on published accounts of other women's memories, we each wrote first and second draft memories of growing up in the 1950s and early 1960s. As part of the same project, we also did a cultural reading of Jessie, the cowgirl doll in the animated feature *ToyStory 2*, a film that can itself be regarded as a cultural reading on memory and children's play. In that chapter we include an account of working with a single photograph, where I am pictured reading an Annie Oakley novel *Danger at Diablo* one Christmas day. While that analysis also points out some of the gendered aspects of girlhood (the good girl sitting quietly reading on Christmas day), there are other memories and objects that might be considered in relation to gender. The account which follows, focusing on boy-play, comes from my recollections of gendered objects and things in my own 1950s girlhood:

> All my life I have been watching brothers up close – as an insider, but also as an outsider – and through spaces, objects and things. As the long awaited girl born into a family that had two boys, it became

'Claudia and the boys'. I was placed in a bedroom by myself. They had a room together. They had specially ordered twin beds with headboards ordered for our brand new fifties ranch house with the picture window. They had matching kitten lamps. And although two years apart in age, they received presents in common at Christmas: one year a mechanical hockey game, then huge sets of Meccano, Lincoln logs, and finally the big one – a full size pool table. They had matching heavy machinery tonka-type toys. They had matching two wheelers, some brand that was not CCM; I had the CCM. I seem to recall that my grandmother and mother always tried to remember in the matching gifts that one liked blue and the other green. Or was it blue and red? And which was which? (Fieldnotes, December, 2008)

In this example my own self-imposed memory prompt was actually "brothers" and not toys or objects per se. I began to wonder what it must have been like to grow up "on the inside" as "just one of the boys". Did they like receiving the same presents or sharing presents (such as the hockey game or the pool table)? And why do I know more about their presents that I do about my own? It is the objects them-selves, marked by gender (through smell, touch, sound and so on), that now take on their own "larger than life" status in the memory account and it is the clear recollection of the objects that somehow makes the account workable – an example perhaps of Daston's non-blurriness.

Children's objects and visual culture

As Marina Warner (2005) argues in her introduction to *Things: A Spectrum of Photographys,* clothing, toys, utensils, books are "texts of materiality". And in addition to being marked by kinesthetic qualities, sound and smell, they can of course be seen. Many of the texts that are typically regarded as central to the study of visual culture – photographs, photo albums, films – and the tools of production– cameras, cell phones, and so on – are themselves objects. From the work of Roland Barthes (1982) in *Camera Lucida* to the study of people's everyday uses of photographs in shopping malls – people looking at (holding, touching, shuffling through a collection of) the vacation photos they have just picked up at a one-hour photo shop, or their digital snaps that have been "manipulated" at Walmart – the photograph, as Edwards and Hart (2004) write, is "a three-dimensional thing, not only a two dimensional image" (p. 1). Likewise, in our account of community-based photovoice projects, it is the photographs as objects that are so engrossing and engaging: as we go back through the photographs that we took during the projects, we have visual evidence of "looking at looking" and the ways that participants are handling their own photographs (Pithouse and Mitchell, 2007).

There are many accounts of the materiality of such tools and products within visual studies that highlight their significance in children's culture. These include, for example, studies of the first Kodak cameras (Mitchell and Reid-Walsh, 2002), and the account of Sadie Bening, the young feminist film-maker who received from her film-maker father a Fisher Price Pixel movie camera for Christmas when she was 16, not the camera she was expecting, but the camera she used to convert her bedroom into a visual laboratory for exploring sexual identity (Paley, 1995). Similarly, Michelle Citron (1999), in her study of home movies, refers to the materiality of the reels of film shot by her father in the 1960s.

The materiality of the visual is also significant within art history and photographic studies, for example in the work of Martha Langford (2001), Elizabeth Edwards and J. Hart (2004) and Richard Chalfen (1991) in their study of people's photo albums. Annette Kuhn's (1995) work with single photographs (including captions) in her own family albums demonstrates how the photograph as object can become the subject of family debate and contestation: Who took the photograph? Who wrote the captions? Who has the photograph in their possession?

A fascinating account of the visual dimensions of children's favourite objects can be found in the work of French artist Christian Boltanksi, well known for his recycling work in which he uses items of clothing, photographs and other objects of material culture in his installations.

A few years ago, Boltanski invited 264 students from La Lycee, a school in Chicago, to choose "the single favourite object of his or her lifetime" to be photographed and incorporated into a large installation that was eventually exhibited at the Museum of Modern Art in New York. Over the course of several days, he set up each object (in most cases, a play object such as a Barbie, stuffed toy or Transformer) to be photographed at exactly the same scale and angle and under uniform lighting. While Boltanksi positioned some of the objects into some sort of pose, the uniform treatment contributes to a democratization of the relationship between camera and object. The full installation, "Favourite Things", is made up of 264 black and white 8½ by 11 inch individual photographs. What is interesting is how all the objects have a similar intimate look. Even the commercial objects become personalized in their appearance, as they maintain their brand new "in the package" look. In so doing, the artist has managed to capture something of the relationship between the child and the object (see also Mitchell and Reid-Walsh, 2002).

Stephen Riggins (1994), a socio-semiotician, also explores the visual in studying the denotative and connotative meaning of things and objects. Using the case of his parents' living room, he methodically photographs each object in the living room, starting at the doorway and ending up back there: the wall hangings, photographs, lamps, television set, easy chairs, books in the book case and so on. For each object there is its denotative meaning (the first television set exhibited in the 1940s), and its connotative meaning, the stories of that particular television set. Riggins uses the term "referencing" to describe "all of the content which is about the history, aesthetics, or customary use of the objects" (p. 109). He claims this information is often "brief and superficial." It is also often taken for granted, as for example in the fact that refrigerators or washing machines are coded as gendered objects, or their history is forgotten or simply not known.

To explore connotative meaning, Riggins (1994) uses the term "mapping" to describe how objects serve as entry points for the telling of stories about the self: "...the self uses the displayed objects (gift, heirlooms, photographs, etc.) as a way of plotting its social network, representing its cosmology and ideology, and projecting its history onto the world's map, its spatial spread so to speak" (p. 109). He goes on to write that the taking of the photographs is central to the process of visual ethnography:

> Many of the subtleties of domestic artifacts will elude the researcher unless it is possible to closely examine photographs. Consequently each room must be thoroughly photographed. Unlike the practice followed by the professional photographers employed by decorating and architectural magazines of removing all ephemeral traces left by users and inhabitants in order to avoid dating the photographs, ethnographers should make an effort to include the permanent as well as the ephemeral. Both are relevant to the research. (p. 110)

Similarly, in relation to written accounts, he emphasizes the importance of being systematic rather than impressionistic:

> One might want to begin the written account of a room with the first object visitors are likely to notice upon entering (something directly opposite the door or some other highlighted space) and from that

point proceed systematically around the room. The same procedure should be applied to the contents of cabinets or shelves. Begin with the object farthest to the right or left and proceed down the shelf. (p. 110)

Elsewhere, Riggins's (1994) work is applied in our own study of children's bedrooms, where the focus is on ideas of "the baby's room", particularly in Western contexts (Mitchell and Reid-Walsh, 2002). We analyse the contemporary marketing obsession with the perfect room for baby (with matching gender-coded wallpaper, crib pads, crib sheets and the like), and how this has developed from a time when babies would have slept in the parents' room (the family bed), through to modern child psychology and the idea of one child = one bedroom, and then to the idea of the child as a commodity in itself, when the child's bedroom becomes an extension of the parents' spending power and taste (Mitchell and Reid-Walsh, 2002).

In an essay on dolls and doll play in *Depicting Canadian Childhood* (Reid-Walsh and Mitchell, in press), I include a section called 'curatorial play" where I revisit the various dolls that I played with in the 1950s, according to the various materials used in their construction: the rubber doll, the composition doll, the hard plastic bride doll, and the vinyl doll. Each of these genres of dolls has its own denotative meaning (albeit a taken-for-granted aspect of dolls to a little girl growing up on a farm in Western Canada in the 1950s) which flows into the connotative meanings now attached to the specific dolls within each genre. Here, for example, is my denotative and connotative account of the bride doll:

Somewhere in my doll-play I managed to acquire a bride doll. This hard plastic 14 inch bride doll (now selling on e-Bay for $129) still exists in the family though her head now is attached to her neck with surgical tape. I am not quite sure when I received the bride doll, though like the Eaton's Beauty doll of my Aunt Viv and Cousin Joan, she existed within a state of awe and amazement, spending most of her life (at least during my childhood) in a plain cardboard box with a cellophane window in our linen closet, to be taken out only on special occasions. In some ways she might be taken as a precursor to Barbie in that she was shapely, with slight breasts. She came dressed in an off white satin down, satin underpants which to this day have never been removed, tiny white leather shoes and mesh white socks. With her beautiful shock of thick dark hair, I always thought she looked like my Aunt Joyce in her wedding photo. To the best of my knowledge there was never a photo of me taken with my bride doll and she never had a name. She was just 'my bride doll'. In the accompanying photo (fig. 3) we see that she did eventually leave the cellophane box – and is now THE worse for wear.

In terms of my earlier discussion of the various gender markers associated with children's toys, smell and touch are clearly significant here, but there are few sounds, except for the crinkle of the early-day cellophane on the box where the doll is stored. Joanne, the vinyl doll, did emit a cry when her stomach was pressed but because of the wire construction it was not easy, I seem to recall, to get a sound out of her.

This approach need not be confined to the past, but can also be applied to new media and contemporary childhoods. For example, Staldt's (2007) work on 'me and my mobile phone' demonstrates the centrality of technological objects as objects of desire within childhood and youth identities. An essay by Sandra Weber with her niece Julia

Illustration 6.1   Bride Doll, from the collection of Claudia Mitchell, McGill University. Photographer, Lewis Wosu, McGill University.

Weber (Weber and Weber, 2007) offers a fascinating social history of new technologies in the life of one child. The look of the objects, their place within visual culture (as in the case of the cell phone), the textures and even sound, are all critical. In a short exchange with my seven year old grandchild, Jakob, in another conversation on the topic of the sounds of his toys and which were his favourite, his immediate response was "there is this cool video game that has great sounds". Obviously sound is part of the design in the first place, but understanding the particular appeal of sounds and the users at whom they are directed is an important aspect of the study of objects and things.

Towards a new materialism within childhood studies

Whether objects actually speak (or need to speak) in order to be important is a point that is somewhat contested between disciplinary domains. Ian Hodder (2003), an archeologist, refers to the interpretive potential of working with the mute evidence of artifacts and written documents: "Such evidence, unlike the spoken word, endures physically and thus can be separated across space and time from its author, producer or user. Material traces thus often have to be interpreted without the benefit of indigenous commentary" (p. 155). Hodder goes on to point out that too often the spoken word is privileged over the written and artifactual, even when we know the limitations of the various actors. As he notes: "...actors often seem curiously inarticulate about the reasons they dress in particular ways, choose particular pottery designs, or discard dung in particular locations" (p. 155). Informants in a study may even say something quite different in an interview when asked the same question a day later. While the point here is not to discredit qualitative studies that rely primarily on interviews and focus groups, it is worth considering the interpretive possibilities of objects, documents and other texts.

A study by Buchli and Lucas (2000) indicates the potential for studying objects (things, photographic images, artifacts) as representational agents of change. The study focuses on a council flat in the UK abandoned by a single mother. The researchers offer a reading of "the remains" – the toys and things scattered throughout the house, Christmas decorations, family photographs, and items of clothing. In particular, they attempt to read the significance of the Flintstones wall paper in the children's room – along with the blue stenciled figures of little bears – as a "neverland". They study the motif of the family portrait depicted in the wallpaper – Fred Flintstone, his wife Wilma and daughter Pebbles – in the context of the circumstances under which the single mother had access to the flat, and the material circumstances of her children:

> The mother of the household clearly attempted to produce the segregated and highly differentiated "other" realm (neverland) in devotional anticipation of a familial ideal (ironically embodied by a prehistoric fantasy), whose reiteration was flawed in a crucial way – the lack of a viable opposite sex partner, the father (who would be the phantasmagorial Fred Flintstone). If this ideal were indeed successfully reiterable, she would have obtained, according to British housing policy, preferential access to care, protection and support as a "wife" or cohabiting partner in addition to being a mother. (Buchli and Lucas, p. 26)

The researchers analyze a child's drawing left on the wall of four figures, a mother, father and two children. They note that there are other visual signs of the biological father having been in the flat, and of the mother having come back once or twice to collect items. The archaeological "dig" of the researchers suggests that objects carry meanings which can extend even into policy analysis – for example in relation to housing and maternity benefits and the procedures that determine which mothers are worthy of benefits. The fact that the mother loses all access to benefits because of her abandonment of the flat (even though she is not in arrears with her payments) suggests that there may be a very serious state of disorder here. Critically, the textual evidence contributes to a much richer policy analysis of what needs to happen within the social welfare system for this mother and the protection of her two children.

A further example arose when a group of our graduate students toured an exhibition called "Growing up in Montreal" at the McCord Museum in Montreal (http://www.mccord-museum.qc.ca/en/exhibitions/1422. html, retrieved 1.2.09). Some of the most provocative comments they made were related to what they saw as "presence and absence" and whose childhoods were preserved and whose, by virtue of class, geographic location, religion, ethnicity, gender and so on, were not. "Where am I?" they ask, many of them having grown up outside of the elite social sphere of the McCord Museum, which serves largely as a repository for artifacts of the upper class (mostly Anglophone) population in Montreal. What this discussion opens up is a recognition of the unique features of childhoods (in this case Canadian childhoods) that should be studied by future scholars across a wide range of disciplines, and in particular the need for greater attention to the social meanings of the objects.

Given the ephemerality of children's toys and other objects, and the potential of new technologies for creating digital archives, this work points to the need for meta-data systems. Meta-data, or data about data, describes and documents the subject matter: when, where and by whom the data was generated, size, textures, sounds, smells and so on, along with access and copyright. In one of our meta-data projects in South Africa around the use of community-based photovoice artifacts in addressing HIV and AIDS, a digital archive offered a way to engage communities themselves, including children (see for example Park *et al.*, 2007). As a tool (or set of tools) that can help to document and interrogate the materiality of childhood and the meaning of things, digital archiving seems an appropriate first step for putting into practice the analysis of children's objects I have discussed.

Conclusion

This chapter has highlighted a variety of methodological approaches to exploring the rich historical and cultural meanings of children's objects and things, and their potential for studying child and teen consumption. There are several broad areas that call for more exploration here. Working with the past, as the studies noted above suggest, highlights the significance of what Andreas Huyssen (2003) calls "productive remembering". This is more than just acknowledging the 'after-life' of children's text (Mitchell and Reid-Walsh, 2002): it also points to the possibility of understanding more about contemporary childhood and children's consumption through the lens of memory – and perhaps of reframing how as adults we regard childhood, our own as well as contemporary childhood. A second area, also drawing on the past – what might be described as "deep memory" reaching back into infancy – relates to childhood and space. In a fascinating visual study by the archaeologist Joanna Sofaer and her brother Joshua, a visual artist (Sofaer and Sofaer, 2008), the focus is on trying to "dig up" the infant self through a re-engagement with "the places they were before they can remember", and working with family photographs from the same time period. Their idea was to use the practices of archaeology in order to explore their forgotten past, and in particular to explore how children might be included in archaeology. In their installation work they draw on various research tools and texts including aerial photographs and "the object biography" (Sofaer, 2002). What their work suggests is a vast and untapped area of study that contests, in a sense, the boundaries of childhood consciousness (as well as adult consciousness about early childhood) as viewed through the materiality of objects (including photographs), spaces and things – not to mention suggesting new uses for Google Earth. As Sherry Turkle has argued, "We live our lives in the middle of things" (2007, p. 6). The work on memory and childhood in such studies suggests new perspectives on when the life of things within childhood really begins.

References

Barthes, R. (1982) *Camera Lucida*. London: Vintage Classics.

Brown, B. (ed.) (2004) *Things*. Chicago: University of Chicago Press.

Brown, B. (1998) "How to do things with things", *Critical Inquiry*. 24, 935–64.

Buchli, V. and G. Lucas (2000) "Children, gender and the material culture of domestic abandonment in the late 20th century". In J. S Derevenski (ed.), *Children's Material Culture* (pp. 131–8). London: Routledge.

Chalfen, R. (1991) *Turning Leaves: The Photographic Collections of Two Japanese American Families*. Albuquerque, NM: University of New Mexico Press.

Christian-Smith, L. (1990) *Becoming a Woman Through Romance*. New York: Routledge.

Citron, M. (1999). *Home Movies and Other Necessary Fictions*. Minneapolis: University of Minnesota Press.

Crawford, J., S. Kippax, Onyx, J., Gault, U. and P. Benton, (1992) *Emotion and Gender: Constructing Meaning from Memory*. London: Sage.

Daston, L. (2004) *Things That Talk: Object Lessons from Art and Science*. New York: Zone Books.

Edwards, E. and J. Hart (eds) (2004) *Photographs Objects Histories: On the Materiality of Images*. London: Routledge.

Feld, S. and D. Brenneis (2004) "Doing anthropology in sound". *American Ethnologist*, 31:4.

Friedman, A. and R. Haddad (1995) *Maisons de reve, maisons jouets/Dream houses, toy homes*. Montreal: Canadian Centre for Architecture.

Fleming, D. (1996) *Powerplay: Toys as Popular Culture*. New York: Manchester University Press.

Glenn, J. and C. Hayes (2007) *Taking Things Seriously: 75 Objects with Unexpected Significance*. Princeton: Princeton Architectural Press.

Hampl, P. (1996) 'Memory and imagination'. In J. McConkey (ed.), *The Anatomy of Memory: An Anthology*. New York: Oxford University Press.

Haug, F., S. Andresen, A. Bunz-Elfferding, K. Hauser, U. Lang, M. Laudan, M. Ludemann and U. Meir (1987) *Female Sexualization. A Collective Work of Memory*. London: Verso.

Hodder, I. (2003) "The interpretation of documents and material culture", in N. Denzin and Y. Lincoln (eds), *Collecting and interpreting qualitative materials* (pp. 155–75). Thousand Oaks: Sage.

Huyssen, A. (2003) *Present Pasts: Palimpsests and the Politics of Memory*. Stanford: Stanford University Press.

Kirkham, P. (ed.) (1996) *The Gendered Object*. Manchester: Manchester University Press.

Kuhn, A. (1995) *Family Secrets: Acts of Memory and Imagination*. London and New York: Verso.

Langford, M. (2001) *Suspended Conversations*. Montreal: McGill-Queens Press

Miller, D. (1998) *Material Culture: Why Some Things Matter*. London: UCL Press.

Mitchell, C. and J. Reid-Walsh (2005) "And I Want To Thank You Barbie: Barbie as a Site of Cultural Interrogation". *The Review of Education/Pedagogy/Cultural Studies*, 17(2), pp. 143–56.

Mitchell, C. and J. Reid-Walsh (1998) "Mail-order memory work: Towards a methodolog of uncovering the experiences of covering over", *Review of Education/Pedagogy/Cultural Studies*. 20 (1), 57–75.

Mitchell, C. and Weber, S. (1999) *Reinventing Ourselves as Teachers: Beyond Nostalgia*. London and New York: Falmer.

Mitchell, C. and J. Reid-Walsh (2005) "Seven Going on Seventeen: Tween Studies in the Culture of Girlhood. New York: Peter Lang.

Mitchell, C. and J. Reid-Walsh (2007) *Girl Culture: An Encyclopedia*. Westport, Conn.: Greenwood Press.

Mitchell, C. and J. Reid-Walsh (2002) *Researching Children's Popular Culture: Childhood as a Cultural Space*. London and New York: Routledge/Taylor Francis.

Paley, N. (1995) *Finding Art's Place: Experiments in Contemporary Education and Culture*. New York: Routledge.

Park, E., Mitchell, C. and N. De Lange (2007) "Working with digital archives: Photovoice and meta-analysis in the context of HIV & AIDS". In N. De Lange, C. Mitchell and J. Stuart (eds), *Putting People in the Picture: Visual Methodologies for Social Change*. Amsterdam: Sense. (pp. 131–40).

Pink, S. (2004) *Home Truths: Gender, Domestic Objects and Everyday Life*. New York: Berg.

Pithouse, K. and C. Mitchell (2007) "Looking into change: Studying participant engagement in photovoice projects". In N. De Lange, C. Mitchell, & J. Stuart (eds), *Putting People in the Picture: Visual Methodologies for Social Change* (pp. 25–48). Amsterdam: Sense.

Reid-Walsh, J. and Mitchell, C. (2004) "Girls' web sites-a virtual 'room of one's own". In A. Harris (ed.), *All About the Girl: Culture, Power and Identity* (pp. 173–82). New York and London: Routledge.

Reid-Walsh, J. and C. Mitchell (in press) "Doll-play: A study of Canadian girlhood". In L. Learner (ed.), *Depicting Canadian Childhood*. Waterloo: Wilfrid Laurier University Press.

Rice, T. (2003) "Soundselves: an accoustemology of sound and self in Edinburgh Royal Infirmary". *Anthropology Today* 19(4), 4–9

Riggins, S. H. (1994) "Fieldwork in the living room: an autoethnographic essay" In *The Socialness of Things: Essays on the Socio-semiotics of Objects*. Berlin: Mouton de Gruyer.

Sofaer, J. (2002) "Disinter/est: Digging up our childhood. Performance research". Vol. 1 Spring. www.joshuasofaer.com/texts/write_dduoc.html (retrieved 24 April 2009).

Sofaer, J. and J. Sofaer (2008) "Disinterest, digging up childhood, authenticity, ambiguity and failure in the autobiography of the infant self". In D. Arnold and

J. Sofaer (eds), *Biographies and Space: Placing the Subject in Art and Architecture* (pp 169–93). London: Routledge.

Spence, J. (1994) *Cultural Sniping: The Art of Transgression*. London: Routledge.

Stald, G. (2007) "Mobile identity: Youth, identity, and mobile communication media". In D. Buckingham (ed.), *Youth, Identity, and Digital Media* (pp. 143–64). Cambridge: MIT Press.

Turkle, S. (ed.) (2007) *Evocative Objects: Things We Think With*. Cambridge: MIT Press.

Warner, M. (2004) Introduction. In Haworth-Booth, M. (ed.), *Things: A Spectrum of Photography 1850–2001*. London : Jonathan Cape in association with the Victoria and Albert Museum.

Weber, S. and C. Mitchell (eds) (2004) *Not Just Any Dress: Narratives of Memory, Body and Identity*. New York: Peter Lang.

Weber, S and J. Weber (2007) "Technology in the everyday lives of 'tweens'". In S. Weber and S. Dixon (eds), *Growing Up Online: Young People and Digital Technologies* (pp. 49–66). New York: Palgrave Macmillan.

Weber, S. and C. Mitchell (2007) "Imaging, keyboarding, and posting identities: Young people and new media technologies". In David Buckingham (ed.), *Youth, Identity, and Digital Media* (pp. 25–48). Cambridge, MA: MIT Press.

Part III

Practices of Contemporary Marketers

7
Children's Virtual Worlds: The Latest Commercialization of Children's Culture

Janet Wasko

The Internet has been praised for offering an unlimited means of accessing and sharing information, as well as new forms of entertainment and diversion. While a good deal of attention has been directed at adult role-playing games (such as *World of Warcraft*), social networks (such as MySpace and Facebook), and virtual communities (such as Second Life), less is known about websites aimed at children.

This chapter considers a recent instance of the commercialization of children's culture by analyzing virtual worlds aimed at young children. While much research has focused on the effects of media use and content on children, the political economic factors involved in this area are often underplayed or ignored by academic researchers. This chapter argues that it is necessary to incorporate forms of critical political economic analysis, especially for new products and media forms that have incorporated marketing and advertising strategies targeted at children.

A brief overview of these developments is followed by detailed case studies of two leading virtual world sites, Neopets and Webkinz. The analysis focuses on the appeals of these sites to children, and how they define children as consumers. This will involve looking at the economic models used by these sites, and the ways in which they are connected with other forms of marketing and commercial activity.

Studying children's media culture

Many agree that the commercialization of childhood and youth has accelerated dramatically with new forms of media and marketing. Not only are children and youth avid consumers of a growing array of media and other cultural products, but the process of targeting children for consumption through the media and advertising has become increasingly more developed and sophisticated. New methods of advertising and marketing to children are emerging with new forms of communication, while the control of children's media is largely in the hands of a few transnational media conglomerates that dominate the rest of the media landscape.

The perspective adopted in this chapter is generally referred to as the political economy of media or communications. In *The Political Economy of Communication*, Vincent Mosco has defined this approach as "the study of the social relations, particularly power relations, that mutually constitute the production, distribution and consumption of resources" (Mosco, 1996, p. 25). He explains that political economy is about survival and control, or how societies are organized to produce what is necessary to survive, and how order is maintained to meet societal goals. Political economic analysis is crucial in understanding children's culture these days, especially the proliferation of products and new media forms, and of diverse forms of advertising.

The internet and virtual worlds

In addition to attracting children and teens to a myriad of resources and activities, the internet is developing into a unique marketing tool for children's products. Advertising expenditures online continue to grow, with the global market for internet advertising estimated at $45 billion in 2006. Though this represents only 7.4 per cent of the total global advertising market, this amount is expected to grow.

In 2001, Kathryn Montgomery identified several strategies used in online marketing related to children:

- Integration of advertising and content.
- Viral marketing that takes full advantage of instant messaging and other peer-to-peer forms of digital communication popular with children and teens.
- Branded environments where users can spend hours interacting with the product.
- Web-based cross promotions that are designed to "drive" kids to advertising sites on the Web.

Among the more recent developments that Montgomery discusses in her later work (Montgomery, 2007) are virtual worlds targeted at children and young people. A virtual world is defined as "...an interactive simulated environment accessed by multiple users through an online interface." (http://www.virtualworldsreview.com/info/whatis.shtml). Virtual worlds are also called "digital worlds" or "simulated worlds" and overlap with "MMOG's" (massively multiplayer online games). There are many different types of virtual worlds, although six common features are identified by the Virtual Worlds Review:

1. *Shared Space*: the world allows many users to participate at once.
2. *Graphical User Interface*: the world depicts space visually, ranging in style from 2D "cartoon" imagery to more immersive 3D environments.
3. *Immediacy*: interaction takes place in real time.
4. *Interactivity*: the world allows users to alter, develop, build, or submit customized content.
5. *Persistence:* the world's existence continues regardless of whether individual users are logged in.
6. *Socialization/Community*: the world allows and encourages the formation of in-world social groups like teams, guilds, clubs, cliques, housemates, neighborhoods, etc.

The virtual worlds business is growing rapidly, not only with new websites such as those discussed here, but also businesses related to the exploitation of those sites. For instance, K Zero is a British company describing itself as "the industry-leader in understanding the marketing dynamics relating to virtual worlds" (http://www.kzero. co.uk/blog/?page_id=2092). Several websites are devoted to the virtual worlds business, while a Virtual Worlds Conference and Expo has been organized during the last few years by a company called Virtual Worlds Management, and features a special "Kids Track" (http://www. VirtualWorldsManagement.com).

One industry analyst has estimated that 8.2 million children were members of a virtual world in 2008, predicting that the number would increase to 20 million by 2011 (Barnes, 2008). While it is difficult to estimate the number of virtual worlds aimed at children and young people, a list of over 200 youth-oriented worlds, live or in development as of January 2009, is provided at the Virtual Worlds Review site (http://www.VirtualWorldsManagement.com/2009/youth-01-26-2009. html). Meanwhile, another source estimates that over 200 children's virtual worlds were in development at the beginning of 2009 (Takahashi, 2009).

These online worlds are based on several different business models. The first type features advertising, in the form of both overt messages (like banners) and messages imbedded in content. The Neopets site, discussed below, is one example of this model. Other virtual worlds are organized around a subscription model. An example is Disney's Toontown, which claims to be "...the first massively multiplayer online game designed specifically for kids and families." Limited play is free, but most activities require a monthly or yearly subscription. Other sites owned by Disney and organized similarly are Club Penguin, Pirates of the Caribbean Online, and Pixie Hollow. Meanwhile, other virtual worlds require some kind of purchase. The Webkinz site, discussed below, is an example of this model, and has been imitated by other toy companies, including Hasbro (Littlest Pet Shop), Russ (Shining Star), Ty (Beanie Babies and Ty Girlz) and Build-a-Bear (Build-a-Bearville).

Some other sites appear to be free: for example, AngelsOnline boasts "Free to play forever." However, advertising sometimes creeps into these sites as well. For instance, the free "educational" site, Whyville, introduced promotions for Toyota's Scion cars as part of the "content" of the site (Nelson, 2007). Some "free" sites tie in to other media or brands. For example, the Nicktropolis site focuses on Nickelodeon-trademarked characters and franchises, without advertising (at least at the moment). A similar example is the FusionFall site, which introduces players to the Cartoon Network Universe. Still other virtual worlds are free but entirely sponsored by one brand, such as General Mills' Millsberry.

The attraction of virtual worlds aimed at children is obvious to many businesses. As a representative of K Zero (mentioned above) explains: "The motivation for these companies to create virtual playgrounds is simple: It's an extension of the real world toy play and keeps the children in a 'branded' frame of mind" (de Mesa, 2008). Media conglomerates, in particular, are interested in these sites for similar reasons: they "can deliver quick growth, help keep movie franchises alive and instill brand loyalty in a generation of new customers" (Barnes, 2008).

While there are numerous virtual worlds aimed at children, the next sections of this chapter provide case studies of two sites that represent a particular subset of these sites. Neopets and Webkinz are virtual pet sites that feature a range of animals – although other pet sites are devoted to specific species, from virtual horses and camels to virtual chinchillas and poultry (see virtualpet.com for an extensive list of virtual pet sites.)

Neopets – a neophyte entertainment franchise

Neopets.com is a "virtual pet community" that can be described as a combination of Tamagotchi (the virtual pet craze of the mid-1990s), The

Sims, and Pokemon, with a little bit of Disney thrown in.[1] It is a "free" site supported by advertising – lots of advertising, which is often integrated into the other content. Members are allowed to create or adopt up to four pets from a wide array of unique animal species. The pets must then be fed and entertained. Although this sounds simple enough, the site is quite complex and includes a wide range of activities.

There are 10 different themed lands around Neopia, such as Faerieland, Mystery Island, the Lost World, etc. These include a wide range of features, including stores and shops where you can buy food and other items (toys, books, clothes, weapons) for your pets using Neopoints, which can be earned in various ways. Neopia has its own post office, newspaper, hotel, concert hall, restaurants, and bank. Pets can own their own pets, called PetPets.

Communication is possible through neoboards, neomail, greetings and other forms of messaging. There are guilds (which are actually clubs with different themes). Other interactive features include members' art work, poetry, coloring pages, and so on. The site boasts that "Neopet members are not merely passive visitors." Many of these features are organized as competitions, including beauty contests, caption contests, pet contests, and Neohome competitions. There are also over 160 different games revolving around competitive battles, puzzles, luck/chance or action activities. The emphasis is on "safe and friendly" entertainment, with various safeguards in place for protecting young children. The company boasts that it adheres to government regulations on children's sites, and is proud of its monitoring of language use.

The website was created in November 1999 by Adam Powell and Donna Williams, sometimes described as two "bored" British college students.[2] Doug Dohring, described as "a marketing executive," bought the site and formed Neopets Inc. in February 2000. Only a few months later (April 2000), NeoPets, Inc., a privately held corporation based in Glendale, California, began business operations as the owner and operator of Neopets.com. By July of the same year, the company was said to have "reached profitability," with annual revenue of "eight figures" from advertising (60 per cent) and merchandising (40 per cent).

While Neopets membership has continued to climb, the reported membership numbers are often contradictory. Statistics on the site are updated regularly and reported over 170 million owners, nearly 251 million individual Neopets, and over 752 billion pageviews in May 2009. The demographics were reported as follows: under 13 years old – 39%, 13–17 years old – 40 per cent, 18 and older – 21 per cent. Around 57 per cent of the members are female and 43 per cent are male.

Neopets is claimed to be "the stickiest site in the world," enticing its members to remain online for long periods of time. According to one source, members spend an average of 6 hours and 15 minutes per month at the site, which was ranked second on the entire Internet. The same source claimed that over 2.7 billion pages were viewed per month.[3]

Neopets matures: ownership and diversification

The Neopets company's goal is stated clearly in its press material: "Continue development as the largest global youth entertainment network on the Internet, and further its revenue generation through opportunistic offline ventures." As Neopets Chairman and CEO Doug Dohring explained: "Since early 2000, when we founded the company, I felt that we could create a strong connection between the youth of the world and our Neopets-created characters and storylines, which we would ultimately extend into television, movies, merchandise, publishing and other offline vehicles in a very significant way."

In March 2005, Neopets made a deal with Warner Bros. Pictures to develop Neopets characters and stories into several feature films. A few months later in June 2005, Viacom purchased the Neopets company for $160 million. Viacom is a huge diversified conglomerate, which incorporates numerous well-known brands including Nickelodeon, MTV and Paramount: it amassed revenues of over $14.6 billion and net earnings of $1.2 billion in 2008. A month after the sale of Neopets, Nickelodeon launched TurboNick, a broadband video platform that allows children to watch full length shows online at any time. The company explained: "As the first kid's network to provide full length video programming online, combined with the recent acquisition of Neopets,® a global online entertainment network ... Nickelodeon now offers more multiplatform experiences than any other kids' entertainment company." Not surprisingly, links to TurboNick, Nick.com and Nick.shop have appeared on the Neopets site. As this suggests, such developments are part of broader trends towards the convergence of different media platforms and brands, and the concentration of ownership within the contemporary media industries.

Neopets and advertising

The Neopets company claims to have pioneered the idea of "immersive advertising," defined more specifically as "creative programs that integrate the advertisers' commercial products, services, brands and names into existing or customized activities and scenarios within the site, thereby making the product an important part of the activity or game."

Although not all activities on the site are sponsored, there have been a significant number of sponsored locations and games. For instance, McDonalds, Disney, Oscar Mayer, and General Mills have sponsored a number of games and locations in Neopia, while other games appear periodically that are connected to current films or television programs, or other sponsors (these are sometimes known as "advergames"). While the company admits that this is "an evolution of the concept of traditional product placement," it is debatable whether or not Neopets invented the idea.

The company typically downplays the effects of immersive advertising, but their press material boasts that the process "...produces lasting awareness, retention and brand affinity, with impressions that effectively and repeatedly convey the advertiser's message to the intended consumer." Advertisers have responded positively to Neopets, as indicated by Courtney Lane, Director of Mattel Girls Online, who explains: "It becomes addictive... It has tremendous stickiness, and that helps us gain the exposure we need." However, not all of Neopets' advertising is "immersive," and much of it stands alone from the games. Advertising banners and other advertising messages accompany nearly every page, and some games are preceded by commercial announcements that cannot be skipped.

The Neopets site is thus the base for a broad entertainment franchise: it represents copyrightable properties or concepts that can be repeated or continuously remade in multiple media platforms or outlets with merchandising and tie-in potentials. The site promotes and sells a wide variety of Neopets merchandise, including hand-held games, mobile phones, trading cards (and a trading card magazine), and video games. Tie-ins are frequent and include McDonald's, Disney, Limited Too, and many others. With various global activities, including translation of the site into 10 different languages, the "free" Neopets site has developed as an entertainment franchise that works especially well with Viacom's other franchises (MTV, Nickelodeon, etc.), and it seems likely that it will continue to expand.

Neopets ideology

The Neopets site is not just about adopting and caring for a pet – it can easily be interpreted as a training ground for capitalist consumer culture. While other values or ideas are represented on the site, themes related to materialism and consumption are particularly overt. Neopia is organized as a capitalist society, as is apparent, for example, in its bank and stock market, as well as the game "Plushie Tycoon" where one can become a successful manufacturing tycoon. There are lots of shops; and while many are created by the site, members are also encouraged to open their own shops, which sometimes come together in malls or markets. In many ways, players are encouraged to acquire (buy) items and sell them for Neopoints. The company explains that "through smart purchases and trades with others, members can turn a 'virtual' profit, increase the size of their shops, and thereby increase their visibility on the site." A recent addition is the NeoCash Mall, where items are available for "real world" money. Customized clothes and decorations can also be purchased through Neocash Cards, which can be purchased through PayPal or at participating stores.

A huge number of "neoitems" are available, both for Neocash or "real" cash. Over 31,736 items were accounted for in early 2009 on one of the fan sites.[4] When pets do not "own" anything, they are portrayed as desperately sad and dejected (often crying), and encourage their owners to purchase something. Even when one feeds or plays with pets, they may still request the owner to buy something else.

To participate in many of the activities on the site, one must pay in Neopoints. You can own a home (for a fee), and furnish it with items purchased with Neopoints (or "real world" money), as well as paying to attend concerts, or visit restaurants and pubs. Even when a pet comes down with a disease, the hospital diagnoses the problem and sends the owner to the pharmacy where drugs and cures must be purchased. There is the possibility to "work", and an employment agency, although these features play only a minor role compared to other activities.

Games of luck and chance are prominently featured – including some overt gambling activities such as slot machines. The battledome is an attraction for many members, who purchase various kinds of weapons or strengths to wage battles with other members. There are also ongoing narratives featured on the site, often involving wars between different lands, complete with heroes and villains.

Overall, the company claims that "...the only limitation of the site is the member's own imagination." However, the site appears quite a lot like the "real world" with many boundaries set and numerous limits on imaginative activities. (This is reminiscent of Disney and its theme parks, where imagination is promoted, but limited by a variety of control mechanisms: see Wasko, 2001).

Neopets and market research

The site encourages its members to spread the word about Neopets, with various incentives provided as part of the Neopets Referral Program.

Numerous offers are also available for earning Neopoints by filling out surveys for Neopets, as well as for other companies. A "Survey Shack" features a "youth panel" and games related to the survey activities. While the company's revenues have been mostly from advertising and merchandising, it also receives funds for its market research activities. Indeed, the Neopets company has become known as an expert in market research through its relationship with OpinionSurveys.com, the online marketing research division of The Dohring Company, which has been listed as one of the top 100 market research firms in North America in *Advertising Age* magazine. Neopets' annual youth survey is used by numerous other marketing companies and publications.

Webkinz – online cuddling

In 2005, a new strategy for linking virtual worlds with actual products was introduced with a line of plush animals called Webkinz. The collection currently includes over 200 different animals (with new ones constantly introduced) that include a "secret code" allowing owners to enter the online Webkinz World and play with the digital version (or avatar) of their toy.

The toys and the Webkinz site have been growing in popularity since their introduction, much to the consternation of some parents, who were initially unable to find the popular products, especially during some Christmas seasons. With demand high, some retailers reported that some children were tearing off the tags in order to access the Web site. Originally, the stuffed animals were sold only in select specialty stores, although distribution has expanded to include larger chain stores and mall stores. By midyear 2007, more than 2 million units had reportedly been sold to retailers and 1 million users were registered on the Webkinz site.[5] Traffic on the site grew more than 800 per cent in 2007, totaling more than 7 million unique visitors per month. Its success has led other companies, including Mattel and Russ Berrie, to copy its approach.

The stuffed animals and the site were created by Ganz, a privately-held family company with headquarters in Toronto, Canada. Ganz was founded in 1950 by Sam Ganz and his two sons. The business began as Ganz Toys and distributed licensed products created by other companies, such as Disney and Sesame Street. The company expanded by offering a wide range of "giftware, fashion accessories, fragrant candles, and finishing touches for the home," and changed its name to Ganz. Its brands include Time & Again, Bella Casa, Treasured Memories, MaggiB, and Heritage Collection. The company is still owned and operated by the Ganz family. Sam Ganz remains active within the company, while his son Howard serves as president and daughter Mindy heads the Webkinz Foundation (see below).

The Webkinz world

Webkinz site is not quite as complex as Neopets, and states that it is intended for users aged 6–13+. (A newer site described below is aimed at younger players.) Webkinz World has its own currency (KinzCash), products for sale, and a range of activities. Daily and hourly giveaways and games attract players to the site. While there is a variety of games, no real "action" or overtly violent games are included and many of the games and activities are considered educational.

Pets are monitored for their health, happiness and hunger. They must be fed food items that must be purchased or won, as well as receiving attention and exercise. The hunger monitor only drops when a player is online, although the happiness monitor drops when pets are ignored. Pets cannot die, but can become sick and must be treated at Dr. Quack's clinic, where prescriptions are paid for with KinzCash.

A major feature of the Webkinz experience is building and furnishing homes (which may include outdoor, underwater and tree top rooms). Players' virtual pets are able to walk around their homes and can invite other players to visit. Other activities are connected with items purchased for the home that include interactive features. Games and toys are available, including exercise equipment (and even swimming pools). Pets can grow their own food, which can be prepared with kitchen appliances. Food, clothing and other items can be stored in refrigerators, dressers and toy boxes. Bathroom items include bathtubs where pets can be bathed and groomed, while toilets actually flush. Televisions feature short animations, but players can also purchase equipment ("Webkinz Studio") plus actors and backgrounds that allow them to produce "shows." In addition to working for Webcash, pets can also attend classes (for a fee) and earn badges at the Kinzville Academy. Competitions are held at the Webkinz Stadium, including Beauty Pageants and Cooking Challenges, but winning is dependent on the badges earned.

Players can communicate with each other through the Kinz Post or in chat rooms, where they can interact and play games. These are carefully monitored and controlled, as explained in the parents' information section:

> In our KinzChat area, the chat is entirely constructed. There is no way for users to type what they want, exchange any personal

information, ask or say anything inappropriate. We control everything the users are able to say. In the KinzChat PLUS area, children may type using their own words and phrases as long as they are not on the excluded list of words and phrases developed for this form of chat. We try to exclude inappropriate words and phrases, including proper names and numbers to avoid the disclosure of personal information. If you do not want your child to chat in the less restricted KinzChat PLUS area, you can block their access in the Parent's Area.

While there is no actual gambling, as in Neopets, roulette-type wheels and scratch cards are integrated into various luck or chance activities.

Another feature similar to Neopets is a room where pets can answer survey questions (and view the results). Sometimes the questions are about activities on the site, but they often also pertain to real life activities, such as "Have you ever been on a cruise liner?" (72% said no) or "what kind of pet do you have in real life?" The surveying is much less prominent than on the Neopets site, and it is also unclear how the information is actually used.

Promotion of Webkinz products

The Webkinz site is not supported by advertising,[6] although it shares some of the same features of the Neopets site. There are many ads for Ganz ("Get your hands on a GANZ™") and Webkinz products, and for retail locations where specific Webkinz plushies can be purchased. There is constant encouragement to buy additional pets, and new creatures are regularly introduced as older ones are retired. The Webkinz of the Month encourages the purchase of a new plushie each month for added bonuses. Other lines of pets have been introduced: L'il Webkinz are smaller versions of the original Webkinz, while Signature Webkinz are bigger, more realistic, and approximately three times more expensive than the regular plushies. Accounts also need to be renewed after one year, by buying a new pet, and the push to sell more plushies is ongoing.

Other Webkinz merchandise is constantly promoted on the site, including trading cards, figurines, pet carriers, bookmarks, school essentials, clothes, purses, knapsacks, cosmetics, Christmas ornaments, and so on. Most of these products include online prizes or Kinzcash bonuses, while some allow access to restricted areas of Webkinz World. Kinz Klips (smaller animals on clips, sold for around the same amount as regular Webkinz plushies) allow entry to ZumWhere; Webkinz charms are needed to enter Fairy Falls and search for virtual charms; and Woodland figures allow entry into the Woodland Wonders forest.

Webkinz has added the opportunity to purchase an online pet without purchasing the actual stuffed animal. Various online or computer-simulated pets or items are available for eStore points, which are purchased with "real money" at the Webkinz e-store. Purchases are restricted to those 18 years old and above, and the site claims to sell to over 60 countries. A recent addition to the site is a subscription feature called "Deluxe Membership." Subscriptions are available for one month ($5) to one year ($45) and include exclusive features, such as monthly eStore points, which then draw users to the store. Yet another new development is a separate site called Webkinz Jr. aimed at 3-6 year olds. The Webkinz Jr. pets are pricier than the originals, selling for around $24. The newer site is definitely aimed at younger children, with much simpler and fewer activities and no interaction with other players. There are numerous educational opportunities for young children and less emphasis on buying items, either virtual or otherwise.

Webkinz ideology

Overall, Webkinz seems considerably more "parent-friendly" than similar sites. For instance, in Webkinz World, healthy food is cheaper, exercise is encouraged, and educational games are promoted. Interaction with other members is strictly limited and special activities are organized only during after-school hours. "Webkinz Cares" announcements appear on many pages and include messages such as: "Fruit is good! Fuel your body!" and "Explore the Outdoors! Take a Break! Spend some time outside!" The parent's guide also places great emphasis on its "age-appropriate" and "educationally based" activities covering areas such as addition, spelling, and logical thinking. For these reasons, the site has won awards from groups such as the iParenting Media Award, which honors products for outstanding achievements in the children's and juvenile marketplace.

Webkinz Philanthropy

Some of the profits that Ganz is accumulating from Webkinz are apparently being directed to charitable causes through The Webkinz Foundation, created in late 2007 to develop programs and donate funds to programs that improve "the welfare, development, health, and safety of children." In fall 2007, Ganz initiated the "All About The Kids" campaign, which involved donating Webkinz pets and laptops to children in hospitals. As of May 2008, it had donated over 17,000 Webkinz pets and 100 laptops to 39 hospitals in the US, and 17 hospitals in Canada.

The program has recently expanded to include the donations of items to family shelters. The Foundation also involves players in its philanthropic activities through a new area on the site called The Caring Valley. Entrance requires purchase of a specially-tagged stuffed animal, after which players can choose from several different themes that relate to charitable organizations. Webkinz Foundation promises to donate $1 million to child-focused charities based on members' choices. In yet another campaign, Webkinz partnered with Walgreens stores in the US to donate a portion of the sale of specially marked Webkinz pets.

Analyzing children's web worlds

Celebrating online freedom and virtual worlds

While this study has not included specific analysis of website audiences, one can identify several potential reasons why these virtual worlds are so popular. One of the key attractions is their interactive and participatory characteristics, which have been lauded by a wide range of observers. Many scholars have pointed to the empowerment and independence associated with participatory and interactive media (for instance, Jenkins, 2006; Benkler, 2007; Shirky, 2009), and online gaming in particular (Castranova, 2008; Taylor, 2009). These new media are praised for encouraging creativity, allowing enhanced social interaction, and offering freedom from centralized media sources.

Of course, the creators of these sites are well aware of these points. In discussing why they started Webkinz, the Ganz company explains:

Where are young people spending their entertainment time? More and more, kids are going to the Internet. Why? It's interactive. Instead of passively watching television, the Internet gives kids choice. They can play games, chat with friends and express themselves. They decide how to have fun. (http://www.ganz.com/corporate/media/ press_release/StoryOfWebkinz.pdf)

The children's sites described above certainly offer a good deal of interactivity, which could be viewed as "empowering". As the Ganz company's communications manager, Susan McVeigh, explains:

. . . there's such diversity when you're on the site. You can focus on the educational element, or you can play in the arcade; if you have a child that likes detail-oriented activities, they can be designing their room and moving furniture around. We've really managed to capture the independence of the Internet where kids control what they do instead of being told what they do.

Many internet activities are considered educational, providing opportunities for learning skills and enhancing knowledge. In the case of Webkinz, the attraction of fun and pleasure is sometimes accompanied with overtly educational opportunities. More commercial sites such as Neopets provide some learning experiences as well – as one observer has noted, they "can teach young people about typing, communicating, caring for pets, and budgeting" (Jesdanun, 2007). Pleasing parents by engaging in these kinds of activities may be an added attraction for children who use the sites.

These virtual worlds also provide appealing ways to connect with friends and interact with other users online; and as some have argued, this may provide opportunities to learn about citizenship and community. The personal nature of the activities may also offer a special attraction. Creating, naming and caring for individualized pets online provides a kind of personalized appeal. Thus, Neopets offers an especially wide variety of activities, in addition to the imaginative, humorous, and creative creatures that populate the site. Meanwhile, Webkinz offers children the fun of owning their own plush pet(s) and playing with them online, in addition to (possibly) gaining an appreciation of philanthropy.

Critiquing children's online worlds

However, other observers of these new media developments have expressed concern about a range of issues pertaining to children's health and welfare – such as the amount of time that children spend playing online, the potential for online stalking, and so on. Yet the commercial dimensions discussed here have received rather less attention.

As I have argued, digital media increasingly offer new marketing potential, especially for reaching audiences that are difficult to connect with through other media. An industry representative has described virtual worlds for children as "…a very powerful medium for marketing because it involves this huge engagement. It's more powerful than a sugar cereal commercial" (Olsen, 2007). Whether "immersive" or not, advertising on children's sites is a particularly controversial practice (see Schor, 2004; Seiter, 2005; Montgomery, 2007). Seiter (2004) found that children did not immediately recognize advertising as part of the Neopets site. More recently, in a study of websites used by UK children, Nairn (2008) found that only 37 per cent of the advertisements were labelled as such and almost one quarter of the ads were integrated or embedded into the content. The study also concluded: "While children gradually learn how to tell entertainment from commerce, the true nature of advergames was not even understood by 16-year-olds."

As noted previously, the internet has opened new avenues for obtaining information about consumers, including techniques to gather data about children who use websites such as Neopets and Webkinz. Indeed, one of the interesting characteristics of pet websites is that children return often, in order to care for and play with their pet(s), thus establishing an ongoing relationship with the site and enhancing the potential for data-mining. The strategies employed in gathering and using information about children in this way are considered by many to be deceptive and highly problematic (CME, 1996).

Much of the literature on new digital media celebrates their liberating and empowering characteristics. While the phenomenon of virtual worlds is far more complex than one-way, mass mediated forms of communication, many (if not most) of these popular sites are still controlled by private, for-profit companies. How much "independence" and "empowerment" they offer is certainly debatable. While Jenkins and others are right to argue that new media engage the imagination of fans, it is still important to ask who is ultimately in control, and to consider how specific ideas, values and meanings are represented here.

This is particularly apparent in the emphasis on consumption at the Neopets site. As Healy (1999) has observed, these sites teach how to be "a good consuming member of the consuming culture." While Webkinz may be less commercial and potentially more educational than Neopets, both represent examples of commercial children's culture, and ultimately reinforce consumer ideology. Though these sites may provide "safe" (Webkinz) or "free" (Neopets) entertainment that is sometimes embraced by parents and educators, they also naturalize the commercial process that is at the core of advanced capitalism. While these sites may represent more participatory forms of media, they also represent the latest example of new technologies being driven by commercial imperatives. Of course, further research is needed to fully assess and understand the impact and effects of these complex forms of new media; but a complete account will need to integrate political economic analysis of the kind provided in this chapter.

Notes

1. This analysis draws strongly on an excellent study by Grimes and Shade (2005).
2. The information describing business aspects of Neopets is taken from the press kit, offered on-line at http://info.neopets.com/presskit/press01.html.
3. comScore Media Metrix, February 2005.
4. http://www.neoitems.net/idb/stats.php

5. The company declined to share more recent data.
6. Around Christmas 2008, the Webkinz site included an ad for a movie, received a good deal of negative feedback from parents and advocate groups, and promptly removed it.

References

Barnes, B. (2008) "Web Playgrounds of the Very Young," *New York Times*, December 31.

Benkler, Y. (2007) *The Wealth of Networks: How Social Production Transforms Markets and Freedom*. Yale University Press.

Castronova, E. (2008) *Exodus to the Virtual World: How Online Fun Is Changing Reality*. New York: Palgrave Macmillan.

Center for Media Education (CME) (1996) *Web of Deception: Threats to Children from Online Marketing*. Washington, DC: CME.

De Mesa, A. (2008) "Toy Brands Don't Play Around in Virtual Worlds," brandchannel.com, July 14. Online at http://brandchannel.com/start1.asp?fa_id=430.

Grimes, S. and L. Shade (2005) "Neopian Economics of Play: Children's Cyberpets and Online Communities as Immersive Advertising in NeoPets. com," *International Journal of Media and Cultural Politics* 1:2.

Healy, J. (1999) *Failure to Connect: How Computers Affect Our Children's Minds – and What We Can Do About It*. New York: Simon & Schuster.

"Hottest Products of 2007: Kids Face Webkinz Shortages" (2007) http://www.bloggingstocks.com/2007/11/24/hottest-products-of-2007-kids-face-webkinz-shortages/

Jenkins, H. (2006) *Convergence Culture: Where Old and New Media Collide*. New York: New York University Press.

Jesdanun, A. (2007) "Sites Introduce Preteens to Online Networking," *USA Today*, 13 July. Accessed online at http://www.usatoday.com/tech/products/2007-07-12-3370531937_x.htm.

Montgomery, K. (2001) "Digital Kids: The New On-Line Children's Consumer Culture," in Dorothy G. Singer & Jerome L. Singer (eds), *Handbook of Children and the Media*. Thousand Oaks, CA: Sage Publications, pp. 640–643.

Montgomery, K. (2007) *Generation Digital: Politics, Commerce, and Childhood in the Age of the Internet*. Boston: The MIT Press.

Mosco, V. (1996) *Political Economy of Communication*. London: Sage.

Nairn, A. (2008) "'It Does My Head in … Buy It, Buy It, Buy It!' The Commercialisation of UK Children's Web Sites," *Young Consumers* Vol. 9, No. 4, pp. 239–53.

Nelson, M. G. (2007) "Virtual Worlds Aren't Just for Reaching Adults Anymore," *Clickz*, July 5. Accessed online at http://www.clickz.com/3626340.

Olsen, S. (2007) "Are Kids Ready for Ads in Virtual Worlds?" CNET, Oct. 16. Online at http://news.cnet.con/Are-kids-aready-for-ads-n-virtual-worlds/2009-1024_3-6213661.html.

Schor, J. B. (2004) *Born to Buy: The Commercialized Child and the New Consumer Culture*. New York: Scribner.

Seiter, E. (2005) *The Internet Playground: Children's Access, Entertainment, and Mis-education*. New York: Peter Lang.

Shirky, C. (2009) *Here Comes Everybody: The Power of Organizing Without Organizations.* New York: Penguin.

Takahashi, D. (2009) "More than 200 Kids Virtual Worlds in Development," *Venutre Beat,* Jan. 26. Accessed on line at http://venturebeat.com/2009/001/26/more-than-200-kids-virtual-world-in-development/.

Taylor, T. L. (2009) *Play Between Worlds: Exploring Online Game Culture.* Boston: MIT Press.

"Tweens: A Consuming Army," (2005) *Playthings,* September, pp. 42–50.

Wasko, J. (2001) *Understanding Disney: The Manufacture of Fantasy.* Cambridge: Polity Press.

8

Creating Long-lasting Brand Loyalty – or a Passing "Craze"?: Lessons from a "Child Classic" in Norway

Ingunn Hagen and Øivind Nakken

> Children (like adults) are vulnerable to media manipulation and to clever marketing plans. But for each carefully orchestrated product launch that succeeds, many others fail. Children may be prone to consumer crazes, but they choose which crazes, and they decide when a craze is over (Tobin, 2004: 10).

This chapter explores the popularity of a Norwegian "craze" centred around a fictional pirate called *Captain Sabertooth (Kaptein Sabeltann)*. As a series of theatrical performances, TV shows, books, music, toys and other merchandise, and now an animated feature film, *Captain Sabertooth* is distinctively different from most global crazes. As Ellen Seiter (2008) has noted, it represents "a rare success story of a brand that has survived despite being restricted to one nation of less than five million people". Indeed, it is a phenomenon that has sought to establish itself as a long-lasting "children's classic" rather than merely a passing "craze". In this chapter, we explore the strategies that have been used by the producers of *Captain Sabertooth* to create and maintain brand loyalty, and to ensure its longevity, among Norwegian children and their parents.

Captain Sabertooth – a national craze

Captain Sabertooth has been a national "craze" almost since the figure was first created in 1989. This pirate and the stories, songs and products related to him have been enormously popular among Norwegian children – especially boys. The producers of *Captain Sabertooth* have been able to create and sell a set of products that have become a widespread "cultural practice", something children (and their families) actively consume, enjoy and play with.

The original story of *Captain Sabertooth* was created by Terje Formoe, the former Director of Marketing and Entertainment of Kristiansand Zoo (see Hjemdahl, 2003). He started to develop annual summer shows (theatre performances) for the Zoo, featuring himself as Captain Sabertooth. In Kristiansand Zoo, where *Captain Sabertooth's* famous nightly summer shows still take place, there are now several areas dedicated to this pirate: the *Black Lady* (his ship), his castle, and the "pirate harbour/village" called *Captain Sabertooth's World*, with restaurants, cafés, and souvenir stores, where daily small shows take place in the summer.

However, from the beginning this character moved beyond Kristiansand Zoo. Soon the creator himself and a growing number of other companies were selling numerous *Captain Sabertooth* media products like films (on video and later DVD), an animated movie, books, music (CDs and audio tapes), TV series, "activity magazines", and computer games. Accompanying the media products, there are numerous spin-offs: swords, pirate robes, T-shirts, nightgowns, toys such as *Captain Sabertooth's* ship, plastic pirate figures, purses, food boxes, bags, pirate jewellery, and so on. It almost seems as though Norway has become "piratized", with *Captain Sabertooth* everywhere and in all forms; as ice-cream, potato chips, bread, cod liver oil, on children's bed linen, and so on. In his "search for gold", the pirate and his creator have conquered a large audience in Norway, perhaps especially through the rather catchy songs.

In her analysis of Nordic theme parks and how the figures from them are present in children's everyday lives, Hjemdahl (2003) found *Captain Sabertooth* to be the dominant popular cultural phenomenon in the Norwegian preschools (kindergartens) she visited. The presence of the pirate was especially apparent in the sword battles taking place all over the preschool playgrounds. Boys aged from two to six years were the most eager *Sabertooth* fans, with this figure forming a permanent part of their role play. Most children also knew the stories and the songs very well. As this implies, the Captain has become an important identification figure and part of preschool (boys') play culture in Norway.

Ingunn's own son was no exception. It was through his and his friends' embrace of *Captain Sabertooth* that she became aware of the intensity of the children's relationship to this figure. Dressing up like *Captain Sabertooth* and having sword battles was a favourite leisure activity during their preschool years. In addition, young boys (and girls) in her son's preschool pretended to be Captain Sabertooth or one of his men and constantly involved themselves in sword battles and play fights. Through this experience, she became a bystander and also a participant in this cultural practice.

Commercial Childhood and "CRAZES"

As the other contributors to this book make clear, consumer culture is present in the lives of today's children from a very early age (Kline, 1993; Cook, 2004). This issue has been frequently discussed in Norway in recent years, in the media, in academic literature and in public reports (e.g. BFD, 2001; Hagen, 2001; and Tingstad, 2006). As these debates make clear, marketing to children invokes larger questions related to contemporary childhood. What does children's participation in the intensified global, mediated consumer culture mean for the continuity between generations? And how can we theorize the relationship between structure and agency here – between market forces and children's active negotiation of these forces and the identity definitions available to them (see Buckingham and Sefton-Green, 2004)?

Trends like globalization and media convergence have led to increased market competition as different commercial actors look for new customers and market niches. By creating brand loyalty among children at an early age, companies seek to secure a profitable future. Thus, marketers will try to identify children's desires, fears (like their fear of the dark), and group norms: their worshipping of (often very masculine or feminine) heroes, their fantasies and dreams, their (often slapstick) humour and their peer group identities (wishing to be "cool" and included, fearing exclusion) (cf. Kline, 1993; Seiter, 1993; Wasko, 2001). For the *Captain Sabertooth* products, the primary target group is 2–8-year-old children, mainly boys. However, efforts are also made to target the whole family, something we will address later on.

Our case study of *Captain Sabertooth* is part of a broader research project exploring the strategies of the media, advertisers and related industries in the children's market. One of the aims here is to understand how marketers respond to often fragmented markets by developing global strategies and multimedia "synergies", where successful products are adapted to several media platforms like TV, film, computer games and printed material. Products targeted at children often become short-lived "crazes", of which well-known examples include *Pokèmon* (see Tobin, 2004), a number of the *Disney* movies and characters, *Teletubbies, Bob the Builder, My Little Pony, Teenage Mutant Ninja Turtles, Barbie, Bratz, Super-Heroes* and *Harry Potter*. These crazes are brands or multimedia trends that spread rapidly on a global scale, across countries and across media and product categories, based on inter-textual references and integrated marketing (cf. Lindstrom and Seybold, 2003). In these ways, successful crazes become part of children's everyday lives and play practices.

Unlike these other examples, *Captain Sabertooth* remains a national craze, despite some attempts to introduce the products in other countries. It is also noteworthy that the character was created by one person – the singer and former Director of Marketing and Entertainment at Kristiansand Zoo Terje Formoe – while most global crazes have large global media conglomerates (like Nintendo or Disney) behind them. *Captain Sabertooth* has expanded gradually from its beginnings as a theatre show and enjoyed almost constant growth for the last 18 years. While he has yet to achieve global popularity, Captain Sabertooth is a figure of central importance in the lives of pre-school boys in Norway. However, this craze has received little academic attention, with the exception of forming part of Hjemdahl's study (2003).

Captain Sabertooth and brand loyalty

In order to understand how brand loyalty may be created among children (and their families), and to explain the relative longevity of *Captain Sabertooth* compared to similar crazes, one needs to examine the encoding processes related to the brand. According to Blindheim (2003), branding is so important because there are often very few real differences between products. Control over a brand is a way to play on the desires, aspirations and fears that consumers have, often unconsciously (for example: "What do I need to have?" or "Who should I be?"). The creation of brand loyalty has become a key goal of contemporary marketing. Brand loyalty means that consumers will buy products related to the brand numerous times (repurchase behaviour), often without considering alternative brand choices. An indicator of brand loyalty is when positive experiences with the brand lead consumers to recommend the brand to family and friends (word-of-mouth).

The concept of "brand equity" is often discussed in relation to brand loyalty, referring to the extra value a brand can add to products. The brand itself will create certain associations and expectations: in the case of toys produced by Disney, for example, these typically relate to a nostalgic view of childhood innocence (as described in several of the articles in Wasko *et al.*, 2001). *Captain Sabertooth* undoubtedly possesses high brand equity, at least in children's culture in Norway. But what is particular about these stories, songs and products that makes them appeal so much to young children? How are the qualities and associations of the brand constructed and managed by the organizations that produce them? Through our analysis of interviews with central actors behind the *Sabertooth* phenomenon and the numerous products and texts, three key themes emerge: synergies, inclusion and brand control (Nakken, 2007). These themes will be elaborated below, as they also shed light on mechanisms present in the marketing of other products and brands to children.

Synergies

The concept of synergies includes the cross-media properties of a brand like *Captain Sabertooth* and the organizational structure and networks surrounding the products. In many respects, it is easy to understand why children feel at home in this brand culture or universe. The same – simple and almost archaic – pirate stories are told over and over again in different ways and in various forms. This reuse of the stories and also the songs may be crucial in making the different products recognizable to small children (who often love repetition).

Moreover, it is possible for the audience to consume the texts and products through a number of channels and via several sensory modalities. As Lindstrom and Seybold (2003) argue, appealing to different senses – like sound, sight, smell, taste, and touch – is an important part of brand building in the children's market. Thus, the *Sabertooth* products appeal to several senses, and also create synergies between them. Sound, in the form of both music and talk, is available both on CDs, in the theatre show, in movies, in the theme park, in audio books and in computer games. Visually, there are powerful images, characters, costumes, and settings. However, in this case, songs, music and sound effects often make the images subordinate. On the official website, the familiar music and Captain Sabertooth's voice are very prominent (www.captainsabertooth.com). Being able to sing along is an important and integral part of the appeal, and the songs seem especially suited to inspire bodily movements, battles and role-play (Hjemdahl, 2003).

Other senses are stimulated by other *Captain Sabertooth* products. Especially in the theme park in Kristiansand Zoo, children may have physical contact with the whole pirate adventure experience. Children (and their parents) can eat "pirate dishes", hear the familiar songs, and even meet their heroes for photo opportunities. An important part of the Kristiansand pirate experience is the fact that this is a family event, something children enjoy together with their parents. Children and their parents can also enter Sabertooth's ship, the *Black Lady*, which when crossing the "Grass Ocean" fires at the "enemy ship" it meets. When the children come home with their newly acquired (and old) *Sabertooth* gear, like movies on DVD, songs and sound books on CD, and costumes, these things serve to remind them of the whole sensory experience of the theme park, and inspire them to continue the play. For children the Sabertooth character and spinoffs offer a "room for action" (Hjemdahl, 2003). If one only pays attention to the textual aspects of this phenomenon (as stories), it is difficult to grasp children's fascination. For children, *Captain Sabertooth* is not only a text, or a collection of texts, but a *cultural practice* (cf. Buckingham and Sefton-Green, 2004). The significance of swords, for instance, relates to the use of swords for fighting and "being" the pirate, and the appeal of the pirate songs may relate to their rhythm and their ability to deepen the adventurous immersion, or to accompany the children's play.

Synergies may be explained in terms of two inter-connected notions: "synergies of production" and "integrated marketing". "Synergies of production" refers to the structure of the production network related to *Captain Sabertooth*. Terje Formoe, the author and copyright owner, estimates that his network consists of 24–25 different companies of various sizes. Formoe owns Captain Sabertooth A/S, which is at the centre of the network. He also has shares in Piratprodukter A/S and Seven Seas Production A/S. Piratprodukter A/S manages *Captain Sabertooth's World* (in Kristiansand Zoo), and owns the restaurants and the spin-off shops in the theme park. Until recently, the majority of spin-off products were also licensed to Piratprodukter A/S. This integration appears to create stronger and more profitable companies than if they had worked independently, or sold licenses to external franchise-holders.

Kristiansand Zoo is a popular location where "good parents" take their offspring for summer trips, and is still the site of the nightly theatre shows. In 1995, there was a dispute between Formoe and Kristiansand Zoo about the *Sabertooth* copyrights and royalties. When the originator then moved the summer shows to Asker (near Oslo), both he and especially the Zoo experienced fewer visitors. The following year, Formoe and his pirate returned to Kristiansand Zoo, and so did the visitors: unsurprisingly, the Zoo has been rather cooperative since that time. This cooperation may thus result in equity transfer between two strong brands: the pirate and Kristiansand Zoo. Brands also rely heavily on the indirect effects of press coverage and "word-of-mouth". Media coverage is secured by Kristiansand Zoo's role as a major cultural institution in Norway, so the cultural context is ideal for promoting the *Sabertooth* brand. Terje Formoe's own growing position as a national celebrity also adds brand value, leading in turn to further positive media coverage.

Such organizational networking is also valuable when it comes to the next theme, integrated marketing. Cross-promotion or marketing in several channels is increasingly important in order for brands to survive (cf. Lindstrom and Seybold, 2003). Organizational networking such as that around the *Captain Sabertooth* brand usually provides a basis for more flexible communication and marketing strategies (cf. Stohl, 2001). The integrated marketing strategies are characterized by cooperation between different companies, in that campaigns in one company may have indirect effects on the others. For example, when Panvision A/S marketed and distributed the computer game (produced by Artplant), or when Svensk Film A/B marketed and distributed the *Captain Sabertooth* animated movie in 2003, these activities would also indirectly market the overall brand. This synergy prevents the marketing of the different media and spin-off products from appearing unduly 'aggressive', which might prove counter-productive, especially in the children's market.

Inclusion

Inclusion here refers to the brand's ability to involve the audience (children of different ages and gender, and their parents) in a variety of ways, through intertextual references, through textual strategies like creating closeness and presence, and through providing characters for identification. We can use Kozloff's (1992) categories of settings, events, and characters to identify the key elements of the *Captain Sabertooth* stories in this respect.

The setting is the Seven Seas, the ocean where several mystical islands are located. The main one is Abra, where the Captain and the other pirates live. The events are typical for pirate stories: Captain Sabertooth and his men sail his ship (the Black Lady) on different adventures and treasure hunts, often assisted by a map. Complications occur when others are searching for the same treasure. The main character is the same in all the stories – the cruel and greedy Captain Sabertooth, described as the most feared pirate of the Seven Seas. He is also feared by his men, Longfinger (also called Captain Sabertooth's shadow), the fat and hopeless twins Wimp and Wally, the often clumsy and foolish Benjamin, and the chef Tully (who uses everything in his cooking, including rats and insects).

Another central character in the stories is Tiny, a small boy who often assists Captain Sabertooth, although the latter would never admit this. Thus, Tiny is often the real hero of the stories and an ideal character for identification. Tiny is the youngest of the Captain's crew. At first, he dreams about becoming a feared and respected pirate. But life is hard since none of the older crew takes him seriously, despite his active role in the successful achievements of the Captain and his men. Tiny misses having someone to talk to who respects him. In several of the stories, Tiny is teamed up with Veronica – a young, cute girl his own age from the cosy village of Luna Bay. This friendly place of "ordinary people" is contrasted with Abra – the invisible island of Captain Sabertooth and his men, where Tiny grew up as an orphan. Despite her nicer environment, Veronica suffers from some of the same problems as Tiny: she is not taken seriously. Through Tiny, the author is able to communicate certain values that are central in all the various cross-media stories: happiness will not be achieved through finding gold – friendship and love are the real treasures of life.

When one reads the different *Captain Sabertooth* stories, one is often struck by the simplicity of their plots. The uncomplicated story structures – with kernels and few storylines involving only some of the characters – seem adjusted to the expected cognitive abilities of the main target audience of children aged 2–8 years. Terje Formoe's skill in simplifying the stories makes them easy to follow, thus facilitating the inclusion process.

Producers are often concerned if there is a discrepancy between the target group and the actual consumers. This was also the case for the production network around *Captain Sabertooth*. Preschool boys are already fascinated by the pirate, but recruiting girls as consumers is more of a challenge, as Formoe admitted in our interview:

> Boys have been the majority so far, probably because boys in general play in a rougher way. Yet, I am working quite consciously and intensively to appeal to more girls. In my next show, I will present more female characters. And actually... I have already noticed more and more girls dressing up like Captain Sabertooth when they come to Kristiansand Zoo... painting their faces white and even painting a moustache. But still... many of the female characters presented in my stories so far have been very traditional girls... in traditional roles. However, in my next show you will meet rougher girls... who can be tough just like the boys. And that is quite important for me... to represent both boys and girls (interview with author, 2006).

Several authors (e.g. Buckingham and Sefton-Green, 2004) have pointed out that the child market is very fragmented according to age and gender. Boys are resistant to anything "girlish", although girls will often consume both what is traditionally feminine and also what is "boy-ish". In this case, Tiny and Veronica represent this blue-pink division. Young boys may find potential identification figures in both Tiny and the Captain or his men. Female characters include traditional, sweet Veronica, and the scary witch Miriam, who are both less prominent characters in the stories; and while girls may identify with them, they may also do so with the male characters.

However, the *Sabertooth* character is not only promoted to children, but also to their parents and grandparents. This is a fruitful strategy, since it is the adult family members who mostly pay for the fun. In particular, going to Kristiansand Zoo and visiting the nightly theatre shows require that children are accompanied by adults. Terje Formoe is clear about this in the interview:

> What is very important in my shows in Kristiansand Zoo is to create not only entertainment for the children, but a happening for the whole family. One of my greatest interests is that the children can experience *Captain Sabertooth* together with adults. I want it to be an experience for several generations. I want parents and grandparents to join in the play. When children watch their parents having fun as well, the intensity of these children's experiences will increase. I try to reach all generations – but everything *through* the children. Because it should all be on their premises (Formoe, 2006).

The summer shows in Kristiansand Zoo have indeed become a tradition for many families with small children. Over almost two decades, Formoe has effectively turned his pirate into a "children's classic", something new generations of children will be introduced to. In some respects, this is similar to the ways in which the Disney Corporation plays on parents' nostalgic childhood associations with their products, despite many parents' feelings that Disney is too aggressive in its marketing (Hagen, 2001; Wasko, 2001). In Norway, there has also been public concern about the commercial nature of *Captain Sabertooth*, especially in relation to the media coverage of the conflict between Formoe and Kristiansand Zoo in the 1990s, where the underlying commercial aspects were illuminated (cf. Hjemdahl, 2003). These critical discourses have also been taken up by certain (often middle class) parents, and also preschool teachers.

But how are the parents invited to become involved in the stories? Different textual strategies are used to include parents, for example by incorporating statements or elements that may amuse adults, such as focusing on the shortcomings of adult characters, gender relations and humorous battles. Humour in *Captain Sabertooth* is often derived from someone trying to appear braver and tougher than he is (and this most frequently applies to male characters), an approach which may appeal to adults as well as children. Moreover, the universe of the pirates is very open to participation by the audience, particularly in Kristiansand Zoo. Here both children and adults can dress up like pirates, take part in the singing and join the pirate characters (Longfinger, Wimp and Wally, and Benjamin), who walk around, participate in photo sessions with the children and enact small shows. Even the Captain himself can occasionally be observed on the roof of his castle. Being in the pirate universe (and the Zoo) with their children and buying them spinoff products they sometimes intensely wish for, may also provide parents with the feeling of being dedicated and generous parents.

The notion of inclusion can also account for some of the indirect marketing strategies used by Terje Formoe and his partners. In addition to the experience of being among the *Sabertooth* figures and places at Kristiansand Zoo, there are also various forms of two-way communication, which happen primarily through the website (www.captainsabertooth.com) and through the "activity magazine". In the latter, children are encouraged to send in pictures of themselves with their pirate heroes or drawings of Captain Sabertooth. One striking example is the very clever creation of the so-called Pacifier Heaven:

> Well… We in *Captain Sabertooth* A/S do not use marketing… I mean direct marketing to children… marketing in its traditional sense. But we communicate in a different way; we get a lot of questions and letters here from children and their parents. For instance, we have a comic named *Captain Sabertooth*, which is a comic/magazine of activities through which we communicate with the children sending us letters and pictures that we put in. And we get a lot of letters from… different people… for instance related to *Captain Sabertooth's Pacifier Heaven*, which is an offer from us to the youngest children at about 4 years who are about to quit using their pacifier. They can send their big treasure here to Captain Sabertooth who promises to keep it and take care of it in his *Pacifier Heaven* – a treasury with seven chests full of pacifiers. Everybody who sends their pacifier to Captain Sabertooth receives a letter from him saying he will keep an eye on their treasure… So we communicate at various levels, but we try to communicate through the stories and the universe that we represent (Formoe, 2006).

This example illustrates some of the efforts that are made to create an emotional bond with small children, by offering to take care of their dearest belonging, and hence to establish brand loyalty from a very early age.

Brand control

Brand control is crucial to the maintenance of brand loyalty: it may be considered as the glue keeping the other components of brand building together and making them work properly. Brand control works at both the organizational and textual level. In relation to brand control, Formoe revealed that he had learnt important lessons from Disney's brand building practices, when as entertainment and marketing director at Kristiansand Zoo he organized Disney weeks and Disney shows in the 1980s. The key lessons were to do with protecting rights through registering the brand and maintaining control over the licensing and quality of products and spinoffs (see also Nakken, 2007). As Gary Cross (1997) suggests, this kind of 'character licensing' implies that the stories and toys are closely interrelated and consumed simultaneously.

Terje Formoe seems to have very long-term ambitions for *Captain Sabertooth*: his aim is to establish it as a "children's classic" rather than merely a passing "craze". According to Hjemdahl (2003), the author is keen to play down the more commercial aspects of his creation, and to focus on the cultural aspects. In our interview, Terje Formoe argued that improving his songs and stories was the only way to develop the brand. His business strategy involves exercising strict control over the development of products related to *Captain Sabertooth*. In order to ensure that the different products stay close to the original concept, Formoe's company *Captain Sabertooth* A/S operates as a kind of quality control police. According to Formoe, only companies that he considers "serious" are given licences.

The wider production network seems to share the understanding that the strict control that Formoe exercises is important for the success of the brand, and especially for its long-term survival. This control is made possible by the fact that the production rights to *Captain Sabertooth* products are licensed to different companies directly by Formoe himself. In the contemporary children's market, such licence agreements have proved to be an efficient way to develop the (economic) potential of a brand (Lindstrom and Seybold, 2003); but carelessness when giving licence rights to different producers may lead to economic losses, as was the case with Nintendo and its *Pokèmon* craze (Tobin, 2004). Of course, brand alliances may strengthen the brand (as in the case of *Captain Sabertooth* and Kristiansand Zoo), but they are also risky. There are also brands one does not want to be associated with, in order not to tarnish one's brand, as Formoe indicated:

> Yes… once I cooperated with *McDonald's*. My publishing house *Cappelen* [a Norwegian publishing house] convinced me. We made two small campaigns with two small books. Actually, those books were quite all right. So… I thought… if they sell out… or give out a bunch of those books – which we already had sold out in the shops – that might be a very good promotion of the whole *Captain Sabertooth* concept. However, these campaigns became such a success for *McDonald's*… that they returned to me and asked for CDs and other stuff as well. But then I was clear on the issue: now it was enough *McDonald's*. In fact, *McDonald's* is not what I want to be associated with first of all… Actually… I think it turned out to be a little bit wrong connecting *Captain Sabertooth* to *McDonald's* (Terje Formoe, 2007).

This strict control also means keeping the stories and products close to the original concept, and ensuring that the universe and characters are predictable and recognizable. However, control is not only a matter of production: it also relates to what is communicated about the brand to the public. The "Sabertooth war" in 1995 – where disagreements between Formoe and Kristiansand Zoo about copyrights and royalties made big newspaper headlines – may illustrate the negative consequences of losing control over public communication about the brand.

Both the concept of "Synergies" and the concept of "Inclusion" should be seen in strong relation to Terje Formoe's brand control, as Figure 8.1 shows.

There are some potential fragilities in the relationship between the three categories outlined above. The other components of the brand-building process may suffer when certain aspects of the brand control fail or are negatively influenced – for instance through disagreements about copyright and royalties. The synergies will fail, at least on a short-term basis. In seeking to maintain synergy, it is crucial that units and companies work together and pull in the same overall direction.

Conclusion

In this chapter, we have discussed some of the strategies used to create brand loyalty to *Captain Sabertooth* among Norwegian children.

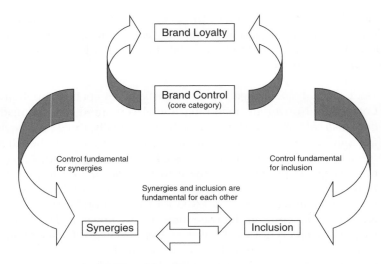

Figure 8.1   Dynamics of brand loyalty

Its long-lasting brand loyalty suggests that there is an effective match between the efforts of the producers (structure) and what appeals to children (agency) (cf. Buckingham and Sefton-Green, 2004). The themes of "synergies", "inclusion" and "brand control" have been discussed as central elements in these strategies. Brand control is regarded as the main foundation for creating brand loyalty, but this category presupposes and is related to the two others.

Synergies are about the relationships between the structures and processes of production. The cooperation between the production networks creates synergies across organizational and media borders, resulting in forms of integrated marketing. Like more global crazes and cross-media products such as Pokèmon and Disney (Tobin, 2004; Wasko, 2001), synergies of production may also lead to synergies between children's senses. In this case, the products' availability in so many forms probably has strengthened the overall experience of the brand.

The *Captain Sabertooth* brand is very inclusive, in the sense that the content and products involve and engage children. The brand is also inclusive in the way it communicates to a broad audience. Both boys and girls are given figures for identification in the stories, enabling them to enter this adventurous pirate universe; while inter-textual associations enable parents and also grandparents to be drawn in as well. In the process, *Captain Sabertooth* becomes a 'cultural practice' which does not only involve buying, reading and watching, but also acting out and playing.

Illustration 8.1   Captain Sabertooth with his sword (photo: copyright Nicolai Prebensen)

Brand control is so central that it can be considered as the glue that holds together all the other economic, organizational, social, psychological, and textual components of brand loyalty creation. Terje Formoe clearly had a good "schooling" in this respect though his earlier cooperation with the Disney company. He has largely succeeded in maintaining control of the *Captain Sabertooth* brand, despite the fact that the content has been spread though numerous media channels; and this has partly been down to his skill in choosing his partners and in creating positive brand alliances.

Brand loyalty among children is not easily created in a rich country like Norway, where globalization and the increased commercialization of childhood create fierce competition from other crazes, media products and toys. The commercial aspects of *Captain Sabertooth* have also have been criticised (Hjemdahl, 2003). It is and has long been a very commercially successful phenomenon; yet Formoe and his partners have been able to create a strong, long-lasting brand that is approaching the status of a "children's classic".

The brand loyalty that has been created around *Captain Sabertooth* casts new light on a classical question in media studies, about the relative power of media and marketers versus that of the audience. It is often presupposed that powerful structures go along with passive audiences (cf. Hagen, 2004/1998). But this case suggests that the power and success of the producers relates to their ability to *activate* their primary and secondary audience. Since the *Sabertooth* figures are able to stimulate playfulness, children's engagement, and their families' active participation, the producers can continue to sell their products to new generations of children and their parents. This continuing brand loyalty is an important asset in further brand building. Terje Formoe seems to have based new successes firmly on earlier successes and what has been proven to work before. Again and again, he has improved the quality of the brand, and thus its equity, thereby ensuring its long-term survival and growth.

The question is whether and how this 'virtuous circle' can be maintained, if *Captain Sabertooth* is now to go global as its originator hopes. It is doubtful that this Norwegian pirate character will be able to compete with Disney's main contemporary pirate, Jack Sparrow in the recent *Pirates of the Caribbean* films. This new popular culture version of the pirate has also reached Norway, and seems to be gaining popularity in the age group somewhat above the primary *Sabertooth* fans (with PEGI recommendations for the films at 11 years+). The slogan of the most recent *Pirates of the Caribbean* game *At World's End* is "Live & Die by the Sword". The slogan for *Captain Sabertooth* could easily have been "Live & Play by the Sword".

Note

1. This chapter is a revised version of the paper Hagen and Nakken wrote for the 3rd International Child and Teen Consumption Conference, held in Trondheim, 24 and 25 April 2008. It is also based upon the paper Hagen presented at the Nordic Consumer Research Conference in Finland, 3–5 October 2007 and Nakken's thesis (2007). Hagen was academic advisor for Nakken's case study of *Captain Sabertooth*, which forms his MA thesis (Nakken, 2007). This work forms part of the wider research project "Consuming Children: Commercialization and the Changing Construction of Childhood" (see Buckingham and Tingstad, 2007, and also http://www.svt.ntnu.no/noseb/Consuming/).

References

BFD (2001) *Oppvekst med prislapp? Om kommersialisering og kjøpepress mot barn og unge.* NOU 2001: 6, Barne- og familiedepartementet.

Blindheim, T. (2003) *Hvorfor kjøper vi? Om forbruk og reklame.* Oslo: Abstrakt Forlag A/S.

Buckingham, D., and J. Sefton-Green (2004) Structure, Agency, and Pedagogy in Children's Media Culture. In J. Tobin (ed.), *Pikachu's Global Adventure. The Rise and Fall of Pokémon* (pp. 12–33). Durham and London: Duke University Press.

Buckingham, D. and V. Tingstad (2007) Consuming Children. Commercialisation and the Changing Construction of Childhood. A Project Description. *Barn,* 2, 49–71.

Cook, D. T. (2004) *The Commodification of Childhood. The Children's Clothing Industry and the Rise of the Child Consumer.* Durham & London: Duke University Press.

Cross, Gary (1997) *Kid's Stuff. Toys and the Changing World of American Childhood.* Cambridge/London: Harvard University Press.

Hagen, I. (2001) "Norway: Norwegian Memories of the Disney Universe". In: Janet Wasko; Mark Phillips and Eileen Meehan (eds): *Dazzled by Disney? The Global Disney Audiences Project.* (pp. 222–57). London and New York: Leicester University Press.

Hagen, I. (2004/1998) *Medias Publikum. Frå mottakar til brukar?* (Media Audiences. From Receivers to Users?) Oslo: Ad Notam, Gyldendal.

Hagen, I. (2007) "Playing on Children's Desires and Fears: On Creating Brand Loyalty among Norwegian Children." Paper to the Nordic Consumer Policy Research Conference, Helsinki, Finland, 3–5 October 2007.

Hjemdahl, K., M. (2003) *Tur-retur temapark. Oppdragelse, opplevelse, kommers.* Kristiansand: Høyskoleforlaget.

Kline, S. (1993) *Out of the Garden. Toys, TV and Children's Culture in the Age of Marketing.* New York, NJ: Verso.

Kozloff, S., R. (1992/1987) Narrative Theory and Television. In R. C. Allen (ed.), *Channels of Discourse, Reassembled. Television and Contemporary Criticism* (pp. 67–101), 2nd edn. London and New York, Routledge.

Lindstrom, M. and P.B. Seybold (2003) *Brand Child. Remarkable Insights into the Minds of Today's Global Kids and Their Relationships with Brands.* UK: Kogan Page.

Nakken, Ø. (2007) *Captain Sabertooth – Adventurous Brand Loyalty.* MA Thesis, Department of Psychology, Norwegian University of Science and Technology (NTNU).

Seiter, E. (1993) *Sold Separately: Parents and Children in Consumer Culture.* Brunswick, NJ: Rutgers University Press.

Seiter, E. (2008) "Of Pirates, Pacifiers and Protectionism", http://flowtv.org/?p=1298

Stohl, C. (2001) Globalizing Organizational Communication. In F., M. Jablin, & L. Putnam (eds). *The New Handbook of Organizational Communication.* (pp. 323–75). London: Sage Publications.

Tingstad, V. (2006) *Barndom under lupen. Å vokse opp i en foranderlig mediekultur.* Oslo: Cappelen Akademisk Forlag.

Tobin, J. (2004) *Pikachu's Global Adventure. The Rise and Fall of Pokèmon.* Durham and London: Duke University Press.

Wasko, J. (2001) *Understanding Disney. The Manufacture of Fantasy.* Cambridge, NJ: Polity Press.

Wasko, J., M. Phillips and E. Meehan (eds)(2001) *Dazzled by Disney? The Global Disney Audiences Project.* London and New York: Leicester University Press.

9
The Cute, the Spectacle and the Practical: Narratives of New Parents and Babies at The Baby Show

Lydia Martens

This chapter considers how "elusive childhood" (Honeyman, 2005) and early parenthood are imagined at the site of The Baby Show, a UK consumer show targeted at new parents and other interested adults. The forms of consumer culture that surround the very young child have not received much scholarly interest to date. Yet this phase in the life course, in which new families are formed and in which adults develop a parental identity, is of interest in part because it illustrates how adult imaginings become interspersed with the complex voices and narratives coming from the marketplace. The Baby Show is an excellent site for an examination of how adults, diverse in terms of their objectives for taking part, construct the young child and the new parent. My arguments draw on ethnographic immersion at this site over several years.

After outlining in more detail the theoretical rationale for the study, and providing a discussion of the ethnographic research, the chapter moves on to the essence of my argument. This is that The Show has a binary reality, as a location for both the celebration and the anxieties of new parenthood. The Show's character as a community of parenthood and its display of the aesthetics of 'the cute' connect with the pleasurable and celebratory aspects of the early parenting experience. An opposing narrative sketches new parents as learners of practical parenting craft and, associated with this, consumers of appropriate parenting commodities (Cook, 1995, 2000). Parent craft connects with notions of child safety, health and education, which cohere with narratives of the young child as in need of care, as unpredictable and in need of training in the practices of everyday life (Martens 2005a; Nelson 2008). These things in turn indicate some of the potential anxieties new parents may suffer as they enter this complex domain, when they need to judge the implications of their choices for themselves and their offspring. In my concluding comments, I argue that these two aspects – the utilitarian concerns of practical parenting and the pleasurable elements of early childhood and parenthood – come together to shape the specific generational personae of the new-parent-adult and the young-baby-child.

Becoming parents and babies: identity (trans)formation and generational culture

This chapter builds upon my earlier argument (Martens *et al.* 2004; Martens 2005b) that research into children's consumerism should pay more attention to familial relations of consumption and to an examination of the interplay between the culturally constructed categories of 'adult' and 'child'. My concern here is with consumerism, consumption and consumer culture around the very young child – babies and even those yet to be born. I focus on the ways in which 'what it means to become a parent' in contemporary British society are culturally constructed alongside and in relation to 'what it means to become a baby'. An associated argument is the need to expand our attention to include all children, even those who as yet show little by way of consumer agency in their own right.[1] The rationale for this is partly to gain greater insight into the specific familial consumer culture (and material culture) into which the young child is received upon birth and through which it receives its early socialisation. Because the arrival of a baby is often connected with the establishment of a new family, the investigation of these consumer practices also allows us to trace the forms of cultural categorisation and transformation in people's self-identification as they move into parenthood.

This specific facet of generational consumer culture has not yet received much scholarly attention. Consumer scholars have examined the ways in which motherhood cultures and identities are forged through consumption practices, and how, through rituals with objects, mothers make sense of their own experiences. Such studies demonstrate how mothering remains a diverse set of experiences. Work by Pugh (2004) and Vincent and Ball (2007), for instance, illustrates how differential access to monetary resources affects the ways in which mothers can participate in consumer culture. Life course experiences also inform the ways in which mothers engage with material and commodity cultures, and how markets approach them. Layne (2004), for instance, has researched the rituals of loss engaged in by mothers of stillborns, whilst Martens (2005a) has focused on how early parenthood is sketched as risky and dangerous in commercial pedagogies. Studies of older children indicate how mothers and children actively negotiate around fashion (Boden *et al.* 2004), whilst Clarke (2007) discusses how mothers create normalised and localised "mothering cultures" through the adoption of similar consumption orientations around children's birthday parties. In relation to "empty nester" families, Hogg *et al.* (2004) have illustrated the memorialising rituals mothers engage in to make sense of the departure of their children from the parental home.

However, very little of this work has focused specifically on the experiences of very young children and new parents, and the commercial endeavours that surround them. Whereas children, teenagers and young adults have been shown to engage actively in creating generational culture through the medium of consumption (e.g. Miles *et al.* 1998; Croghan *et al.* 2006; Henderson *et al.* 2006), the cultural characterisation of 'the baby' is essentially an adult creation. Greater understanding of consumption in this phase of the life course also allows insight into the dimensions of consumer and generational culture that older children come to struggle against when they become more agentive.

The Baby Show

The Baby Show is a consumer exhibition which made its first appearance in London in 2002. It now takes place in five different locations in the UK at different times of the year[2] and is organised by Clarion Events, an events organisation company, which (according to its website) specialises in 'high value, difficult-to-engage markets' through the creation of 'environments that stimulate consumers to interact with our clients'.[3] My investigation of The Baby Show started in 2005 in Glasgow. I have visited six shows since then and my time has been spent walking around the show, talking with and observing visitors, exhibitors, their interactions, and activities on The Baby Show Stage and other 'entertainment'. Twenty semi-structured interviews have been conducted with parents-to-be and mothers-to-be, sometimes visiting with their own mums, and at each show photographic material has been generated.[4] I participated in The Show as a visitor and exhibitor, as a researcher and a mother of young children myself. Whilst this provided insight into the varying roles adopted by the people present,[5] my autobiographical reality as a mother of young children came into play through continuous reflection between my observations and my own mothering experiences and knowledge (Ellis and Bochner 2000; White 2003) and in my communications with exhibitors and visitors. This autobiographical dimension was also important when I piloted the 'shopping with consumers' approach advocated by Otnes *et al.* (1995) with my colleague Dr Emma Casey,[6] who was pregnant during the Earls Court 2007 show.

Visiting the exhibition was initially something of a novelty for me.[7] Like other consumption scholars, I had never consciously considered 'the exhibition' as a consumer event. How interesting, I noted during my first visit, that visitors pay £9 to enter the show, to then be offered a very diverse range of products, consumer advice and information on early parenting, freebies and entertainment. Apart from the big brands (such as Fisher Price, Mothercare, Huggies, Pampers, Phillips Avent, Comfort), exhibitor stands were populated by midwives and by the National Childbirth Trust; and there was a show area where the audience could, for instance, listen to the good parenting advice of the 'super nanny' and child behaviour expert Jo Frost or watch a fashion show for pregnant women and the young child. For the purposes of the new parent, this show could work very effectively, because high-street retailers in goods for the young child do not carry all the articles that can be found in the niche markets that currently exist, and that were present in abundance at the Show.

Of considerable interest to me was also the fact that the Show brings together a range of different actors with diverging and converging interests, including parents, prospective parents, babies and young children, other family members and interested outsiders, entrepreneurs from the market that caters for babies and their families, 'experts' and health professionals who work in the field of pregnancy and the young child, and entertainers. The Show therefore offers exactly what Clarion Events outlines on its website: the possibility for representatives from the commercial and non-commercial sectors to talk and engage with an otherwise hard-to-capture audience – that of new and prospective parents.

Unlike the relatively streamlined and organised mode of representation found in Mothercare, the UK's main retailer for the new and early parent, The Baby Show brings together exhibitors, brands, niche market products, visitors, freebies, services, displays, entertainment and parenting advice. It offers a mixed and at times bewildering array of potential experiences and first time encounters that demonstrates its character as a spectacle. This very element makes The Show excellent for moving beyond the uniform or streamlined message of the brand, as reflected in Mothercare. Through the diverse 'medical', 'health', 'scientific', 'educational', 'safety', 'care', 'memory', 'fun', 'cute', 'needs' and 'must-have' discourses employed by the various commercial and non-commercial agents at The Show, one here finds a more comprehensive and complex set of stories about new parenthood and the young child than in other commercial endeavours targeted at this population group. In this sense, too, The Show offers a rich environment in which prominent discourses about impending parenthood and the young child can be investigated.

The pleasures of early parenthood

The consumer-trade show has not received a high level of interest from cultural scholars commenting on consumption and consumer culture. More prominent foci for investigation have been inner city and out-of-town shopping centres and malls (Jackson *et al.* 2000; Woodruffe-Burten *et al.* 2006), department stores (Falk and Campbell 1997) and supermarkets (Humphery 1998). By contrast, historians have conceptualised the exhibition as a significant feature of modernity. In Rosalind Williams' *Dream Worlds* (1982), for instance, the phenomenon of the exhibition connects with historical developments in technologies of display, which she relates to the growth of the department store as a new mode of retailing in the late 19th century. Williams' emphasis on display, the orchestration of exhibits and visual aesthetics, and their connection to the manipulation of desires, are themes which have subsequently been elaborated upon by consumer behaviour scholars (e.g. Belk *et al.* 1989).

In the spectacle of The Baby Show, the visual and experiential orchestration is complex, deriving in part from the fact that the overall organisation of the Show by Clarion Events comes together with the more micro-level orchestrations and priorities of exhibitors. In addition, a diverse experiential and visual resource comes from the visitors, mostly people who are about to become parents, or who are already parents with young children. There is a temporal dimension to the 'crowd' experience, with a clear ebb and flow pattern discernible. Saturday is the busiest day, and Friday the quietest. In the early afternoons the crowd can become so dense that it is hard to walk through the Show at anything but a very slow pace, inducing one pregnant couple I interviewed to comment on the dubious safety aspect – how were so many parents going to get out with their prams and babies in an emergency? It is at this time that visitors end up sitting on the floor at the edges of the exhibition, when it is hard to find an empty place in any of the seating areas. These multiple temporal dimensions are evident in the short hand field notes written by Liz Ellis, who accompanied me to the Birmingham 2006 Show:

> Calm and relaxed as you enter. Soft pastel blue carpet underfoot, pink stands. Although quite busy with lots of pushchairs everywhere,

sense of calm. (Our) stand looks good with children's pictures – hope we get people. From the main entrance no clear path to follow – go where you feel – explore. Distinct areas at the ends e.g. Fairy non-bio stand, Huggies play bus, areas sponsored by large, successful companies. Ask a Midwife. Many different stands – busiest "Magic Custard" bronze casts of babies' hands and feet, Huggies free booty bag with nappies and baby wipes, Babylicious frozen baby food – free samples.

There is also an element of explicit and implicit 'on-show-ness' amongst visitors, with 'the bump' serving as a clear visual identifier for exhibitors, who targeted pregnant women with their sales tactics – something which some interviewees commented upon as being tiring. The events on The Baby Show Stage and the explicit call for visitors to consider the possibility of showcasing their 'cute child' also reflect the 'show' market relating to this phase of life – after all, the photographs of half-clothed babies found on the pages of magazines, in brochures and on packaging were mostly real life images.

The spectacle of 'the cute' was omnipresent at the Show, inviting adults into a world of innocence, cosiness and cuddliness (Harris 2000; Cross 2002, 2004). My photographic materials abound with examples of cuddly looking bunnies, bears, mice, ducks, often in subdued pastel (rather than primary) colour schemes, draped in specific ways over nursery furniture, or incorporated into baby clothing. Bunny shapes decorate the feet of baby grows, and clothing features slogans like 'made with 100% love', 'little monkey', 'don't wake me, I'll wake you', and sport flowers and other decorations, often in pastel colours incorporating light blues and pinks. A stall selling clothing for older girls (3–6 year olds) was notable for going against this aesthetic. On the other hand, 'cute' as a word did not often appear in the vocabulary of the parents-to-be I interviewed, unless they were explicitly asked to comment on it.

> LM: "Are you into cute?" Mum-to-be: "Yeah, definitely." LM: "What sort of things?" Mum-to-be: "I bought today... as we got a rocker and I definitely went for one that, well, as well as it being able to rock and being nicely padded and everything, I did go for the cutest one as well. There is an element of that. It is funny, as the practical side of me says 'It doesn't have to be cute, they don't really care if it is that cute or not' but then of course there is that need. I do definitely feel the need at the moment for things to be quite sweet and quite cute, so yeah..." LM: "What about you?" Dad-to-be: "Less so I think,

I am more practical. But if it is not much more money then yeah, you have got to get something that looks that little bit nicer." LM: "What is it about cute? This place is full of cute!" Mum-to-be: " Don't know." LM: "It is like you go round and you have to smile and..." Dad-to-be: "Babies, they do things to people!"

There was a clear common understanding amongst exhibitors at The Show about the visually desirable qualities of babyhood; and this was shared by the visitors who were frequently seen approaching certain stands exclaiming: "Ohhh, how cute!"[8] Exceptions also exist, as evidenced by the 'non-cute' dad-to-be in the above quotation and some other interviewees who rejected this desire for 'the cute'.

The aesthetic of the cute is an interesting, though insufficiently examined, phenomenon linking generational and gender imaginations with consumer culture in contemporary societies. It is clear that there is a huge market for the cute that defies age and parental relations, in the sense that people of different ages buy into it, in addition to those who are not parents. It is gendered in the sense that the cute appeals more to women and teenage girls than men, and connections may be identified between cuteness and various stereotypically feminine characteristics such as small, beautiful and desirable. Historically, these associations are evident in the small shoe and foot treasured in Chinese culture and in Western fairy tales like Cinderella (Martens 2004). There are indications that cuteness is a more universally appreciated aesthetic in Japanese society (Tosca 2003), but in the West its cultural significance is also apparent, for instance, in the animal and child imagery used extensively in the card and poster industry, and found in the photographic material produced by Anne Geddes and Betsy Cameron (Higonnet, 1998). Although it can be hard to define, the cute is visually easily identifiable and clearly generates a sense of desire and emotional affect in certain people.[9]

At The Baby Show, the cute and the use of specific colour schemes are clearly seen as the aesthetic best suited to the commercial and advisory space of the new parent and the young child. Through its connections with innocence, cosiness and cuddliness, it encourages the experience of pleasure in visitors at the Show, although these orchestrations are at times jeopardised. Crowd density, tired infants and visitors, and noise from the stage, for instance, all create distance from the subdued aesthetics of early childhood. In this sense, then, the Show offers a mixed, rather than a uniform and predictable aesthetic experience.

The Baby Show also functions as a commercial "community of parenthood" in the sense that it offers an opportunity for people to move in a crowd of parents and parents-to-be, surrounded by those with a similar interest and focus. At various stages, visitors will rub shoulders, whether whilst waiting in the queue to purchase their entry ticket; observing amongst others the antics of exhibitors; sharing a table or floor space to take a rest and have a drink; partaking in the baby crawling competition organised by Huggies, as parents of a crawling toddler or as spectator; or sitting and observing activities that are happening on the Baby Show Stage. These seem in varying ways to offer a shared parenthood experience, as expressed by Emma Casey after our 'shopping with consumers' experience: 'The event definitely perpetuated for me a sense of community and belonging' (Emma's notes, Earls Court Baby Show, London, October 2007).

Participation in a social gathering with like-minded others is typically a stimulus for pleasure (Warde and Martens, 2000), yet opportunities for new parents to come together like this are rare. Some examples of contemporary communities of parenthood include ante-natal classes, baby massage (and other) classes, National Childbirth Trust meetings, parent and toddler groups and Sure Start groups.[10] While some of these are provided by the state, others are commercially run. Other commercial agents have also recently appealed to the 'club' spirit of early parenthood, and various internet sites now offer virtual communities of parenthood, with active blog and discussion forums. At The Baby Show, however, new parents meet with others in a real life event and it could hence be seen as a rather unique experience.

The show as a 'practical' information conduit

As a commercial community of parenthood, The Baby Show also functions as an information conduit, providing opportunities for adults to come together as 'parents', to exchange ideas, and provide and receive advice on parenting practice. A related point of interest here is that there appears to be a strong presence of mothers amongst exhibitors. 'Being a mother' seems to be an important credential for offering 'good' advice and products to other mothers. In this sense, too, The Baby Show works as a community of parenthood, as it does not matter whether you are seller or buyer, exhibitor or visitor; parenthood gives participants an authority to advise others and functions as a reason to place trust in the advice given.[11]

Contemporary parents of young children are a particular group of adult consumers. As I have argued elsewhere (Martens 2005a), like their young children, parents, especially new ones, are essentially learners.

They are learning what it means to be a 'good' parent, and in the process they also learn about the product world that shapes and facilitates (and obstructs) parenting practices. Parents-in-the-making are established consumers before they enter parenthood, but the advent of a baby requires familiarisation with a new product world and a new set of everyday practices. In becoming parents, they are essentially in a transitional phase of identity formation (see also Taylor *et al.* Layne and Wozniak 2004). In comparison to other markets, this transitional quality of early parenthood makes early childhood a potent breeding ground for commercial innovation and experimentation. In this market, commerce can (and does) engage with and draw upon narratives from a range of knowledge communities which come together in informing this phase of the life course. These include medical, scientific, health, safety, environmental, and educational narratives. Many of the diverse products offered to people here thus tap into the parental and child 'needs' associated with these narratives.

During one of my visits, I concentrated on narratives around child safety, and found there to be multiple products and product features connected with this theme. In Martens (2005a), I analysed how the baby products market features different product groups that reflect safety concerns, including so-called child safety products, child safety conscious products and child safety advice products. In the first group belong such products as baby and toddler monitors, car seats, UV protective swim and beach wear, and a whole range of products from a company called Clippasave, which sells such diverse products as the bump belt (to avoid the car safety belt digging into the bump of a pregnant woman) through to safety clips for kitchen cupboards and windows. Perhaps the epitome of ascribed parental concern is represented by the new stem cell 'insurance' company, which stores cells from the baby's umbilical cord in the event of these being of use when the child develops certain illnesses in later life. In the second group belong those products whose design and production are guided by safety standards, or whose innovation narrative is based in an explicit aspect of progress in safety. These include baby chairs and rockers, prams and other 'travel systems', which come with labels that indicate the fire-resistance of the materials, warnings about and advice on how they ought to be used to avoid risks to child safety. Meanwhile, documentary products like parenting magazines, advice books and literature, fall into the third product group. The Show also features some products which carry dubious child safety credentials. Examples of these included the bed bumper (a decorative padded lining used to surround the inside of a cot bed, and associated with baby suffocation) and the baby sleeping bag (associated with overheating and baby cot death). Changes in these product groups also illustrate the intensification (and relaxation) of safety concerns over time. Stair gates, for instance, have moved through different formulations of safety standards over the years, rendering older versions unsafe to contemporary parents.

The Show's diverse safety products received some positive commentary from visitors. In an interview with a prospective mum, accompanied by her own mother, the latter said:

> I think what is out there for new mums is fantastic [compared] to when I was a mum. They didn't do baby shows when I was pregnant. You didn't see what was available and things, so it has been great today 'cause there's been lots of things that you think "Yeah, that will really give peace of mind" and I would have loved, like there is a little technique that you put on the baby's nappy and if the baby stops breathing for so many seconds it would give it a little shock and it would restart. If it didn't then it would give a longer bleep. So it would... certainly make you aware that the baby had stopped breathing. When I had my first, I was always worried about cot death.

Discussing the matter further, however, they had not bought one, but had taken away the web-address to think about it. Of course, with a price tag of £75, this new child monitoring device, which was showcased at the Birmingham 2006 Show for the first time, did not come cheap. Knowing about it now, however, the two mothers continued:

> Mother-to-be: "It is something that I want to think about, but I would like to [buy it]. God forbid if anything happened, I would feel guilty for not getting one." Her mother: "Yeah, after being shown it."

However, parents also expressed apprehension about the varied range of products on show. A new mother who was attending the Show for the second time commented that when she had been for the first time when she was pregnant, she 'was overwhelmed by how much stuff there was to buy.'

In my discussion with parents-to-be, it was clear that The Baby Show was regarded as an informational resource. One couple had attended the show twice, once when they were thinking about becoming parents, and this time when the woman was pregnant. They said they would come again, because they clearly thought the Show was excellent for learning about parenting products and practices:

> Mother-to-be: "I am interested in expressing."[12] Father-to-be: "That is one of the reasons why we are here today, you see, to find things out like that, aren't we?"

The Show thus provides a shop window for an extensive range of informational and instructional resources that characterise this transitional phase of the life course: these include a growing number of pregnancy and early parenting websites, magazines, advisory services, parenting manuals and advice books, as well as products with accompanying information. In this pedagogic terrain, the distinction between non-commercial and commercial is not clear cut. Midwifery information, for instance, comes as a free resource at the Show, whilst various exhibitors employ midwives to work on their stands alongside the company's own representatives. Moreover, the informational and parent networking websites, which have seen such growth in recent years, are set up as free (albeit branded) resources by companies as diverse as Bounty and Tesco (Martens 2009). Especially interesting is how, in their 'introduction speeches' to new parents, many companies draw on scientific and medical-health knowledge. Emma Casey, speaking from the position of a consumption scholar who attended as my pregnant companion, reiterated this:

> The thing that mostly left an impact on me was the sheer volume of complex pseudo-scientific information which we seemed to encounter at every stall... I felt I was given a lot of information which was intended just to make me buy products which I previously would never have thought I needed.

These types of comments illustrate how the narratives circulating at The Show around the practical aspects of parenting shape a specific understanding of what it means to be a "good parent" in contemporary society. Visitors clearly pick up on these messages and they have a diverse emotional response to them.

Conclusion

Through its celebration of the young child, the pregnant woman and the new parent, The Baby Show provides a diverse and complex range of informational resources and emotional appeals, not only for parents, but also for me, a consumption scholar making sense of it all. Though many scholarly narratives could no doubt be written about it, in my analysis here I have focused on the binary reality of the Show as celebratory and fun on the one hand, and utilitarian and practical on the other. The Show exhibited 'show-specific' features that emphasised its character as a spectacle, and that helped draw in visitors and create an expectation of fun, enjoyment and entertainment. The aesthetic of 'the cute' played a key function in merging 'what it means to be a new parent' with the qualities of 'early childhood', and tapping into the cuddliness, closeness and cosiness of the parent-child bond. 'The cute' is an interesting form of pleasure in the sense that it is a subdued form of joy experienced by adults focusing in on the world of the young child. It stands in contrast to the more 'extrovert' fun offered, for instance, by events happening on The Baby Show Stage, that reflect another facet of adult pleasure, and that at times dominated the impact of the cute at the Show. Gary Cross (2002, 2004) has described the opposition between the cute and the cool in children's consumer culture, and the pleasure that adults can gain from both dimensions (see Chapter 1 in this volume). However, we know little about how children use these different resources as they grow older, and how they move from the cute towards the type of 'cool' fun which scholars like Kenway and Bullen (2001) have identified as symptomatic of the opposition between older children and the significant adults around them.

As an aesthetic experience for the new parent, the subdued pleasure offered by the cute also apparently stands in contrast to the more serious aspects of new parenthood. It is clear that a number of prominent contemporary discourses, around health and safety, education and environment, inform product innovation and sales discourses at The Show; and in this consumer event, these diverse narratives are not sequestered or strait-jacketed. Exactly how exhibitors talk with visitors is entirely unconstrained, and notwithstanding the morality that surrounds parenthood, this inevitably means that new parents may be guilt-tripped into purchasing by being made to feel a 'bad parent' if they do not buy. Having a baby thus translates into an experience which must be simultaneously pleasurable, serious and even anxiety provoking. In the end, these facets work together to identify the young child as precious, making the parental duties of safeguarding, protecting and nurturing those youngsters all the more pertinent. 'What it means to become a parent' in contemporary society is therefore culturally constructed alongside and in relation to 'what it means to be a baby'. This chapter has emphasised that these constructions are essentially built by adults, working discursively on the cultural distinction between adulthood and childhood.

Acknowledgements

Many thanks to Liz Ellis and Dr Emma Casey, who have generously given their time to accompany me to The Baby Show during my research there; Liz as an active research assistant and Emma during her pregnancy so I could pilot the 'shopping with consumers' research technique. Both wrote some notes for me, and I have taken these into my discussion here. Nevertheless, any shortcomings in this chapter remain entirely my own.

Notes

1. This may be taken to mean different things. It is for example true that the assumed 'child' in much consumption-related research has the wherewithal to consume (i.e. that they are affluent), and whilst researchers have been interested to examine whether children from poorer backgrounds behave differently from those of affluent backgrounds when it comes to consumer agency and preferences, this distinction is often forgotten in the formulation of a uniform 'child' consumer. The difference I point to here is that of age, since another feature of such studies is to talk about the child as an agentive consumer, giving too little attention to the fact that age matters.
2. London Excel and Earls Court; Birmingham NEC and Glasgow SECC. In 2008, The Show made its first appearance in Manchester. Each show lasts three days, providing certain challenges for continuous ethnographic work, though offering an excellent temporality for iterative research.
3. From the company's website: http://www.clarionevents.com/?page= whatwedo consulted on 26 January 2008.
4. The exception was the Manchester 2008 show, when visitors were warned not to take photographs on entry into The Show.
5. It was for instance easier to talk with other exhibitors whilst being at the show as an exhibitor. As exhibitor, I was also confronted with the Show's regulations and the fees structure for exhibitors.
6. Dr Emma Casey is Senior Lecturer in Sociology at Kingston University (UK) and works around themes of gender, leisure and consumption. She had her first baby in February 2008.
7. Some 10 years earlier I had visited the modern homes exhibition at Glasgow's SECC, but apart from this, consumer shows had never been part of my repertoire of activities.
8. When we were exhibiting at the Birmingham Show, our little stand was positioned alongside the much larger fashion stand of the company Blooming Marvellous. It had a 'washing line' of baby grows with 'cute' logos hanging alongside the entrance to our little cubicle, and during time spent there, this observation was frequently heard.
9. See also Harris (2000) for a description of the features of 'the cute'.
10. National Childbirth Trust is a UK based charity supporting new parents. Sure Start is a recent UK government initiative targeted at children and parents in deprived areas, and connects with its social inclusion programme.

11. Practical Parenting, a magazine targeted at this life course phase also has its participating staff explicitly introducing themselves as parents.
12. 'Expressing' is the term used for breastfeeding mothers who express some of their own milk to store and feed to their babies through a bottle at a later date.

References

Belk, R. W., Wallendorf M. and J.F. Sherry Jr. (1989) 'The Sacred and the Profane in Consumer Behavior: Theodicy on the Odyssey'. *The Journal of Consumer Research*, 16, No. 1: 1–38.

Boden, S. C. Pole, J. Pilcher and T. Edwards (2004) 'New Consumers? The Social and Cultural Significance of Children's Fashion Consumption'. Cultures of Consumption Working Paper Series, No. 16: 1–26.

Clarke, A. (2007) 'Making Sameness: Motherhood, Commerce and the Culture of Children's Birthday Parties.' In E. Casey and L. Martens(eds) *Gender and Consumption: Material Culture and the Commercialisation of Everyday Life*, 79–98. Avebury: Ashgate.

Cook, D. T. (1995) 'The Mother as Consumer: Insights from the Children Wear Industry, 1917–1929'. *Sociological Quarterly*, 36, No. 3: 505–22.

Cook, D. T. (2000) 'The Rise of "The Toddler" as Subject and as Merchandising Category in the 1930s'. In M. Gottdiener (ed.). *New Forms of Consumption: Consumers, Culture and Commodification*. Lanham, M/ Oxford: Rowman and Littlefield.

Croghan, R., Griffin C., Hunter J. and A. Phoenix (2006) 'Style Failure: Consumption, Identity and Social Exclusion'. *Journal of Youth Studies*, 9, No. 4: 463–78.

Cross, G. (2002) 'Valves of Desire: A Historian's Perspective on Parents, Children, and Marketing'. *Journal of Consumer Research*, 29: 441–7.

Cross, G. (2004) *The Cute and the Cool: Wondrous Innocence and Modern American Children's Culture*. New York: Oxford University Press.

Ellis, C, and A. Bochner (2000) 'Autoethnography, Personal Narrative, Reflexivity. Researcher as Subject.' In N. K. Denzin and Y. S. Lincoln (eds). *The Handbook of Qualitative Research.*, 733–67. Thousand Oaks, CA: Sage Publications.

Falk, P. and C. Campbell (1997) *The Shopping Experience*. London: Sage.

Harris, D. (2000) *Cute, Quaint, Hungry and Romantic: The Aesthetics of Consumerism*. Da Capo Press.

Henderson, S, J. Holland, S. McGrellis, S. Sharpe and R. Thomson (2006) *Inventing Adulthoods: A Biographical Approach to Youth Transitions*. London: Sage/Open University Press.

Higonnet, A. (1998) *Pictures of Innocence: The History and Crisis of Ideal Childhood*. London: Thames & Hudson

Hogg, M. K., C. F. Curasi and P. Maclaran (2004) 'The (Re-)Configuration of Production and Consumption in Empty Nest Households/Families" *Consumption Markets & Culture*, 7, No. 3: 239–259.

Honeyman, S. (2005) *Elusive Childhood: Impossible Representations in Modern Fiction*. Columbus: Ohio State University Press.

Humphery, K. (1998) *Shelf Life: Supermarkets and the Changing Cultures of Consumption*. Cambridge: Cambridge University Press.

Jackson, P., M. Lowe, D. Miller and F. Mort (2000) *Commercial Cultures: Economies, Practices, Spaces*. London: Berg Publishers.

Kenway, J. and E. Bullen (2001) *Consuming Children: Education-Entertainment-Advertising*. Buckingham/Philadelphia, Open University Press.

Layne, L.L. (2004) 'Making Memories: Trauma, Choice, and Consumer Culture in the Case of Pregnancy Loss'. In J. S. Taylor, L. L. Layne, and D. F. Wozniak (eds). *Consuming Motherhood.*, 122–38. Rutgers University Press.

Martens, L. (2004) 'Comfort, Colour, Brand, Style and Size – Which Shoe Fits You? An Excursion into the Sociology of Shoes'. Paper presented to the 'Step-on-It Programme of Public Readings', Clayport Library, Durham, December.

Martens, L. (2005a) 'Safety, Safety, Safety for Small Fry: The Conjoining of Children and Danger in Commercial Communities of Parenthood'. Unpublished conference paper presented at the Childhoods 2005 conference, Oslo, June.

Martens, L. (2005b) 'Learning to Consume – Consuming to Learn: Children at the interface between consumption and education'. *British Journal of Sociology of Education*, 26, No. 3: 343–57.

Martens, L. (2009) 'Creating the Ethical Parent–Consumer Subject: Commerce, Moralities and Pedagogies in Early Parenthood'. In J. A. Sandlin and P McLaren (Eds). *Critical Pedagogies of Consumption: Living and Learning in the Shadow of the "Shopocalypse"*. New York: Routledge.

Martens, L., Southerton, D. and S. Scott. (2004) 'Bringing Children (and Parents) into the Sociology of Consumption: Towards a theoretical and empirical agenda'. *Journal of Consumer Culture*, 4, No. 2: 155–82.

Miles, S., Cliff, D. and V. Burr (1998) 'Fitting In and Sticking Out': Consumption, Consumer Meanings and the Construction of Young People's Identities'. *Journal of Youth Studies*, 1, No. 1: 81–96

Nelson, M. K. (2008) 'Watching Children: Describing the Use of Baby Monitors on the Epinions.com.'. *Journal of Family Issues*, Vol 29 (4): 516–38.

Otnes, C., M. A. McGrath, T. M. Lowrey. (1995) 'Shopping with Consumers: Usage as Past, Present and Future Research Technique'. *Journal of Retailing and Consumer Services*, 2, No. 2: 97–110.

Pugh, A. J. (2004). 'Windfall Child Rearing: Low-Income Care and Consumption'. *Journal of Consumer Culture*, Vol. 4, No. 2, 229–49.

Taylor, J. S., Layne, L. L. and D. F. Wozniak (2004) (eds). *Consuming Motherhood*. Rutgers University Press.

Tosca, Susana P. (2003) 'The appeal of Cute Monkeys'. In *Proceedings of Level Up*. Digital Games Researchers Association Conference, Utrecht, the Netherlands, November.

Vincent, C. and S. J. Ball. (2007) '"Making Up" the Middle-Class Child: Families, Activities and Class Dispositions', *Sociology*. 41, No. 6: 1061–77.

Warde, A. and L. Martens (2000) *Eating Out: Social Differentiation, Consumption and Pleasure*. Cambridge, Cambridge University Press.

White, S. (2003) 'Autoethnography – An Appropriate Methodology?'. *Qualitative Research Journal*, 3:22–32.

Williams, R. H. (1982) *Dream Worlds: Mass Communication in Late Nineteenth Century France*. Berkeley, California, University of California Press.

Woodruffe-Burton· H., S. Eccles and R, Elliott. (2006) 'Towards a Theory of Shopping: A Holistic Framework', *Journal of Consumer Behaviour*, 1, No. 3: 256–66.

Part IV

Social Contexts of Children's Consumption

10
The Stuff at Mom's House and the Stuff at Dad's House: The Material Consumption of Divorce for Adolescents

Caitlyn Collins and Michelle Janning

> Caitlyn: Why are some of the items that you've mentioned at one place rather than the other?
> Paige: Um, like all the pictures and memory stuff is over here 'cause my life is over here...

Our life-stories as social actors can be told through our objects, our places, and our consumption practices. Once told, these stories can reveal the active individual and collective meaning-making processes that are at stake in home consumption, and they can illuminate the many intersections between identities, interactions, and the material culture of homes (Hurdley 2006). The first decade of this millennium has seen an increase, albeit slow, in multidisciplinary research and theorizing about home consumption, defined recently by Reimer and Leslie (2004:188) as 'the purchasing, acquisition, and display of furniture and other domestic goods' in homes. Missing from this body of knowledge are the stories of consumption practices of young family members, and specifically stories of consumption practices that are part of a process of family dissolution. As the above quotation illustrates, after a divorce, a child's life is split between two places, but often one place feels more representative of her identity than another. Examining what children and adolescents consume and display (or are given no choice but to display) in their dwellings during and after their parents' divorce can shed light not only on their own identity formation, but also on the dynamics of the shifting familial relationships contained within those dwellings. Consuming material culture and displaying it in the 'critical spaces' (McCorkel 1998: 227) of homes has been seen as constitutive of the identities and relationships in those homes (e.g. Goode 2007;

Hurdley 2006). As such, analyzing the process of home consumption for adolescents whose parents have divorced can tell us how the process of family dissolution can be manifested in the material culture of a home divided.

The life-stories of adolescents whose parents have divorced form the foundation of the research reported in this chapter. Extensive research has been conducted on the significance and repercussions of divorce for children and adolescents (e.g, Wallerstein 2005). We seek to tie this body of work to its manifestations in material culture and home spaces for children. By analyzing in-depth interviews and surveys from twenty-two young adults from the Pacific Northwest in the United States (9 male and 13 female; ages 18–22), we seek to unite these two bodies of knowledge. We ask the question: How does the consumption of material culture in adolescents' home spaces reflect their identity formation and their perceptions of and relationships with each parent after their parents' divorce? More specifically, we seek to find out how the consumption of goods and use and display of these goods in home spaces (and in the transition between two home spaces) are manifested in these adolescents' lives post-divorce.

While our research does not aim to establish any causal relationships between identities, relationships, and material culture, it does aim to situate the consumption of material culture more prominently in the discussion of children's experiences with divorce. Our retelling and organizing of these young people's narratives, then, has utility not only for researchers in the fields of family studies, geography, material culture and consumption studies, and social sciences generally, but also for practitioners (attorneys, mediators, counsellors, child advocates, and judges) who work directly with families that are splitting up. Discussions initiated by adults in the divorce process that are meant to seek out what is 'in the best interest of the children,' we argue, need to include recognition that children's sentiments about their belongings and their spaces matter. As our research findings demonstrate, adolescents talking about their consumption of material culture may tell us as much about their post-divorce sentiments as would traditional measures of identity formation and relationship satisfaction.

Homes, material culture, consumption, and identity

In a home, objects and spaces are markers of stability for its inhabitants and, for some, 'being at home mean[s] being surrounded by familiar things that mark... a home as "my home"' (Whitmore 2001:61). Homes are sites for active consumption practices, whereby the objects that we choose to buy and display (and where we display them) are part of a social process that produces meanings, rather than static symbols that merely reflect our role as passive consumers (Csikszentmihalyi and Rochberg-Halton 1981; Hurdley 2006; Miller 2001; Reimer and Leslie 2004). Narratives about aesthetic choices in the seemingly private sphere of the home tell us that home objects actually play a big role in people's accomplishment of social identities (Hurdley 2006; Suter *et al.* 2008). Things (and the spaces those things occupy) are thus useful signifiers of personal and social identities.

Autoethnographic research by Goode (2007), specifically related to the material cultural manifestations of the divorce experience, suggests that the meanings of home objects can change over time and vary between household members. This is especially visible throughout the emotional negotiations over possessions during and after a divorce:

> When a marriage breaks down, what has been 'taken up' and what 'projected' is laid bare and becomes subject to competing claims of 'how it was'. Here, contested claims of ownership of items…, made while 'dividing the spoils', render the organization of social, cultural and aesthetic relations more visible (367).

Thus, for the adults in a relationship that has dissolved, the objects of the marriage undergo a transition into the objects of divorce, and it is during this transition that the objects' meaning changes to express the shifting identities of spouses as they become ex-spouses. Identities change during a divorce, and so do the 'spoils' that represent those changing identities. If an object is lost or taken away, part of one's identity that is attached to that object may be changed, if not eliminated, even if the object becomes more important to those who are involved. Although adolescents do not 'divide the spoils' in quite the same way as their parents after a divorce, the displacement, loss, and division of their personal possessions between two homes has similar implications for changes in identity.

Adolescents, space, and consumption

There is now extensive research on adolescent 'room culture' which has looked at its embodiment of larger patterns of identity, consumption, and culture (Baker 2004; Steele & Browne 1995). Children's consumer culture is manifested here through their choices regarding what to include, decorate, and do in their bedrooms. In their patterns of consumption, children are not passive receptacles; rather, they are social actors who actively appropriate culture (Cook 2004). According to Childress (2004), it is important to study the appropriation of space by teenagers and young adults because very little public or private space is deemed theirs in today's society. Disenfranchised groups who lack access to publicly (or privately) valuable spaces, and who are often under more surveillance than powerful groups, sometimes create and use 'critical spaces' to establish their own identities, which run counter to dominant institutional identity claims (McCorkel 1998: 227). Critical spaces for adolescents can serve as locations whereby individuals question adult claims about what their self-identities are 'supposed' to be. Without access to critical spaces like bedrooms, adolescents may find it more difficult to construct identities that resist the identity demands of adults. So, if the divorce experience for adolescents consists of them reconfiguring their individual identities in light of changing family identities, and if identity construction is manifest in material culture, then researchers need to pay attention to the spaces where this process takes place: namely, the adolescents' bedrooms and other domestic spaces and objects that they utilize.

Children's divorce experiences

Changes in family structure as a result of divorce most often mean changes in family living arrangements as well. Wallerstein (2005) points out that children are rarely consulted about their wishes regarding the visitation schedule when the plans are originally drawn up. For this reason, she claims that the child has in fact 'disappeared from the equation and become mere property' (409). Research on the topic of the implications for children of divorced families is widely varied and often contradictory. A wealth of research has concluded that divorce has a deleterious effect on children in numerous ways (Amato and Cheadle 2005; Juby *et al.* 2005; Kowaleski-Jones and Donifon 2004; Sigle-Rushton *et al.* 2005; Wallerstein 2005). Conversely, other studies have found that parental divorce sometimes leads to positive outcomes for children (Cartwright 2006; Strohschein 2005; Wallerstein 2005). Ahrons (2004) claims that 'good divorces' in which family members actually benefit from the experience of divorce are rarely discussed because they call into question the nostalgic image of the traditional American family. Many researchers have determined that every divorce has both positive and negative effects on children and later, adults, and that the impacts are rarely *all* harmful or *all* helpful (Cartwright 2006). It is evident, then, that there is no clear-cut, all-encompassing set of consequences that manifest themselves for all children growing up in divorced families. However, there is a gap in the existing research relating to the importance of material culture in the divorce experiences of children. As we shall argue, these indicators can help us understand the positive and/or negative outcomes of divorce for adolescents.

Methods

The survey and in-person interview data discussed in this chapter were collected as part of a larger study on adolescents from divorced families. Eligible participants included those whose parents were divorced and who had grown up splitting their time between two parents' homes. In addition, photographs were taken of willing participants' bedrooms, and each participant completed a short demographic survey. The majority of the twenty-two participants were White, Non-Hispanic (86 per cent) and from the middle and upper classes, both in terms of parents' income, education, and occupational prestige levels and self-reported social class. In the interviews, respondents were asked about the function, use, and perception of their home spaces (specifically, bedrooms), as well as questions about their favorite possessions and use of technology. Finally, we asked participants about the time spent and the quality of their relationship with each parent. Pseudonyms are used for all respondents.

Bedroom decorating as symbolic of attachment, belonging, and identity

While the interview data for this project revealed over a dozen themes related to identity and relationship dynamics, we focus here on two. The first of these is highlighted by the stories of a handful of our respondents, which reflect on the role of bedroom decorating as symbolic of attachment, belonging, and identity.

Pink (2004:42) argues that home decorating (or 'home creativity,' as she terms it) is a process of 'the constitution of self that involve[s] embodied performative actions [and] material objects.' Accordingly, adolescents' rooms and decorations in those rooms are representations and material manifestations of who they feel they are. For example, when Paige was asked to describe her room, she said,

> It's like a collection of, I don't know, like, high school, well now, a little bit of college, and kind of like my activities, and what I do, what I'm interested in... It's just definitely a reflection of me.

Paige surrounded herself with decorations that are reflective of her activities and interests, and hence of aspects of her identity that she values.

While many if not most people decorate their spaces to reflect their identities, what is significant for children of divorce is often their choice to decorate and personalize their rooms *at one home and not the other*. Paige specifically chose to put up all these decorations in her room at her mother's house because it was where she spent the vast majority of her time:

> Caitlyn: Why are some of the items that you've mentioned at one place rather than the other?
>
> Paige: Um, like all the pictures and memory stuff is over here 'cause my life is over here...

Paige decorates her room at her mom's house because it's where her 'life' is, where she feels a sense of belonging. Conversely, when Paige was asked to describe her room at her father's house, she said, 'it's a lot more barren.' Another respondent, Molly, reported similar feelings when discussing her rooms at both homes. She said, 'I guess it's just all very much mine' when she described her room at her mom's house, using the adjectives 'warm,' 'comfortable,' 'welcoming,' and 'safe' to describe that room and 'sad,' 'unfamiliar,' and 'forced' to describe the room at her father's house. She said: 'It more feels like an obligation when I go [to my dad's house] than comfort.' Apparent in Molly's description is her identification with her room at her mother's and her discomfort in and detachment from her room at her father's. Following Pink's (2004) line of reasoning, then, one might argue that the adjectives she uses to describe her room at her mom's are reflective of how she sees herself: comfortable at Mom's house and unfamiliar at Dad's.

Some respondents seemed to understand in explicit terms the connection between their room decorations and identity characteristics and explained how they consciously decorated their rooms in a particular manner in order to reflect certain aspects of their personality or identity, and to indicate different identities in the two homes. Kelsey, for instance, said, 'Um, my room at my mom's house, I felt like, it really explained my personality, like I'm a really bright and bubbly person' and she explained how she had laid out a very careful game plan with her mother for what she wanted the room to look like so she felt at home in the space. The adjectives she used to describe this space were 'beautiful, pink, yellow, blue, flowers, spacious, I have a window, it's very bright,' which can be seen as paralleling the way she described her personality. In contrast, Kelsey was not allowed to make the decisions about the appearance of her room at her dad's house and described it in this way: 'Pretty confined, I don't know, it was dark, and um, I just, I don't know, it seemed like it was a little cluttered, not well organized as much. It was like different mismatching things that kind of just filled the room.' Kelsey understood that her feelings of belonging and connection at each parent's home were impacted by, and expressed through, the extent to which the space seemed to reflect her identity. Her room at her mother's house was well planned out, bright and bubbly, whereas the room at her father's was dark, unorganized, and full of 'mismatching things.' Among other reasons (involving stepparents), this impacted on Kelsey's decision to eventually spend all of her time at her mother's house and to only visit her father at his home rather than live there a portion of the time.

Another respondent, Ben, chose to decorate his walls only with the paraphernalia of the sports and activities in which he participated. He decorated his walls with objects that can easily be understood as concrete symbols of his identity, perhaps indicating an athletic, adventuresome, no-nonsense nature. When asked to describe this room, he explained:

> Uh, I like the word utilitarian... Because, there's like, there's nothing around that I don't use, like, everything has, like a purpose, like there's nothing on the walls that are, like, hanging around for me to stare at, like the stuff on the walls are like, like, this is going to sound really stupid but, uh, I have like, a scuba spear, and like, my, like, lacrosse sticks are all, like, hanging on the walls, I have like, stuff that I use you know, and like, my stereo's on my dresser...

Ben spent roughly the same amount of time at both houses and put up decorations of value and use at both places. His lacrosse gear was displayed at his mother's house and his cycling gear was displayed at his father's.

Paige seemed to sum up what many respondents said when they were asked to describe in adjectives all the decorations in and feelings related to their rooms: 'It's just definitely a reflection of me. I don't know how to put it in an adjective.' Many stories like these are present in the interview transcripts, where it is evident that the consumption of material culture, specifically via bedroom decorating, plays a role in both adolescent identity development and relationships with both parents after a young person experiences his or her parents' divorce. Not only do these objects and spaces get put to use in terms of creativity and convenience, they serve as indicators of the ways that adolescents see spaces and things as being important in their everyday lives and relationships.

Technology and consumption

In the same way that adolescents' practices of bedroom decorating tell us about the important dynamics taking place within their 'divided homes,' children's consumption of technology post-divorce also reveals how material culture is related to and impacted by their parents' divorce and subsequent home lives.

The consumer culture surrounding technology for children in divorced families is unique in that it exists not in one home setting, but in two, where the differing functions, availability, and significance of technology become clearer as a result of the comparison between the two homes. So, here we elaborate on our second theme, examining adolescents' consumption of technology within their 'critical spaces' (McCorkel 1998) and its relation to their perceptions of home, their awareness of agency, and the division of time between parents' residences. Every individual mentioned the use of multiple forms of technology in their daily lives while living in two different houses in their adolescence. Respondents discussed the significance of computers, Internet connection, cellular phones, video and computer games, television, and portable games, laptops, and music. Our results here demonstrate that adolescents' use of technology at both homes following their parents' divorce is both a social process and an active consumption practice, with implications for their home lives and relationships with their parents.

Views of parents and home

'Fun' vs. 'not fun.' When asked what words came to mind when they thought of 'my space at my mom's house' and 'my space at my dad's house', a number of individuals mentioned the words 'fun' and 'not fun.' They qualified these terms by explaining that certain 'fun' objects, activities, and technology were disproportionately available at one house compared with the other. Michael explained,

> ... my dad's house in high school, and before that, [had] like a nicer PC computer that had like games and stuff and that became another reason that was the 'fun' place to be and I probably spent too much time doing that. At my mom's there was just a shitty old Mac [computer] and my mom would complain a lot about how much I was

playing video games at my dad's. There's also a Playstation [video game system] at my dad's; at my mom's there's just TV.

Individuals considered the more 'fun' house and parent to be the one with more television channels, faster Internet connection, more compu-ter/video games, and bigger/nicer/newer/more televisions or computers.

Incentives/one upmanship

Parents occasionally offered their children enticements to come over and spend more time at their house. Kate described, 'I had a TV in my room at my dad's house, which was his big, like, incentive... I think I probably liked spending time there because I had a television and when you're 10, that's real cool.' Similarly, Daniel recalled, 'I remember one time we got some super nice computer on the West coast and my stepbrother... said something to the effect of, "You know they only got that new computer to entice you to move out there."' Another respondent, Sam, explained that his mother refused to let him play or own video games or watch a lot of television, but his dad bought him a Playstation video game system and let him watch TV often. He said 'there's a definite difference in my amount of technology I was allowed to intake.'

Virtual connectedness

Respondents often stressed the importance of feeling 'connected' and 'reachable.' The lack of this connectivity at one parent's home or the other often resulted in adolescents feeling bored, annoyed, and lonely. Sarah explained that at her dad's house, 'I would just feel kinda stuck, especially with no Internet, I just get really antsy there unless I go there specifically to hang out but otherwise I think I'm like, "there's nothing to do."' Conversely, respondents seemed satisfied when their ability to connect was equal at both houses. Elsa said, 'Well we both had internet at both houses, thank goodness. I don't think I'd be able to live without Internet. I'm a 21st century girl.' Respondents also used technology, mainly laptop computers and iPods, to help them feel connected wher-ever they were. When asked if he had any favorite items he brought back and forth between houses, Daniel said, 'Well my computer because it's my life...the laptop's easy, because I take it wherever I go.' Kate got a laptop so she could easily do homework at both houses: 'I started to need to type things up and write papers and they were on different computers and there were times when I would like, need to work on a paper and realize it was saved on the computer at my mom's house and I was at dad's house and it was due the next day.' Technology was used, then, to help respondents feel more organized and connected, and to help create a virtual space whereby homework could be transported from home to home.

In sum, then, the consumption of technology performed functional and entertainment roles for these adolescents, but it also influenced, or at least represented, the status of the relationship between children and parents at the two houses. In the eyes of these respondents, parents provided technology for their children in order to create spaces that would seem more enticing – a process that influenced the quality of parent–child relations. It is important to note, however, that not all respondents were clearly aware of this practice and its influence on their identities and relationships, which is the subject of the next section.

Agency and technology

Technology played an important role in these adolescents' sense of agency, or freedom to enact the social identities that they chose, after their parents divorced. More specifically, respondents who had very little to say about the significance of technology in their lives as children growing up in a divorced family were those whose houses had *no discrepancies* in the amount or types of technology. Because they had no basis for comparison, they had little consciousness of the amount or extent of their agency. When a disparity in availability, use, or access to technology existed between two houses, however, respondents were very aware of their agency. In other words, respondents' awareness of the role that technology played in their relationships with both parents after a divorce, as well as their awareness of how that technology affected their everyday freedom to use their time as they wished, were more likely to arise in cases where the two homes had different levels or types of technology available for their use. Becky, for example, had an equally nice computer at each house: 'It was never like, "I need to stay at mom's this weekend because I need to write a paper" type thing, we could always just take that to the other house and work on it there. And just take the floppy disk it was on, you know.' In contrast, Jeff explained that it was a big inconvenience and source of discomfort that there was a disparity between the computers at his parents' homes:

> Because the computer at my dad's house was like the family com-
> puter and it was also a lot slower and the Internet worked sparingly,
> I couldn't do schoolwork on it, well I could do schoolwork on it of
> course, but it was trying and took way more time and all sorts of stuff

like that. So, yeah, during a lot of high school, one of the big things I would say is, 'I'm going over to mom's house to work on a report'... And he'd say, 'Why don't you do it here?' And I'd say 'um...' because I didn't want to say 'the stuff over there is nicer'...

Another respondent, Elsa, explained that the restrictions placed on technology at one parent's home had a significant impact on her emotionally:

My dad's house, we would have a family computer but the only thing is is that he would password it off and you had to ask him to sign [onto] it which is kinda odd because even if – it made you automatically suspicious, my dad's very suspicious and growing up in a very suspicious household made me be a very suspicious person when I was older. Recently, I was with my girlfriend and we went to China together and she kept a diary about it and I was like, 'Do you mind if I, like, read it?' and she was like, 'Why would I mind? Of course not!' and I wasn't used to ever being around someone where they would be so open about something like that. So just that, just a little thing like passwording off the Internet has made me really suspicious about everything.

The language used by respondents who were more aware of their agency, as a result of having dissimilar technology at both homes, is different from those who were less aware. They often discussed their homes not as 'mom's *and* dad's' but 'mom's *versus* dad's', thereby reflecting a somewhat dichotomous viewpoint concerning their two homes rather than a more united, cohesive understanding of them. The consciousness of personal agency played a significant role in how respondents conceived of and interacted with their parents as a result of the technology available in both homes. Some were comfortable, satisfied, and unexpressive when they talked about their access to technology. Others, who experienced discrepancies in the availability of technology at their parents' houses, were very expressive about the related discomfort, frustration, and sometimes sadness they felt stemming from it.

Technology and time

Technology also influenced the amount of time respondents spent with their parents, and ultimately the kinds of relationships they had with them. Thus, a number of respondents discussed how they had distant or uncomfortable relationships with their fathers; when staying at their homes, these individuals reported using television and video games as a means of separating and distracting themselves from being at their fathers' homes. For example, when asked what words came to mind in describing his room at his dad's house, Sam replied, 'Video games... sadly, I would just sit there and play video games. But yeah, that's the first thing that comes to mind.'

Generally, children were more willing and interested to go over to a parent's house if they had the phones, Internet, television, etc. that made it comfortable, convenient, and home-like to them. Sarah, for example, explained that she never spent the night at her father's house as a young adult because '... I need to be using the phone and the Internet and the car every day and I think that it's those that aren't available to me there... [At my mom's the] Internet is here, my clothes are here, the car is here, yeah, it's just a lot of stuff that is really useful for me to use. There's a phone line here, there's not a phone line at my dad's because we both have cell phones.' For another young woman, her father's refusal to get a cell phone or use the one she bought him resulted in her seeing him less often because he was so hard to contact.

Jeff explained how the technology at his mother's house increased his desire to be over there, and actually shifted the time spent proportionally at each house:

> ...it probably became 60/40 in effect. ... [T]he nicer TV was over there, the nicer computer was over there, the faster Internet was over there, so when I was always doing homework and everything like that, it was better, and because it was-- this was shallow and superficial of me-- but I was in middle school and high school, because it was the 'nicer' house and the 'richer' house, it would be what I wanted my friends to see or people to see.

It is important to note, however, that for many interview respondents, the relationship quality with a parent *preceded* the desire to spend time at that parent's house, regardless of how fast the Internet connection was or how fun the video games were. It is not as if the parent with the better technology won – that would be a misinterpretation of these respondents' words. Rather, a discussion of technology is often a tangible way for adolescents and pre-adolescents to talk about their relationships, especially if, as noted above, the technological tools they needed for everyday life were more available at one parent's house than another's. Perhaps cynically, it is also a way for parents to try to encourage their children to spend more time at their houses. Technology is a symbol of how time is spent, and time spent with a parent signifies at least some important component in that relationship. It is clear, then, that the consumption of technology, just as with the consumption of bedroom artifacts, plays a role in how these adolescents view their own social identities, and their relationships with both parents after the divorce.

Conclusion

Adolescents' consumption of material culture has a significant impact on the daily practices, habits, and allocation of time involved with growing up in divorced families. From a child's perspective, it is crucial that parents see how closely connected these issues are in order to make their homes feel comfortable, livable, and inviting to their children. Perhaps because certain elements of material culture played a different role in the adolescent lives of today's parents (for example, in the case of technology), it is especially important to understand the significant impact and importance they hold for children currently. From a parent's perspective, it is important to make sure that children understand the reasons why there may be discrepancies between houses in terms of the material possessions the children use in their everyday lives. Further, the use of objects and spaces is an important, and often under-discussed, topic of conversation between ex-partners that needs to be made more transparent in negotiations over time spent with children, visitation, child support arrangements, and geographic location.

Many adolescents often feel displaced after a divorce. Respondents explained that this feeling of displacement often resulted from their family being split in two, having to move out of the home in which they had lived, and feeling like they no longer had a center or a home because their family did not live under one roof anymore. Adolescents' desires to feel at home, to feel comfortable, to feel that they belong somewhere, to feel connected to friends and school via communication technology, and to feel that they are in control are all tied to the need to counter these feelings of displacement, and to feel 'emplaced'. The process of emplacement, or the attempt to construct a place for oneself both figuratively and literally, is established through the kinds of consumption patterns that have been presented in this chapter.

In addition to exploring the extent to which children have become, as Wallerstein (2005) states, 'mere property' (409), we must uncover the sociological significance of the *property of children*. Children and adolescents are increasingly savvy consumers, and parents are increasingly likely to use consumer goods and services in order to attempt to preserve positive familial relationships, for better or for worse. This chapter has attempted to give some insights into the role of consumption in families post-divorce, and how the bedrooms, belongings and pieces of technology of young adults whose parents have divorced are an important part of the parent-child relationship.

References

Ahrons, C. (2004) *We're Still Family: What Grown Children Have to Say About Their Parents' Divorce*. New York: HarperCollins.

Amato, P. R. and J. Cheadle (2005) 'The Long Reach of Divorce: Divorce and Child Well-Being Across Three Generations,' *Journal of Marriage and Family* 67: 191–206.

Baker, S. L. (2004) 'Pop In(to) the Bedroom: Popular Music in Pre-Teen Girls' Bedroom Culture,' *European Journal of Cultural Studies* 7(1): 75–93.

Cartwright, C. (2006) 'You Want to Know How it Affected Me? Young Adults' Perceptions of the Impact of Parental Divorce,' *Journal of Divorce and Remarriage* 44: 125–43.

Childress, H. (2004) 'Teenagers, Territory, and the Appropriation of Space,' *Childhood* 11(2): 195–205.

Cook, D. T. (2004) 'Beyond Either/Or,' *Journal of Consumer Culture* 4(2): 147–53.

Csikszentmihalyi, M., and E. Rochberg-Halton (1981) *The Meaning of Things: Domestic Symbols and the Self.* Cambridge, UK: Cambridge University Press.

Goode, J. (2007) 'Whose Collection is it Anyway? An Autoethnographic Account of "Dividing the Spoils" upon Divorce,' *Cultural Sociology* 1(3): 365–82.

Hurdley, R. (2006) 'Dismantling Mantlepieces: Narrating Identities and Materializating Culture in the Home,' *Sociology* 40(4): 717–33.

Juby, H., LeBourdais, C. and N. Marcil-Gratton (2005) 'Sharing Roles, Sharing Custody? Couples' Characteristics and Children's Living Arrangements at Separation,' *Journal of Marriage and Family* 67: 157–72.

Kowaleski-Jones, L. and R. Donifon (2004) 'Children's Home Environments: Understanding the Role of Family Structure Changes,' *Journal of Family Issues* 25(1): 3–28.

McCorkel, J. (1998) 'Going to the Crackhouse: Critical Space as a Form of Resistance in Total Institutions and Everyday Life,' *Symbolic Interaction* 21(3): 227–52.

Miller, D. (2001) 'Behind Closed Doors,' in D. Miller (ed.) *Home Possessions: Material Culture Behind Closed Doors*, pp. 1–19. Oxford and New York: Berg Publishers.

Pink, S. (2004) *Home Truths: Gender, Domestic Objects and Everyday Life*. Oxford: Berg.

Reimer, S. and D. Leslie (2004) 'Identity, Consumption, and the Home,' *Home Cultures* 1(2):187–208.

Sigle-Rushton, W., J. Hobcraft and K. Kiernan (2005) 'Parental Divorce and Subsequent Disadvantage: A Cross-Cohort Comparison,' *Demography* 42(3): 427–46.

Steele, J. R. and J. D. Brown (1995) 'Adolescent Room Culture: Studying Media in the Context of Everyday Life,' *Journal of Youth and Adolescence* 24(5): 551–68.

Strohschein, L. (2005) 'Parental Divorce and Child Mental Health Trajectories,' *Journal of Marriage and Family* 67: 1286–1300.

Suter, E., Daas, K. L. and K. M. Bergen (2008) 'Negotiating Lesbian Family Identity via Symbols and Rituals,' *Journal of Family Issues* 29(1): 26–47.

Wallerstein, J. S. (2005) 'Growing Up in the Divorced Family,' *Clinical Social Work Journal* 33(4): 401–18.

Whitmore, H. (2001) 'Value that Marketing Cannot Manufacture: Cherished Possessions as Links to Identity and Wisdom,' *Generations* 25(3): 57–64.

11

The Dao of Consumer Socialization: Raising Children in the Chinese Consumer Revolution

Randi Wærdahl

The rapid economic growth and increasing household incomes that characterized Chinese society during the 1980s and 1990s have transformed consumer habits, particularly in urban areas, resulting in what some have described as a "consumer revolution" (Davis 2000, Hooper 2000, Tilt 2006). Like other revolutions, this one has had revolutionary effects. Guan Ying reports that children's consumption levels are now higher than those of adults, seen in terms of the percentage of total family income allocated to children's consumption (Ying 2003). That children's level of consumption should rise proportionally to a family's income is in itself not very surprising, but it is noteworthy that in the Chinese case it has in fact exceeded the level of adult consumption.

This rapid change in consumer habits has raised some familiar concerns about the place of children in society. In the Western literature, particularly since the 1980s, the possible harmful effects of bad consumption have been tied to ideas about the healthy development of the individual. The development of a materialistic personality and the drive to fulfill an endless desire for more may not only lead children's personalities astray, but also place an economic burden on the family's ability to meet children's growing material desires and needs (Linn 2005, Shor 2004, Quart 2003). Such arguments have also arisen in the Chinese context: Zhao, for example, expresses a similar concern for Chinese children, namely that they "lack a view about appropriate consumption" (Zhao 2006). Such concerns are perfectly understandable, given that the existence of a wide selection of consumer goods is a fairly new phenomenon, as is the economic ability to acquire them. However, within this concern there is an assumption that there is such a thing as "appropriate consumption," which can be taught and learned.

Chinese scholars point to diverging trends in parents' attitudes towards their children's consumption. There are two common explanations for why such a large proportion of family income is spent on children. Some suggest that parents want their children to have everything that they themselves did not enjoy in their own deprived childhood (Ying 2003). This explanation does not point to a view of consumption as purely harmful, but rather as a positive possibility, resembling the optimism of post-war consumer developments in the West. On the other hand, there are explanations that point to the lack of time parents have to spend with their children and their resulting feelings of guilt (Zhao 2006). Money and consumption are again not seen as directly harmful in this view, but rather as somewhat immoral – a view which in many ways echoes studies in the West, where double-work, double-income parents are seen to feel guilty because they do not spend enough time with their children (Jacobs and Gerson 2004).

Both explanations resonate with responses to consumer society in the West. On the one hand, the possible harmful psychological effects of a consumer society fuel a need for the *protection* of the vulnerable child. On the other hand, the economic challenges posed for children and families by an expanding market and new demands on social participation require a new kind of *preparation*, or new socialization practices. In the West, the challenge of protection and preparation has most commonly been met by a combination of legislation, consumer awareness initiatives and economic education for the young.

The conclusions and explanations in the Chinese studies mentioned above are drawn from family consumer statistics at the household level. The similarity to the general tendencies in Western society over the last fifty or so years makes it tempting to describe the challenges to Chinese families as similar to those posed for Western families. But household statistics cannot answer questions about how Chinese parents themselves feel about their children growing up in an increasingly consumer-oriented society. In addition, information about the practices of economic and consumer socialization *within* urban one-child families in China is scarce. The economic and consumer revolution in China is planted and cultivated within a different cultural soil, and we would expect the effects to take a shape and form that is different from the West. Can we identify a distinctively Chinese version of consumer socialization by using a different set of methods? In this chapter, the findings from a questionnaire designed in accordance with Western precedents are compared with the thoughts and concerns expressed in conversations with Chinese parents about their children and everyday socialization. The purpose is to explore how Chinese parents find "a way" (Dao) to meet the new challenges of raising children during the consumer revolution.

Two sets of data will be used. First, I discuss the results from two composite questions from the questionnaires on what parents regard to be the main influences on children's consumer choices (13 statements), along with how they evaluate the latter's knowledge about consumption (14 statements). The questionnaires were distributed through schools to parents of 6th grade children (*n*=149) in urban one-child families in Beijing in the fall of 2006. Children in the 6th grade are for the most part 11–12 years old, with the exception of some, but very few, 13–14 year olds. The schools were all public schools situated in the Dong Chang area (east-center) of Beijing, and they cater to children from families with diverse professional backgrounds, although predominantly from the middle- to high-income groups.

Secondly, I discuss results from conversational interviews conducted in home visits with ten families, selected from the same schools. As a foreign researcher, I depended on an interpreter for the conversations with the families. We were greeted very much as guests during the home visits, but at least one hour of the visits was set up as a formal interview with both the children and their parents present. The interviews were filmed as well as taped; and the films have proved to be very useful since they open up for a "show and tell" function, as well as the interpretation of body language. My different roles as a stranger and outsider to their culture, a guest, a researcher, and a mother and thus an insider as regards parenthood, are all reflected in the data. The language barrier and use of an interpreter has of course added yet another element to the acquisition and interpretation of these data. Nonetheless, two advantages can be emphasized: a stranger to the culture will not let taken-for-granted truths pass without explanation; and good hosts and representatives of a country and its culture will not let their guest leave without one. In particular, given my position as a foreigner and as naïve regarding Chinese cultural heritage, the parents found it necessary not only to explain their personal views, but also give an interpretation of where they thought their values and views originated. This has to a large extent framed the last part of the present analysis, where the Western-style survey questions sometimes came to appear "off target."

The sample is in statistical terms very small. However, it has been strategically chosen as an example of families that are at the epicenter of the social and economic transformations that have taken place in urban China, which is faced with the challenge of sorting out new, and often contradictory, ideas and influences at a rapid pace. These are the kinds of families that Ying and Zhao and other Chinese scholars worry about. The discussion centers around issues of *protection* from and *preparation* for a new consumer-oriented society, and the values parents feel need to be inculcated in the child.

What to expect from a consumer revolution

In the Chinese context, advertisements for children's products on TV and elsewhere emerged in the early 1980s, along with a rapidly expanding market for consumer goods, displayed and marketed for private consumption. This development was also followed very closely by the expansion of the media and access to the Internet. The sources of potential influence on consumer choices and human values thus multiplied greatly over a short period of time. Similar things have also been said about the development of consumer society in the West, although few attempts have been made to define "rapid." But if this development in the West took place at the speed of a car, China has been introduced to consumer society at the speed of a space rocket. And what is to be expected from such a rapid development? How does this influence the way we understand our children in this new context, and not least how we prepare them to deal with this new world?

If the reactions to this development in Chinese society were to mirror the reactions seen in Western countries, we would expect to see a debate about the vulnerability of children, and different modes of preparation and protection would be suggested. When traditional culture and knowledge are challenged by a bombardment of new images of the presumed good life, one likely way of reacting to them is to put up one's guard until one can figure out whether the intruder is a friend or a foe. What is believed to guard children against improper influences will, however, vary both between societies and between social groups. Thus, some Chinese critics have expressed concerns about the psychological effects the new influences have on children (e.g. Zhao 2003). Others have argued that increased child consumption is just an effect of parents embracing the possibilities offered by the consumer society, and their attempts to ensure that their child is on the right path to a materially better life (e.g. Ying 2003). Both concerns and reactions can also be present at the same time, as parents mobilize various agents to protect and prepare their children for the new reality.

An unlikely result: are Chinese parents not so worried about undue influence?

Although the questionnaires I used in Beijing in 2006 were discussed and edited in collaboration with Chinese scholars in the field, the basic outline was the same as one I had previously used in Norway, and thus is very likely to have a Western bias. Parents were asked to rank the importance of thirteen different sources of information when it comes to influencing children's choices as consumers on a scale from 1 "Not important" to 5 "Very important.". Figure 11.1 gives a summary of the results, presented as mean scores.

Looking at the relationships between the different factors, we can see that the family and the school curriculum are both high on the list of agents that are regarded as influential. However, an almost equally high rating is given to the suggestion that children learn about consumer choices through "just buying things". On the one hand, this can be interpreted optimistically: as children acquire experience of making consumer choices, they will learn. On the other hand, if "just buying things" comes before learning about it, this comes very close to being classified as mindless consumption, potentially an effective fuel for worries among those who seek to monitor children's consumer habits.

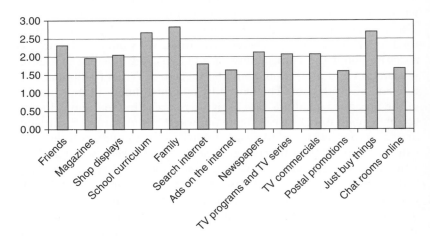

Figure 11.1 Sources of information and influence on children's consumer choices (mean scores of parents' answers: range: 1 = not important, 5 = very important (n = 124 – 38))

However, the most interesting piece of information here comes from the score scale to the left of the figure. In the questionnaire, the scale went from "Not important," via "Of some importance," "Important" and "Quite important" to "Very important." Only four of the listed sources of information influencing children's consumer choices have enough significance to tip the mean scale above 2.5, or the middle of the importance scale. In other words, in mean scores, none of the sources of information and influence mentioned in the questionnaire reaches the status even of "Quite important." In general, one could say that these parents are not too concerned about whether or how children are influenced in their choices as consumers by *any* of the listed influences, whether from magazines, advertisements on the internet or online chat rooms. Shop displays and TV commercials are definitely present in their lives, but according to these answers, neither raises any significant concern about children being influenced when it comes to making consumer choices.

This result seems hard to credit when held up against the amount of scientific and popular literature produced in the West over the past two decades that in different ways has described the dangers posed to children by the consumer society (e.g. Linn 2005, Shor 2004, Quart 2003). As we have seen, even some Chinese scholars have raised concerns about children and families not having sufficient knowledge of appropriate consumer behavior. Does this finding mean that Chinese families are not yet sufficiently informed about the possible effects of consumer culture? Are they not yet exposed to these agents of influence to a degree that raises concerns about the well-being of their children? Or do they have a more elaborate understanding that consumer culture can offer possibilities that outweigh the dangers? Is protection less important for them than preparation? A negative finding like this therefore raises many questions about how Beijing parents are meeting the challenges of their children growing up in a consumer culture. What are the values and attitudes that guide the mobilization of agents to prepare their children for this new reality?

Vulnerable children need guidance from the family and the state

The questionnaire had a list of fourteen statements regarding children's knowledge of consumption and the possible effects of their exposure to consumer culture.

The statements contained assumptions regarding children's competence and ability on the one hand, and their vulnerability and need for protection on the other. The statements also contained assumptions about the condition and constitution of consumer society as either harmful and something children must be protected from, or as inevitable and offering good prospects for the future. In Figure 11.2, the statements are listed from top to bottom according to the relative number of parents who stated either "I totally agree" or "I agree" with the statement. The statements "I totally disagree" and "I disagree" are combined in the same way, while "I don't know" is placed as a middle category.

From Figure 11.2, we can clearly see that children are considered as vulnerable and in need of protection from (and education about) consumption. The four statements that close to 80 per cent of parents agree with are all tied to protection from the market. The responsibility for this protection is seen to lie with the state/government and the family. As the questions were pre-formulated, we cannot be sure whether the state and the family should provide protection through regulation, or through preparation. But as we move further down the list, the latter comes to seem more and more likely. We can see an obvious acknowledgement of the possible danger of being manipulated by the market, but still a belief that children can be taught how to handle market influences. Interestingly, this can be tied to experiences within the family, both in reading and evaluating advertisements and through shopping with children – an approach that again stresses the responsibilities of the family in terms of preparation and education. Children's vulnerability therefore seems conceptually to be more strongly connected to preparation rather than protection.

Statements 5 to 7 express the same kinds of concerns about the undue influences of marketing and consumerism as the questions presented in Figure 11.2. But even though these attitudes are more strongly supported here by 60 to 70 per cent of parents, there is also a tendency for almost half of parents to acknowledge children's competence to understand and use new products, as expressed in statements 8 and 9. Interestingly, very few agree with the assessment in statement 13, where protecting the child from any kind of advertisement or from shopping is offered as a solution to his or her vulnerability. The fact that assertions about children's vulnerability and competence come together in the middle of a ranked list, as well as the 50/30 or 30/50 balance between agreeing and disagreeing with these statements, underlines the overall impression of ambivalence here. Consumer society is seen to offer new opportunities for the capable child, although it is also regarded as a threat to the children's personality and potentially as also harmful to their human qualities.

185

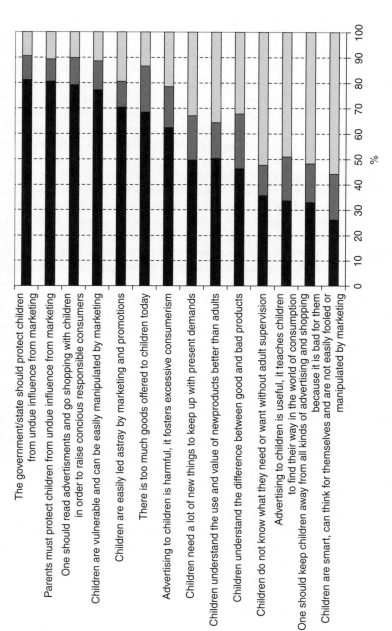

Figure 11.2 Children and their knowledge about consumption (Parents' answers: (n = 149))

So far, the figures have shown that external sources of information and influence on children's consumer choices are not considered particularly important. Even so, parents do believe that both the state and the family have a responsibility to protect and educate children to handle the new commercial influences. However, education and preparation are seen as more important than protection, and totally isolating children from the potential harmful reality of the consumer society is not seen as a preferred solution. Family practices and involvement seem to be important agents in this endeavor to prepare the individual child for a new social reality.

The fact that half of all parents agree that *children need a lot of things to keep up with present demands* underscores the fact that this preparation is happening in a society where the condition of childhood has undergone substantial change. Yet ultimately, parents' worries about undue influence and commercial pressures do not seem so important after all. Ying (2003) might be right to suggest that the importance given to children's consumption within the family is the parents' way of compensating for their own deprived childhoods. Shifting to a more structural explanation, one could also suggest that childhood has become more expensive under the new conditions, and that parents feel they must spend more on their children in order to fulfill the hopes and dreams they have for them.

Growing into a more expensive lifestyle

Thus far, I have used existing research and questionnaire data to explore Chinese parents' responses to the consumer revolution. However, the attitudes, values, fears, concerns and possibilities written into the statements the parents were asked to evaluate were built on experience of Western research and beliefs. The available Chinese research in English is built upon household statistics, and thus equally devoid of parents' own voices. I would therefore like to elaborate on and maybe even contest these findings with data from the conversations and interviews I conducted during my home visits. In particular, I will describe these parents' own interpretations of how the economic, social and cultural changes are affecting their children's lives, how they are adapting to them, and what measures they are taking to prepare their children for a new kind of future.

As with the questionnaires, these ten families cannot be seen as representative of all Chinese parents, and not even of all Chinese parents in Beijing. But they share something which I think is important. They were *not* selected because they display some curiously excessive spending on their children's behalf; nor were they sought out to illustrate popular or scientific conceptions of the only child. They were simply asked to take part in the study because they saw themselves as ordinary families living ordinary city lives in extraordinary times.

TV, computers and the internet were commonplace in these households. One would expect that the increasing use of these channels of influence on the child might have raised some concerns among the parents about inappropriate market exposure. But curiously, and just as in the questionnaire, it was not so much the psychological effects of the new media exposure that worried parents the most: rather, they were all consistently worried about the *physiological* effects such exposure may have on the child's eyes. This was also the case when we talked about reading books or doing crafts. This fear that the child's eyesight might be damaged seemed to be a primary reason for regulating many activities. I was also surprised by a loud and public 'eye exercise break' in one of the schools I visited, which strengthens my certainty that being concerned about children's eyesight was not just a peculiarity of my selected families, but part of a culturally acceptable framework for deciding what is good and bad and when enough is enough.

As the conversations turned to another effect of a more affluent lifestyle, I expected that there would be similar concerns about children's health. But when a changing diet and the increased consumption of meat were brought up, a different worry was voiced. For the most part, the parents were happy to be able to feed their children the meat they wanted. However, they expressed concerns about meat in general being more expensive than vegetables. These were habits that the child would eventually have to pay for itself. Where was the child to earn this money?

It was not the cost of meat, having TVs, computers, musical instruments or other provision for the child *today* that worried them. Rather, parents repeatedly raised more general concerns about their children growing up and adopting a more expensive life-style; and they felt that keeping up with new developments would require well-developed skills if they were to obtain a well-paid job. One of the implications of the new society is that their children's world has become more competitive and meritocratic. And this concern seemed to overshadow all other potential concerns: How is my child going to compete with other children in the future – compete for jobs, for privileges, for love, for money or for status? When I asked Jian's mother if she ever worried about her son's future, she replied that there was no way to predict what the future will bring for him, and that this made her uneasy: "The only thing I can do is to make sure he has a solid foundation. If he does not have a solid foundation, he can never become a good person and achieve his dreams," she said.

The introduction of consumer society in China offers a sense of possibility for the children, but also a sense of responsibility for the family. "We do not want to spoil him," Cheng Lei's mother said: "we will teach him which is the better way to do (things)...," and Cheng Lei's father completed the thought "... so that he can gradually form his own habits." Xiuying's parents felt that teaching their child about the sacrifices you have to make in life would help to balance her mind: "Right now we just emphasize to her to be healthy in mind," Xiuying's father remarked about his twelve-year-old daughter, but hurried to add that they hoped that she would find a good profession in the future and that she needed to study hard to achieve that.

There is no doubt that the cost of childhood is rising, but Chinese parents seem happy to be able to provide all the things that they themselves did not have when they grew up (Ying 2003). However, the implications of this new life-style for the future are much discussed. From the discussions and conversations I had in the homes, it seems that the new economic, social and cultural changes are being received and interpreted as a new framework for the future that fuels another kind of worry: How is my child going to compete?

Preparing children for a new kind of future

An important condition for children's engagement with consumer society lies within the family, its practices and its mediation of values. Family values, family talk and family negotiations are becoming significant as a means to screen consumer information and knowledge. Liu's father said that the best time to communicate was when he took his son to school on the back of his bike every morning: "Then we can chat along the way about our feelings about ordinary life, about art and the works of Confucius."

The idea of preparing for the future that emerged as significant during the family visits has two central aspects: exercising virtues and extracurricular schooling. Interestingly, none of the family activities or extracurricular classes was directly linked to the idea that the child should be prepared for economic participation or for wise consumption. As Western researchers, we tend to think that consumer culture requires training in the symbolic, social and economic values of things, and that this will serve as a means of avoiding reckless spending. Teaching about the equivalence in value between a task performed and a product has been one way of doing this; and children have been encouraged to "earn" the right to certain products in different ways, such as through participation in housework, doing well in school or achieving other goals in their lives.

This concept did not resonate well with the Beijing families. In the very first home I visited, Song's mother started by commenting on the questionnaire that she had filled in earlier in the week. There were some questions that she found strange, she said; in particular, she was wondering what all the questions about children working or earning money were about. "If children help out in the house, it really has nothing to do with money," she said. We ended up having a long but friendly discussion about the issue of children helping and working and whether this had anything to do with money, and she concluded as she had started by saying that children's work in the household had nothing to do with money. I decided to bring this discussion up in the other visits, and was met with either giggling or polite disbelief every time I linked children's work, their efforts and money in the same sentence. Meilin's father said he thought this connection was immoral. He would never even consider giving out prizes for good efforts or school results, nor paying his child for doing housework. For one thing, children were not servants, he said, drawing a clear line between children and domestic workers. But even more significantly, he talked at length about the importance of not mentally or actually connecting money with the child's efforts in school, sports, music or other fields. If you make this connection, you take away the joy, pride and satisfaction of doing well for its own sake: "A child should strive at bettering himself, and the reward should be to become a better person." Diplomas and symbolic prizes were fine, but to reward such efforts with material goods or money would be immoral at best.

This does not mean that Chinese children are exempt from their share of housework. They keep their rooms more or less tidy, as children in the Western world do. They practise their skills in the kitchen, learning to cook for themselves and assisting in cooking for their families. But household chores are not considered work, and should not be associated with money. Rather, this form of labour is connected to developing virtues as a good and capable person.

Exercising the virtues of mankind occupies a central position in raising children in China. One curious example of this was an anthology that all the boys I visited had been introduced to during the past year.

Its title was translated to me as "Fostering the real man," and Jin Jing, one of the boys, took time to go through its list of contents with me. Among the texts, we found Hemingway represented by "The old man and the sea," an Italian author with a text about love, and a British author with a text on what it is to be a gentleman. They all fitted my stereotypical expectations of Western male virtues. The last text in the book was by a Chinese author from the Xing dynasty which discussed ideals for men in the East, and how to cultivate the character and personality of an ideal man. The most interesting thing about these texts is not so much that most of them are non-Chinese, but that most of them are relatively old.

"Education needs a deposit of history," Meilin's father said. He was referring to the fact that his family had moved back to Beijing from the south, from the more modern schools in Shenzhen, a city in Deng Xiaoping's "new economic zone." The schools there were good in terms of pedagogy, he said, but they were lacking in history, tradition and examinations. This was a common sentiment. To prepare yourself or your children for an uncertain future, you needed to root yourself properly in traditions and history, in order to be able to withstand potential moral corruption and make a sound transition and adaptation to the new. In addition, an educational system is needed that produces exams and diplomas that can give entry into the prestigious universities, and therefore economic security in the future.

Chinese parents therefore seem to choose two routes of preparation. By exercising human virtues drawn from Chinese history and traditions, children become sound and good human beings who can face any challenge and still stand up strong. By extracurricular schooling, from lessons in English and advanced maths to learning to be proficient on a musical instrument, a child's chances of competing in a system in which formal education and extraordinary skills are the only available form of exchangeable capital is advanced.

The Dao of consumer socialization

Even though urban parents in China may celebrate their only children by spending a large part of their income on child-related expenses, the things they pay for can only rarely be characterized as mindless or conspicuous consumption, at least from a Western point of view. Expenses for education, from schools to extra-curricular classes, comprise a large part of this spending. In many ways, the children are put into the driving seat of development: they are seen to be in need of new knowledge and skills quickly and of great quality, in order to catch up with the rest of the developed world. Children's levels of consumption are above those of their parents because preparation for the new society requires more and costs more. The formal part of this preparation cannot be done in the family, and even if there are no official fees as such in the public schools, all the extracurricular courses, educational equipment, character-building activities and transport represent a quite substantial cost.

Ernst Engel's famously observed economic law states that as income rises, the proportion of income spent on food falls, even if actual expenditure on food rises. In this context, it is tempting to formulate another law about the effects of rapid social change on the family economy: as a society experiences rapid social and economic growth, the relative cost of childhood as a preparatory phase rises above the cost of adult adjustment to the new social reality, even if actual expenditure on adulthood also rises. Or, to use a more colloquial allegory, "catching up" costs more than "keeping up with the Joneses."

Contemporary Chinese child-rearing practices are still closely tied to traditional values of education and the cultivation of self-control. At first glance, the simplicity of virtues endorsed in the child could be ascribed to the Maoist heritage, where "hard work and plain living" were key ideals (Chen and Sun 2006). However, simplicity is not the first word that comes to mind when a child is truly skilled in playing the Chin or Gu Zheng (traditional Chinese string instruments) at the age of twelve. Hard work, complexity and a balanced mind are values that date back even further in history. The social philosophy of Confucius is one cultural heritage that continues to influence the most strongly held values in contemporary Chinese culture, too (Zhao 1997). In the philosophy of Confucianism, man is by nature good. This means that man can be educated and can strive for perfection. In order to strive for perfection in one, two or all virtues, man needs to exercise self-discipline and self-control. The child-rearing practices I encountered in Beijing are easy to understand within this philosophical framework.

The challenges of bringing up a child in a consumer culture seem to reflect more fundamental changes in society, such as the changing opportunities for securing one's life chances. But when Chinese parents are faced with the challenges of rapid social change and altered opportunity structures, they mobilize their history and traditions in attempting to find a "Way" both to protect and to prepare their children for a new reality. "The Dao" simply means "The Way" (Roberts 2001). In the Chinese way, protection can be found in the exercise of old virtues.

A virtuous and good person cannot be led astray so easily. This strategy differs from those we have seen develop in the West, where understanding the new is a stronger pedagogical idea than securing the old as a shield against the new. The fears evoked by the rapid introduction of a consumer society also seem to be less focused on its psychological effects in the present, and rather more on the difficulties children might face in being able to keep up the lifestyle they have grown accustomed to in the future. Preparation is thus tied to economic rather than psychological vulnerability.

Education and a striving for excellence is another traditional Chinese strategy for bettering one's life chances that was apparent in my research. The increasing amount of time Chinese children spend studying at school, at home and in extracurricular classes is another part of the "Dao" in which Chinese parents are preparing their children to compete in an increasingly meritocratic system. As formal education and skills training have become consumer commodities, the costs of childhood have increased more than the cost of adulthood in those families that aspire to be a part of social progress.

References

Chen, X. and J. Sun (2006) "Sociological Perspectives on Urban China: From Familiar Territories to Complex Terrains" *China Information* 20: 519–51.

Davis, D. (2000) "Introduction: A Revolution in Consumption," in D. Davis (ed.), *The Consumer Revolution in Urban China* (pp. 1–20). Berkeley, CA: University of California Press.

Davis, D. and J. S. Sensenbrenner (2000) "Commercializing Childhood: Parental Purchases for Shanghai's Only Child," in D. Davis (ed.), *The Consumer Revolution in Urban China* (pp. 1–20). Berkeley: University of California Press.

Hooper, B. (2000) "Consumer Voices: Asserting Rights in Post-Mao China," *China Information* 14 (92): 92–128.

Jacobs, J.A. and K. Gerson, (2004) *The Time Divide: Work, Family, and Gender Inequality*, Cambridge Mass. and London, England: Harvard University Press.

Laotzi, translated by Roberts, M. (2001) *Dao De Jing: The Book of the Way*. Berkeley and Los Angeles, CA and London: University of California Press.

Linn, S. (2005) *Consuming Kids: The Hostile Takeover of Childhood*, New York NY: Anchor Books, Random House.

Quart, A. (2003) *Branded: the Buying and Selling of Teenagers*. Cambridge: Perseus Publishing.

Shor, J. B. (2004) *Born to Buy: The Commercialized Child and the New Consumer Culture*, New York: Shribner.

Tilt, B. (2006) "Chinese Children's Consumption: A Commentary," in Y. S. Jienying Xi, Jing Jian Xiao (eds), *Chinese Youth in Transition*, Aldershot, England: Ashgate Publishing.

Ying, G. (2003) "Consumption Patterns of Chinese Children,", *Journal of Family and Economic Issues* 24: 373–79.

Zhao, B. (1997) "Consumerism, Confucianism, Communism: Making Sense of China Today," *New Left Review*, no. 222: 43–55.

Zhao, X. (2006) "Chinese Children's Consumption,", in Y. S. Jienying Xi, Jing Jian Xiao (eds), *Chinese Youth in Transition*. Aldershot, England: Ashgate Publishing.

12

"Those Who Have Less Want More. But Does it Make Them Feel Bad?": Deprivation, Materialism and Self-Esteem in Childhood

Agnes Nairn, Paul Bottomley and Johanne Ormrod

Understanding how consumer culture affects children's wellbeing has recently moved centre stage across the world with concerns growing over the adverse effects of rising levels of materialism. Globally, Unicef (Innocenti, 2007) has painted a bleak picture for the psychological welfare of children living in the world's most materially rich countries. Best sellers from North America, such as *Consuming Kids* (Linn, 2004) or *Born to Buy* (Shor, 2004) and in the UK *Toxic Childhood* (Palmer, 2006) go further by criticizing how marketing organizations, society in general and contemporary family values encourage children to consume more and be satisfied with less. Academic research has also begun identifying the mechanisms by which consumer culture may interfere with the psychological wellbeing of children (Achenreiner, 1997; Buijzen & Valkenburg, 2003; Goldberg, Gorn, Peracchio & Bamossy, 2003; Flouri, 2004; Luthar, 2003; Kasser, 2002; Chaplin & John, 2007). This chapter explores the relationship between materialism and children's self-esteem. In particular, it focuses on one area which has so far received relatively little attention, namely the effects of socio-economic status (SES) on this interaction. In other words, are the links between materialism and feeling good or bad affected by whether a child is living in a household which can afford to purchase consumer goods or one where money is tight?

The research for this chapter differs in two respects from most of the other chapters in this book. It is grounded in literature from psychology and consumer research rather than anthropology or sociology. Within this substantial stream of literature "materialism" is usually conceptualised as a psychological construct and specifically a component of an individual's value-set. It has thus tended to be measured through response to attitude questionnaires. The empirical study reported here is therefore

194

quantitative. This approach is, of course, rather different from, for example, ethnographic studies which examine how individuals interact with the material world in their daily lives or use material objects to symbolise special occasions or feelings. Whilst quantitative research cannot bring the richness and depth of some of these studies, the benefit of using questionnaire based research is the ability to create measurement instruments which can be used to establish correlations between constructs, between different samples of people and across time. In the context of this research it allows us to draw reliable comparisons between children in different economic circumstances and to make measurable inferences about the differential relationships between materialism and self-esteem.

We begin the chapter by explaining the constructs we examined in our research and presenting the measurement instruments used. We then report the study and its findings before discussing the conclusions and suggesting avenues for future research.

Materialism, self-esteem and socio-economic status in adulthood

Most consumer research on materialism has been conducted on adults. Consumer researchers define materialism as "the importance a consumer attaches to worldly possessions" (Belk 1984: 291) and "the importance a person places on possessions and their acquisition as a necessary or desirable form of conduct to reach desired end states, including happiness" (Richins and Dawson 1992: 307). Although the accumulation of material possessions can be an end in itself, most of the research in this area has explored the acquisition of material possessions as a means for achieving higher goals, such as self-definition, self-enhancement and happiness or life satisfaction. Materialistic values reflect the view that acquisition of wealth and possessions is: (i) *central* to life giving it meaning and guiding behaviour, (ii) important for life satisfaction and *happiness* and (iii) crucial for judging *success* of oneself and others. Items measuring these three components make up Richins and Dawson's (1992; 2004) Material Values Scale which is the measure which has been most widely used over the past 15 years to establish links between materialism and a range of other variables including life satisfaction, self-esteem, community involvement and ecological footprint (e.g. Kasser & Ryan, 1993; Cohen & Cohen, 1996; Saunders & Munro, 2000).

A very consistent finding across the consumer research literature is the association in adults between materialism and self-esteem, with lower feelings of self-worth relating to higher levels of materialism

(Wright & Larsen, 1993; Cohen & Cohen, 1996; Ahuvia & Wong, 2002; Burroughs and Rindfleisch, 2002; Kasser & Kanner, 2003). This dynamic is commonly interpreted as a recurring cyclical process where material goods are acquired in the (unfulfilled) hope of compensating for feelings of insecurity and searching for happiness (Fournier & Richins 1991; Richins & Dawson 1992; Mick 1996). The process can be exacerbated by marketing which thrives on selling the notion that consumer goods will fulfil emotional needs. Work by Csikszentmihalyi (2003), and Kasser and Kanner (2003) has shown that a perceived gap between current life status and some aspired future level causes individuals to develop more unrealistic expectations, thus rendering them more vulnerable to dissatisfaction. Other researchers note that an excessive focus on materialistic values is also associated with reduced interpersonal contact and social interaction (Rindfleisch *et al.*, 1997; Solberg *et al.*, 2003).

It should be noted that the direction of the causal relationship between materialism and self-esteem is ambiguous. On the one hand, insecure people may seek to find solace in a new car or new clothes and on the other hand, people who orientate their lives around the accumulation of wealth and possessions may simply end up experiencing feelings of low self-worth when the product fails to deliver emotional benefits. In a way this is a chicken and egg phenomenon: high levels of materialism and low levels of self-esteem are highly correlated and it is difficult to say which came first. Given the reinforcing cyclical nature of the dynamic, this may, ultimately, be unimportant as it is the dynamics within the cycle itself which give cause for concern.

Another consistent finding in research with adults is that those living in social and economic deprivation display higher levels of materialism than their affluent counterparts (Kasser *et al.* 1995; Kasser & Kanner, 2003). Much of the research in this area stems from the work of Ronald Inglehart (1971, 1977, 1979, 1990) who has shown that physical and psychological needs become more salient in the absence of the possibility of meeting them satisfactorily. In other words, the more unobtainable something is, the more desirable it appears. In line with Maslow's hierarchy of needs, Inglehart's work shows that once an individual (or society) has fulfilled their material needs then they will pass into a phase of "post materialism" where goals more allied to ideas and self-actualisation will assume greater importance.

This work on the links between materialism, self-esteem and socioeconomic status in adults is important for children's research because values (including materialism) are propagated and nurtured through people's daily social contact with their immediate social group. This has been shown to be the case in family units where strong correlations have been established between materialism levels in parents and children (e.g. Kasser *et al.* 1995). In other words, materialistic parents are more likely to nurture materialistic values in their children. However, Burroughs and Rindfleisch (2002) have shown that when materialistic attitudes are at odds with the values of the social group then this causes a psychological tension which is in turn associated with negative well-being. Thus if consumer culture more generally nurtures materialistic values in children whose parents are not materialistic, then this may cause family antagonism.

In summary, within the consumer research field a great deal of work has been conducted on adult materialism. Materialism (the importance attached to material goods as a means of achieving desired end states including happiness) is strongly associated with low self-esteem in a circular dynamic; those from lower socio-economic groups tend to be more materialistic; materialism is propagated through the social group (including the family) and conflict can arise when a member has differing levels of materialism from the group.

Materialism, Self-esteem and socio-economic status in childhood

As noted in the introduction to this book, children's place in consumer culture has attracted increasing attention and debate over the past decade. In the light of this, a number of researchers have begun to explore the materialism construct as applied to children and adolescents (e.g. Buizjen & Valkenburg, 2003; Goldberg *et al.*, 2003; Schor, 2004; Chaplin & John, 2007). The most widely used measurement instrument to date is the Youth Materialism Scale (YMS) (Goldberg *et al.*, 2003) which has been specifically designed to reflect the thoughts, feelings and developmental capacity of 9–14 year olds. The scale is essentially an adaptation of the Material Values Scale and includes items related to the happiness dimension such as "I would be happier if I had more money to buy more things for myself"; the success dimension – "I really like the kids that have very special games and clothes"; and the centrality dimension – "I have fun just thinking of all the things I own." Like the Richins and Dawson (2004) measure, the scale consists of a number of items (10 in this case) which can be summed to create an overall materialism score. The YMS has been used over the past 6 years to establish correlations between childhood materialism and self-esteem, school performance, purchase requests to parents and indicators of mental health (e.g. Goldberg *et al.*, 2003, Chaplin & John, 2005, 2007).

Drawing more on literature from sociology and anthropology, Juliet Schor (2004) has also proposed a conceptualization of what she prefers to call children's "Consumer Involvement" rather than materialism. In addition to focusing on the personal values children might use to "interpret their environment and structure their lives" (Richins, 2004, p.209), her intention is to capture how they interact with the consumer world. Thus she includes items such as "When I go somewhere special, I usually like to buy something," and "brand labels really matter to me".

In our study we used the YMS scale in order to be able to compare our results with other research and we also included Schor's Consumer Involvement Scale as it had not previously been tested outside the original study (Schor, 2004).

To measure children's self-esteem we decided to use the Rosenberg Self-Esteem Scale (Rosenberg, 1965). The RSES measures what is known as 'global self-esteem'. Understood as a basic human need, global self-esteem is characterised by an individual motivation to protect and enhance the feeling of self-worth, which is an important element in psychological stability. The dynamics of self-esteem appear to pivot around "hopelessness". It has been noted that children who adopt an attitude of not caring, following the crowd, and attributing events to luck or fate often have a pronounced sense of hopelessness. They gradually come to expect failure and assume that they are less capable in all areas of life (learned helplessness), resulting in low self-esteem, which colours all areas of their lives. It has been argued that this, in turn, renders these children prone to depression. Following the feelings of general hopelessness and worthlessness developed during childhood, individuals can begin to develop negative thought patterns such as "I never succeed anyway", or "I won't be able to do it"' Impaired global self-esteem persisting into adolescence and adulthood causes an increased vulnerability to depression.

The RSES is the most widely used measure of global self-esteem. This is partly because of its consistent reliability over the years and partly because of the ease of administration: there are only ten simple items on the scale, for example "I feel good about myself", "I am able to do things as well as most people" and "I feel that I have a number of good qualities." Moreover, the scale has recently been validated in a 53-country study, giving us confidence that this is a reliable and valid measure of psychological wellbeing (Schmitt & Allick, 2005). Perhaps most importantly, it has also been used in conjunction with materialism in a number of recent studies with children (Fiouri, 2004; Schor, 2004).

Just as children's levels of materialism are bound up with family values, so too is children's self-esteem inextricably linked to family relationships. It was therefore decided to include children's relationships with their parents as a factor in the interaction between materialism and self-esteem. We considered two aspects of this. First it has been shown that children who watch more TV advertising are more likely to ask their parents to buy products for them. Incidence of purchase requests is linked not only to materialism but also to family arguments. (Buizjen & Valkenburg, 2003). Juliet Schor (2004) proposes a slightly different angle. She and other campaigners for less commercialism in the lives of children suggest that the youth culture propagated in the mass media in general, and by advertisers of children's products in particular, drive a wedge between parents and their children:

> It's important to recognise the nature of the corporate message: kids and products are aligned together in a really great, fun place, while parents, teachers, and other adults inhabit an oppressive, drab, and joyless world. The lesson to kids is that it's the product, not your parent who's really on your side (p. 55).

To explore the possibility that children's relationships with their parents may be affected by aspects of materialism and consumer culture we created a scale built on questions requiring children to rate whether their mothers and fathers were cool, boring, understanding and fun. We also measured the correlation between materialism and how much time children spend with TV and computer as well as their attitudes to advertising.

The research

The objective of our empirical research was to explore in more detail the moderating effect of social and economic deprivation on the links between materialism and self-esteem in children.

A questionnaire including the YMS, the Schor CI scale, RSES and children's attitudes towards their parents was distributed to 557 children aged 9–13 from six UK schools (three in deprived areas and three in affluent areas). We also included items recording how much time the children spend watching TV and using the computer and whether they like and believe adverts. Most equivalent surveys simply ask children to estimate how many hours they spend watching TV or using the computer. We felt that children (particularly the younger ones) would be unable to estimate this accurately. We chose, instead, to use a "times of day" approach. We produced 17 items split into weekdays, Saturdays and Sundays, such as "Do you watch TV in the morning before school?" or "Do you use the computer on Sunday evenings after dinner?" We offered four response options: "never", "some days", "most days", and 'every day'. These responses scored one to four respectively, giving a minimum possible score of 17 (all answers being 'never') and a maximum score of 68 (all answers being 'every day'). From this we calculated the children's TV and computer scores.

Given research showing that advertising can fuel materialism and purchase requests (Buijzen & Valkenberg, 2003) we felt that it was important to gather children's views on adverts. We used a standardised and validated set of questions developed specifically to measure the global attitude towards TV advertising among children aged 8–12 (Derbaix & Pecheux, 2003). These assess both whether children like TV advertising and whether they believe it.

Levels of deprivation were measured using the Index of Multiple Deprivation calculated by the UK National Statistics Office (2006) which ranks geographical areas by comparing national and local measures of income, employment, health, education, barriers to housing and services, living environment and crime rates. Half of the schools in our sample ranked in the most deprived 15 per cent and half ranked in the least deprived 15 per cent. In order to reduce bias from differences in geographical area the schools chosen were located only 15 miles apart. Since our main aim was to look at deprivation and affluence, we chose to focus on groups of children at either end of the spectrum: while a "middle" group would have made an interesting control group, we did not collect this data. All children in years 5, 6 (for the 4 primary schools) and 7 and 8 (for the 2 secondary schools) present in school on the day of the survey took part. This survey was designed with the broader purpose of exploring the links between media consumption, materialism and wellbeing and some results have already been published by the UK National Consumer Council (Nairn *et al.*, 2007).

Results

As noted above, adults from deprived backgrounds have consistently been found to be more materialistic than their affluent counterparts (e.g. Kasser *et al.* 1995; Kasser & Kanner, 2003) and these values appear to be passed on to their children. Both Goldberg *et al.* (2003) and Schor (2004) found that children living in areas of socioeconomic deprivation scored particularly highly on materialism. Our study completely supports these findings. The mean YMS score for the deprived area (25.55) was significantly and dramatically higher than that for the affluent area (22.47). Table 12.1 shows that a significantly higher percentage of children from the deprived areas agreed with every single one of the 10 materialism statements – apart, that is, from the statement "I really enjoy going shopping", which appears to be driven primarily by gender. Perhaps most notable is that around half of children from deprived areas said they would "rather spend time buying things than doing almost anything else"; and said they believe that "when you grow up, the more money you have the happier you are" – whilst less than a quarter of children in affluent areas said the same. And whilst less than a third of children in affluent areas said they believe that "the only job I want when I grow up is one that gets me lots of money"; over two-thirds of children in deprived areas claimed to have such career aspirations.

We found strong and significant links between materialism and the TV score, the Computer score and liking advertising. There was no link between believing advertising and materialism. The structural equation models used allowed us to see that the link between the TV score and materialism was the strongest (explaining around a third of the variation in materialism). The computer score explained 19 per cent and liking adverts 10 per cent. There were very great differences in media use

Table 12.1 Youth materialism by SES

	Agree (%)	
	Affluent	**Deprived**
I'd rather spend time buying things than doing almost anything else	23	47
I would be happier if I had more money to buy more things for myself	50	66
I have fun just thinking of all the things I own	50	62
I like to buy things my friends have	44	56
When you grow up the more money you have the happier you are	23	51
I'd rather not share my snacks with others if it means I'll have less for myself	17	25
I would love to be able to buy things that cost lots of money	43	55
I really like the kids that have very special games and clothes	19	34
The only kind of job I want when I grow up is one that gets me a lot of money	28	69
I really enjoy going shopping	63	61

by socio-economic group with deprived children spending a lot more time in front of the TV and computer screen. The average TV score for the deprived children was 46.7 compared with 35.7 for the affluent group. This accords with other studies (e.g. Schor, 2004). The difference in the computer score was not quite so dramatic with the affluent children scoring on average 26.9 and the deprived children 30.9. Twice as many deprived children said they believed adverts (40 per cent versus 20 per cent). Thus we see that watching TV in particular is strongly associated with materialism and that the most materialistic group of children (from deprived backgrounds) also watch most TV.

To explore the dynamics of the moderating role of SES on the interaction between materialism and self-esteem we ran a series of structural equation models. The first model hypothesised a negative relationship between an aggregated score on the YMS scale and an aggregated score on RSES. The model demonstrated a significant and sizeable negative link between the two scores: the higher a child's score on the materialism scale the lower his or her self-esteem. When we ran this model for the affluent and deprived groups separately the links remained sizeable and significant for both groups. This is consistent with prior research on adults and children. It should be noted that although the data fits the hypothesised path from materialism to self-esteem structural equation models cannot claim to show causality. Whether materialism causes low self-esteem or vice versa is open to debate, as noted above.

We then ran three more similar models, this time using Schor's Consumer Involvement scale. Whilst the items in YMS have consistently loaded on a single factor (i.e. the items measure a single construct, "materialism"), we found that this scale consisted of three independent factors which we named Consumer Involvement (including items such as "I usually have something in mind I want to buy or get" and "I care a lot about my games, toys and other possessions"); Brand Attachment (including statements such as "brand names matter to me" and "I like clothes with popular labels"); and Material Dissatisfaction (e.g. "I wish my family could afford to buy me more of what I want" and "I feel like other kids have more stuff than I do"). Interestingly, whilst Brand Attachment and Consumer Orientation did not prove to be significantly linked with Self-Esteem, Material Dissatisfaction did. This is a new finding which suggests a more nuanced interpretation of childhood materialism. Simply being involved in a consumer culture is not necessarily detrimental *per se*, but becomes so when it is implicated in dissatisfaction with what a child owns. These findings have been replicated and, in fact, reinforced since we originally conducted our study: Day *et al.* (2007) found the same three factor structure in the scale and noted a strong association between high Material Dissatisfaction and not only low self-esteem but also high depressive, anxiety, obsessive and behaviour symptoms.

Our next finding was puzzling. We had expected to find lower self-esteem amongst the deprived group of children. Given the strong and significant link between materialism and self-esteem and given that the deprived group were dramatically more materialistic than the affluent group, this seemed the obvious expectation. Moreover, just as is the case for adults, prior research on young people from psychiatry (Collishaw *et al.*, 2004) shows lower levels of mental wellbeing generally amongst deprived children. This is linked to stresses of poverty such as living in overcrowded housing, poor health, parental anxiety about finances, etc. In particular, vulnerability to depression and maladjustment has been demonstrated to be above both normative rates and rates for children in affluent areas (Luthar & Latendresse, 2005). However we found that in fact there was no significant difference in self-esteem scores between the affluent group (28.75) and deprived group (28.85).

In order to investigate this further, we built another series of structural equation models to explore the moderating impact of socio-economic status on the link between materialism and self-esteem. We wanted to test whether there was a stronger relationship between materialism and self-esteem in the affluent or the deprived group. We also included in these models the effects of children's attitudes to both their mother and their father (as defined through statements like "s/he doesn't under-stand what kids need to have these days", "s/he is not cool", and so on). The results are shown in Table 12.2 for the model using Schor's Material Dissatisfaction scale.

As would be expected from the previous models, as materialism increases, a child's self-esteem decreases. We also found that as materialism increases, a child's attitude to their parents becomes less positive: children

Table 12.2   Materialism and attitude to parents by SES

	Materialism → self-esteem	Materialism → attitude to mother	Attitude to mother → self-esteem
Affluent	−0.09	−0.57	0.05
Deprived	−0.07	−0.31	0.09
	materialism → self-esteem	materialism → attitude to father	attitude to father → self-esteem
Affluent	−0.08	−0.49	0.09
Deprived	−0.09	−0.21	0.04

who are more materialistic think their parents are less fun, cool and understanding and more boring. Interestingly this link is very much stronger than the direct link from materialism to self-esteem, which means that materialism has a stronger impact on a child's attitude towards their parent than it does on their own self-esteem. This applies regardless of socio-economic status. Looking at Table 12.2, if we compare the regression coefficient for the link between materialism and self-esteem and materialism and attitude to mother or father we see that –0.09 is much smaller than –0.57 (affluent children and their mothers); –0.08 is much smaller than –0.49 (affluent children and their fathers); –0.07 is smaller than –0.31 (deprived children and their mothers); and –0.09 is smaller than –0.21 (deprived children and their fathers).

We can also see from Table 12.2 that a child's attitude to their parents (mother or father) is positively related to their own self-esteem and that this holds for all groups. We have therefore uncovered an interesting dynamic. Materialism in children appears to work not directly on their psychological state but indirectly through their relationship with their parents. Higher levels of materialism are associated with less positive attitudes towards parents; and this impaired relationship with parents is in turn associated with lower self-esteem. A loosening of parental bonds may well be linked to insecurity, which children are likely to try to mitigate with greater attachment to material goods.

Perhaps most interesting, Table 12.2 also shows us that socio-economic status moderates the strength of the relationship between materialism and children's attitudes towards their parents. As materialism increases, affluent children's positive attitudes to their mothers decrease more than they do for the deprived children (–0.57 vs –0.31), a difference which is statistically significant. Likewise, as materialism increases, affluent children's positive attitudes to their fathers decrease more than they do for deprived children (–0.49 vs –0.21), a difference which again is significant. Another interesting and unexpected finding is that across both groups of children the negative relationship between materialism and positive attitudes towards parents is stronger for mothers (–0.57 and –0.49) than fathers (–0.31 and –0.21).

Conclusion and discussion

Our study shows that materialism (measured in two ways) is linked to low self-esteem in this sample of British tweens. It also shows that this is not a direct effect but appears to work through family dynamics, whereby material dissatisfaction is played out in feelings of disappointment with parents' (particularly mothers') ability to understand the younger generation. These feelings of disappointment with parents seem to be strongly related to children's low estimation of themselves. Meanwhile, whilst the children from households where money is tight have a much stronger desire for money and possessions, it is the children from the affluent households whose relationship with their parents is more negatively associated with materialistic values.

A possible explanation for this latter finding may be found in Burroughs and Rindfleisch's (2002) notion of "conflicting values", mentioned earlier, where the materialistic attitudes of an individual (in this case the child) are at odds with those of the social group (the family), causing a psychological tension which is in turn associated with negative well-being. Adults from more deprived backgrounds are likely to be more materialistic and so it is possible that materialistic children in deprived households share their family values whilst materialistic children of affluent parents are subject to conflicting values. It is possible that for the parents of the affluent group ("post-materialists"), academic achievement, for example, may be seen as of greater importance. The average percentage of children entering further education from middle-class households is, after all, dramatically higher than the percentage from deprived groups. Thus for the affluent parent it may be that the personal value of "doing well at school" takes on more importance than "getting stuff at the shops" whilst for parents in deprived areas "getting a job and getting money" may assume a higher priority. Materialistic children in middle-class households may find the values they have been encouraged to espouse through the heavy commercial inducements in the media all around them stand in stark contrast to those of their parents whose (much lower) levels of materialism have already been fixed as they entered young adulthood in a much less commercialised era.

The work of Luthar and colleagues may also add some light to these findings. They have noted that a number of stressful factors associated with post-materialism and affluence seem to cause depression in wealthier adolescents (Luthar & D'Avanzo, 1999; Luthar & Latendresse, 2005b). These factors might include the expectation to do well at school and the pressure to excel at an increasing number of extra-curricular activities such as music examinations, ballet classes, gaining a place in the first football team etc. Our affluent sample was drawn from a small city where parental involvement in the child's life is high and an achievement orientation is prevalent. These tensions may have resulted in poorer relationships at home and, indeed, self-esteem being lower than might have been expected elsewhere.

Our findings offer a few new insights into the important global debate over the effects of rising material wealth on the mental health of children. It seems that a personal value system which rates the possession of consumption objects and financial wealth very highly is linked to impaired wellbeing in children, as it is in adults. However, it also seems that it is the children whose parents can most afford to purchase consumer objects who are most susceptible to these negative effects. This adds a new dimension to the theory that "those who have less want more". Deprived children may, indeed, want more but this may not necessarily make them less happy than other children because, comfortingly, they may share a value system with their parents. On the other hand, impairment to wellbeing does seem to occur when "those who have more want more", because it may create damaging family value conflict. This offers intriguing new possibilities for future research and theory building.

References

Achenreiner, G. B. (1997) "Materialistic Values and Susceptibility to Influence in Children", *Advances in Consumer Research*, Vol. 24, Marrie Brucks and Deborah J. MacInnis (eds). Provo, Utah: Association for Consumer Research, 82–8.

Ahuvia, Aaron C. and N. Y. Wong (2002) "Personality and Value Based Materialism: Their Relationship and Origins", *Journal of Consumer Psychology*, 12 (4), 389–402.

Belk, R. W. (1984) "Three Scales to Measure Constructs Related to Materialism: Reliability, Validity and Relationships to Measures of Happiness", *Advances in Consumer Research*, Thomas Kinnear, ed. Provo, Utah: Association for Consumer Research, 291–7.

Buijzen, M. and M. P Valkenburg. (2003) "The unintended effects of television advertising, a parent child survey", *Communication Research*, 30, 483–503.

Burroughs, J. & Rindfleisch A. (2002) "Materialism and Wellbeing: A conflicting values Perspective", *Journal of Consumer Research*, 29, 348–70

Chaplin, Lan Nguyen & Deborah Roedder John (2005) "The Development of Self-Brand Connections in Children and Adolescents", *Journal of Consumer Research*, 32 (June), 119–29.

Chaplin, L. N. and D. R. John (2007) "Growing Up in a Material World: Age Differences in Materialism in Children and Adolescents", *Journal of Consumer Research*, 34, Dec.

Cohen, P., & Cohen, J. (1996) *Life Values and Adolescent Mental Health*. Mahwah, NJ: Erlbaum.

Collishaw, S., B. Maughan, R. Goodman and A. Pickles (2004) "Time Trends in Adolescent Mental Health", *Journal of Child Psychology and Psychiatry*, 45(8), 1350–62.

Csikszentmihalyi, M. (2003). "Materialism and the evolution of consciousness", T. Kasser and A. D. Kanner (eds), *Psychology and Consumer Culture*, pp. 91–106.

Day, J., V. Dunn, V. and I. Goodyer (2007) "Results from the ROOTS Consumer Involvement Scale", Working Paper, University of Cambridge, Department of Developmental Psychiatry, 13 November.

Derbaix, C. and C. Pecheux, (2003) "A New Scale to Assess Children's Attitude toward TV Advertising", *Journal of Advertising Research*, 43(4), 390–9.

Flouri, E. (2004). "Exploring the relationship between mothers' and fathers' parenting practices and children's materialistic values", *Journal of Economic Psychology*, 25, 743–75.

Fournier, S. and M. L. Richins (1991) "Some Theoretical and Popular Notions Concerning Materialism", *Journal of Social Behavior and Personality*, 6 (6), 403–14.

Goldberg, M. E., Gorn., G. J., Peracchio L. A., and G. Bamossy G. (2003) "Understanding Materialism Among Youth". *Journal of Consumer Psychology*, 13 (3), 278–88.

Inglehart, R. (1971) "The Silent Revolution in Europe: Intergenerational Change in Post-industrial Societies". *American Political Science Review*, 65, 991–1017.

Inglehart, R. (1977) *The Silent Revolution: Changing Values and Political Styles Among Western Publics*. Princeton, NJ: Princeton University Press.

Inglehart, R. (1979) "Value Priorities and Socioeconomic Change". In Samuel Barnes & Max Kaase (ed.), *Political Action: Mass Participation in Five Western Democracies* (pp. 305–342). Thousand Oaks, CA: Sage.

Inglehart, R. (1990) *Culture Shift in Advanced Industrial Society*. Princeton, NJ: Princeton University Press.

Innocenti (2007) "Child Poverty in Perspective: An Overview of Child Well-being in Rich Countries: A Comprehensive Assessment of the Lives and Well-being of Children and Adolescents in the Economically Advanced Nations. Italy: UNICEF Innocenti Research Centre, Innocenti Report card 7.

Kasser, T. (2002) *The High Price of Materialism*. Cambridge, MA: MIT Press

Kasser, T. and R. M. Ryan (1993) "A Dark Side of the American Dream: Correlates of Financial Success as a Central Life Aspiration", *Journal of Personality and Social Psychology*, 65, 410–22.

Kasser, T., R. M. Ryan, M. Zax and A. J. Sameroff (1995) "The Relations of Maternal and Social Environments to Late Adolescent's Materialistic and Prosocial Values", *Developmental Psychology*, 31, 907–914.

Kasser, T and A. D. Kanner (2003) "Where Is the Psychology of Consumer Culture?". In T. Kasser & A. D. Kanner (eds) *Psychology and Consumer Culture, The Struggle for a Good Life in a Materialistic World*. (pp. 3–8). Washington, DC: American Psychological Association.

Linn, Susan (2004) *Consuming Kids: The Hostile Takeover of Childhood*. New York: New Press.

Luthar, Suniya S. (2003) "The Culture of Affluence: Psychological Costs of Material Wealth", *Child Development*, 74 (6), 1581–93.

Luthar, S. S. and B. E. Becker (2002), "Privileged but Pressured? A Study of Affluent Youth", *Child Development*, 73 (5), 1593–1610.

Luthar, S. S. & D'Avanzo, K. (1999) "Contextual Factors in Substance Use: A Study of Suburban and Inner City Adolescents", *Development and Psychopathology*, Special Issue, 11(3), 845–867.

Luthar, S. S., and S. J. Latendresse (2005) "Children of the Affluent: Challenges to Well-Being", *Directions in Psychological Science*, 14, 49–53.

Mick, D. G. (1996) "Are Studies of Dark Side Variables Confounded by Socially Desirable Responding? The Case of Materialism", *Journal of Consumer Research*, 23 (September), 106–19.

Nairn, A., J. Ormrod, and P. Bottomley (2007) *Watching, Wanting and Wellbeing. Exploring the Links*, London: National Consumer Council.

Palmer, S. (2006) *Toxic Childhood*. London: Orion.

Richins, M. L. (2004) "The Material Values Scale: Measurement Properties and Development of a Short Form". *Journal of Consumer Research*, 31 (June), 209–19.

Richins, M. L. and S. Dawson (1992) "A Consumer Values Orientation for Materialism and Its Measurement: Scale Development and Validation". *Journal of Consumer Research*, 19 (3), 303–316.

Rindfleisch, A., J. E. Borroughs and F. Denton, (1997) "Family Structure, Materialism, and Compulsive Consumption", *Journal of Consumer Research*, 23, 312–25.

Rosenberg, M. (1965) *Society and the Adolescent Self-Image*. Princeton, NJ: Princeton University Press.

Saunders, S., and D. Munro (2000)"The Construction and Validation of a Consumer Orientation Questionnaire (SCOI) Designed To Measure Fromm's (1955) "Marketing Character" in Australia",. *Social Behavior and Personality, 28*, 219–40.

Schor, J. (2004) *Born to Buy*. New York: Schribner.

Schmitt, D. P. and J. Allick (2005) "Simultaneous Administration of the Rosenberg Self-esteem Sscale in 53 Nations: Exploring the Universal and Culture-specific Features of Global Self-esteem", *Journal of Personality and Social Psychology*, 89(4), , 623–42.

Solberg, E. G, E. Diener and M. D. Robinson (2003) 'Why are Materialists Less Satisfied?" In T. Kasser and A. D. Kanner (eds) *Psychology and Consumer Culture, The Struggle for a Good Llife in a Materialistic World*. (pp. 29–48). Washington, DC: American Psychological Association.

Wright, N. D and Larsen V. (1993) " Materialism and Life Satisfaction: A Meta-Analysis", *Journal of Consumer Satisfaction, Dissatisfaction and Complaining Behaviou*r, 6, 158–65.

Part V

Childhood Identities and Consumption

13
Branded Selves: How Children Relate to Marketing on a Social Network Site

Håvard Skaar

During the past few years, the use of so-called social network sites has been a rapidly growing trend in young people's communication on the Internet. This chapter explores how marketing affects a group of 11–12 year old classmates' use of a network site called Piczo. Piczo enables young people to create "sites with multiple pages featuring photos, graphics, guest books, comment boards, music, and more" (www.piczo.com). Social connections are made explicit and social networking emerges when users subsequently link their pages to those of their friends.

The chapter relates the classmates' social and textual practice to a broader debate about the role of digital media in today's commercialization of children's lives. David Buckingham describes this debate as a polarization between "on the one hand, the critical view of children as passive victims of consumer culture; and on the other, the view of marketers themselves, who define children as much more active, competent and powerful" (Buckingham, 2007: 15). Claiming that this polarization is a simplification, Buckingham suggests that researchers need to concentrate on "newer commercial strategies" such as "product placement, peer-to peer marketing, cross-promotion and viral and online marketing" (Buckingham, 2007: 21). The Piczo website is based on these kinds of marketing strategies, which essentially give young people a more productive role than they have as consumers of more traditional media. An analysis of their Piczo productions can therefore inform the debate outlined above.

In the study, the design and content of young people's Piczo pages will be understood as a form of self-presentation. The notion originates from the work of Erving Goffman (1959) and reflects his view of identity as a product of everyday social interaction. Goffman basically analyzes self-presentation as part of face-to-face interaction, so here the notion must be qualified in a way that captures the specific nature of self-presentation on interactive web pages. Indeed, it is precisely the deviation from face-to-face interaction which opens up children's self-presentations on the Piczo website to new kinds of commercial influence. The phenomenon of branding renders these influences visible and traceable. Against this background, the study sets out to answer the following research question: How does branding affect young people's self-presentation on the Piczo website?

Brands and identity

While the content and economic value of brands were previously closely related to the products they stood for, they are now increasingly detaching themselves from this material basis. The most successful brands have acquired a standing that gives them cultural influence and economic value independent of the products they represent. In recent years cognitive approaches, where branding has been understood as a question of gaining effective access to consumers' minds (Ries & Trout, 1980), have been challenged by social and cultural approaches which focus on consumers' identity building (e.g. Belk, 1988). One strand of research uses psycho-sociological concepts to explain the relationships consumers form with brands (e.g. Fournier, 1998). In this perspective, brands gain importance by becoming part of consumers' lived experiences. Another strand of research explores how brands are used to build communities (Cova & Cova, 2001; Muñiz & O'Guinn, 2001) and thereby fulfil consumers' social, mythological and even religious needs and longings (Muñiz & Schau, 2005).

Although brands' increasingly intrusive role in our everyday lives has attracted criticism (Klein 2000) and mobilized a counterculture (www. nologo.org, www.adbusters. org), Holt (2002, p. 87) claims that such a counterculture presents no threat to branding. People have become well aware of the commercial interests associated with brands. As consumers, their only concern will be what contribution the brand can offer as they seek to develop their own identity. They will "look for brands to contribute directly to their identity projects by providing original and relevant cultural materials with which to work."

This study explores what cultural materials a group of 11–12 year olds find original and relevant on a social network site and how they choose to work with them.

Self-presentation on the Internet

Erving Goffman (1959) describes "the presentation of self in everyday life" (1959) as a perpetual process of social performance. The self cannot be grasped as an autonomous entity but only as a function of roles performed in everyday interaction. To be able to interact we must (at least seemingly) reach a mutual understanding of how the situation is to be defined, or else we will not know how to relate to the other participants and they will not know how to relate to us.

The purpose of the young people's self-presentation on the Piczo pages will be understood here in accordance with an assumption underlying Goffman's dramaturgical approach to interaction: "in all interaction a basic underlying theme is the desire of each participant to guide and control the response made by the others present" (Goffman, 1959: 3). Controlling the response means making the audience buy into or accept a specific definition of the social situation. Actors achieve this through their "impression management". Impression management consists of the methods and techniques employed to maintain the impression of a role played out in a social situation. Goffman (1959: 22) describes the performance of roles as dependent on a setting and a personal front, which he further distinguishes as appearance and manners. Lack of bodily presence on the Internet means that presentation of the self requires resources to mediate not only the setting and appearance but also the manners, the dramatic realization.

Goffman (1963: 18) defines a social gathering as "any set of two or more individuals who are in one another's immediate presence". This simple and basic definition, which confines the social situation physically, does not apply to self-presentation on a website. In his discussion of media and social behaviour Meyrowitz (1985: 7) claims that this is because the presence of media deprives us of the ability to have a physical "sense of place". While "Goffman (...) tends to think of social roles in terms of the places in which they are performed, I argue that electronic media have undermined the traditional relationship between physical setting and social situation."

The young people in this study present themselves to a handful of friends, but at the same time they may, at least theoretically, be presenting themselves to millions of unknown visitors as well. Applying Goffman's theatrical approach to the analysis of young people's self-presentation on a web site, the spatial situation might best be described as "distantiated" (Giddens 1990: 27–8). And as space is distantiated, so is time: there are no limits to when and for how long visitors engage in the social situations made possible by the young people's self-presentations on web pages.

Method

The study is based on downloading of web pages, observations and interviews with pupils and teachers in a 6th grade primary school class in Oslo (ages range from 11–12 years old). The class had 23 (later 22) pupils, 9 girls and 14 boys, most typically from middle-class and lower middle-class homes. Around half of the pupils were ethnic Norwegians while the other half had mixed or immigrant backgrounds. All but one of the 22 pupils in the class had Internet access at home, although with a variable degree of personal access.

The pupils were connected online through a school-based blog called eLogg (see Østerud, Schwebs *et al.*, 2006). Some of the pupils were also shown to be Piczo users, and they were interviewed about their production of pages as they appeared consecutively on the net. On this basis their literacy on Piczo pages was compared with their school-based literacy (see also Skaar, 2008). The self-presentations on Piczo and eLogg are the primary data sources. Interviews, observations and non-digital textual production give a real life background for understanding why the children chose to present themselves as they did in these two different web-based surroundings. The analysis is based on a constant comparative method where categories are generated and tested out in a move from small to larger data sets over time (Silverman 2005: 214). The presentation of the findings is not exhaustive but structured in accordance with the research question raised in this chapter.

Branded space, texts and tools

The Piczo brand is not primarily attached to users' self-presentations but rather to the social situation in which the presentation of self takes place. This naturally makes Piczo the paramount brand on the Piczo web site. Piczo profits from branding, as well as allowing other marketers to brand the space, texts and tools their users need to present themselves. Goffman suggests that it is by the use of "frames" that we relate the situations we define in social interactions to the surrounding social world. The space offered to Piczo users relates their self-presentations to brands and commercially produced self-presentations, e.g. the commercial personae exposed in adverts (see Cook & Kaiser, 2004), which inevitably become a point of reference, a frame, when users' own self-presentations are related to the surrounding world.

In addition, Piczo offers its users textual resources for self-presentation (e.g. writing, pictures, music, animations and video clips) which are, or include elements from, brands, promotion and adverts. Brands link the self-presentations to products and/or to websites that have specialized in providing videos, animations and pictures for use on social network sites.

Finally, Piczo offers branded tools that enable users to integrate these selected texts or textual elements on their own pages. For example, users do not have to spell out "Welcome" on their pages, instead they can choose a "Welcome-sign" from the "textual elements" menu. The coding of the word is done, and at the same time thirty different choices of colour, background and so on, are added. In other words, Piczo offers tools that allow its users "shortcuts" in the coding process, while simultaneously expanding the range of brands and branded texts. By their choice of these shortcuts, users inevitably attach their self-presentations to brands, promotion and adverts.

In the Piczo network, branded resources and non-commercial resources become part of the same circuit of space, texts and tools. As they are free to use them at will, Piczo users merge branded resources with non-commercial resources in ways which often make it difficult, and sometimes impossible, to tell the one from the other. When pupils provide others in their local network with commercially manufactured resources, the closer and more personal relationship between the provider and consumer also reinforces identification with the tastes and judgements implied in the resource.

Users and non-users

Experimental studies show that children aged 11–12 years old have reached a level of maturity that enables impression management based on an internalized understanding of how other people will perceive their self-presentation. At this age, however, children are in a phase where their degree of maturity in this regard is unevenly distributed (Banerjee, 2002). However, maturity is only one requisite for being able to present oneself on Piczo pages: the other factor is the existence of a social network.

In this study one group of pupils presented itself on Piczo (13), while another group did not (9). The use of Piczo corresponded largely to the pupils' social position in the class circle. It had spread from one of the class's most popular pupils, originally introduced to Piczo by an older sister, to a cluster of correspondingly popular and trend-setting pupils and from there gradually to a cluster of pupils of intermediate standing. Conversely, Piczo use never reached those pupils who had greatest difficulty in asserting themselves and their social interests in the classroom context. In interviews, it became clear that this was either due to total lack of familiarity with Piczo, i.e. they were not part of the practice in any way, or because, although they knew about Piczo, they had insufficient social standing or interest to become Piczo users.

In comparison, the school-based learning platform eLogg is based on principles designed to prevent this form of social selection. All pupils have equal access to the website because this is channelled through teacher-initiated writing tasks. Pupils' comments on each other must be related to the responses they publish on the website. In many cases this response is teacher-controlled. Although these norms are exceeded in a way that allows the social hierarchy described above to manifest itself on eLogg, the social ranking in the class makes itself felt much more strongly on Piczo.

The struggle for coolness

Both Piczo and eLogg encourage their users to complete a default profile headed "About myself" and the subordinate fields "interests" and "favourites". The way pupils choose to complete these three fields on eLogg and Piczo show that in the written mode the same interests are expressed on eLogg and Piczo. The difference between the two websites is that Piczo also allows its users to express their preferences and interest through the use of branded texts and tools. During interviews, the pupils in the study gave two reasons for producing Piczo pages: it was either "fun" or "cool". In comparison, they described their production of eLogg pages in more moderate terms, the most typical being "ok". In the comments the pupils made on each other's Piczo pages, "fun" and "cool" were also among the main evaluation criteria. On the commercial web site they used brands to associate the self with fun and coolness inaccessible in their real life:

> In RL, association is limited; consumers often run up against financial, space, or proximal limitations in associating themselves with brands. For example, consumers may feel Gucci expresses their identities but may be unable to own Gucci items in RL. In personal web space consumers' brand associations are limited only by their

imaginations and computer skills. They can literally associate themselves with any brand by digital appropriation and manipulation of digital symbols. (Schau & Gilly, 2003: 400)

Piczo is a brand that gains in currency through users introducing it to each other (many to many) rather than by the marketers presenting the brand to a large public (one to many). Because viral branding (see Holt, 2004: 28) makes it is important to gain access to trend-setting users, this form of marketing has also been called "coolhunting" (Gladwell, 1997).

On eLogg the class teachers have laid down rules for how pupils are expected to behave towards each other. The intention is that everyone should be included. Piczo, on the other hand, constantly encourages its users to say which user pages they rate as being most cool. This competition is based on the forms of distinction consumers strive for in identity-relevant domains, which also explains why too much popularity can make brands uncool (Berger & Heath, 2007). Based on the results of the children's own rating of each others' self-presentations and other factors, Piczo offers the children what they need in order to be favourably rated themselves. In this way, Piczo lays the foundation for social competition among the children, based on the same mechanisms that make some brands attractive and others less attractive, some cool and others uncool.

Collectors and elaborators

On eLogg, pupils' networks are predefined by the school community, while Piczo limits itself to offering young people the resources they need to create their own networks. According to the way they use these resources, the Piczo users in this study can be divided into two categories: collectors and elaborators. Elaborators use branded resources in active and continuing network building. Collectors do not. Elaborators hence produce more Piczo pages over a longer period of time than collectors, which gives them an opportunity to gradually develop more skilful digital design (see also Skaar, 2008). This design reinforces their social position in the network.

Although the terms collectors and elaborators are used here to distinguish between two categories of Piczo users, they can also be seen as stages in the development of a practice. All elaborators began as collectors. To move from one production mode to the other, however, requires time and effort. Elaborators are characterized by a lasting interest in designing self-presentations that give them the best possible basis for social life on the Piczo website. Collectors, on the other hand, give up before they have succeeded in mastering the necessary skills for developing a Piczo design capable of convincing their peers that they are well worth relating to (see Table 13.1).

Schau and Gilly (2003: 391) identify exploration of other selves, the desire to meet expectations based on increased exposure to feedback and to increase and display technical competence as motivating factors behind the production of self-presentations on the web. In the case of elaborators all these three motivational factors are present, whereas one or more is missing in the case of collectors. Collectors' production of Piczo pages is therefore limited and their digital design less advanced. In interviews, they often report that they have grown tired of producing Piczo pages. The most skilful Piczo users in the study, on the other hand, have a declared wish to become ever better designers of Piczo pages.

A collector's use of brands

Tobias was introduced to the possibility of making a self-presentation by the first Piczo user in the class. He made two successive versions of his web pages. The first time, he used NIKE as his address. The Nike brand was also centrally positioned on his opening page. It could also be seen on several of the other pages where Tobias collected brands and other texts he himself perceived as cool or funny. In the interviews, he explained what lead him to choose brands and branded resources on his Piczo pages:

I. Piczo is the name of the people who provide you with the pages to use. But they give you more than that, don't they? Ideas as to what you could put on your pages and so on?

T. Sure. You can find all sorts of things here. As soon as I went in, there were things like "Welcome" and "Enter". I get those from Piczo. There's one page you can go into which is... it's Piczo who's made it...

I. What about these ideas of Piczo's... do you think they're good?

T. Yes.

I. You think so? Because I can see here that you've got some (brand) names... Nike... and is that a brand you're specially keen on?

Table 13.1 Production modes

| | Production volume | | | | Production mode | |
| | Production persistence | | | | | |
	Less than 10 pages	More than 10 pages	Less than 12 months	More than 12 months	Collectors	Elaborators
Amina	X		X		X	
Nadia	X		X		X	
Safdar	X		X		X	
Kent	X		X		X	
Ann	X		X		X	
Hilda	X		X		X	
Tobias		X	X		X	
Benny		X	X		X	
Freddy		X	X		X	
Peter		X		X		X
Dorthe		X		X		X
Jenny		X		X		X
Henry		X		X		X
13	6	7	9	4	9	4

T. Mm.

I. Why do you like it so much?

T. Don't know.

I. It's just that you like it? You like Nike better than Adidas?

T. Yes. It's because... I've got lots of Nike things and... I just like it better.

I: Where did you get the Nike logo and stuff from, then?

T. Just on Google. You just ask it to search for Nike and up it comes.

His first self-presentation attracted some negative feedback in the shout-boxes on the page. These negative comments had nothing to do with the brands and branded resources Tobias has collected on his pages, however, but concerned the way he presented himself under the heading "a little bit about myself":

Anonymous: Lol. You must have a small brain.

A few months later, Tobias deleted the entire contents of the pages he had made and left a new address:

Hi! My home page has now moved to the address "Jejeparty" because this page sucked.

On these new pages, Tobias's written description of himself was no longer there and there was only a completed profile list. His page design was more carefully thought through and was at a higher level. Tobias has developed his digital skills. For example, he had managed to incorporate his own name in the logo of the football club he was a fan of. However, these new pages were also abandoned before they were completed. In the interview, Tobias said he was interested in meeting people on the web but that he had grown tired of making home pages. He preferred communicating on MSN: "I'll always be there, like." When he was interviewed together with a classmate, Tobias said he thought writing was boring, both at school and on Piczo, but when interviewed alone he said writing was fun. When writing was required to form part of his Piczo page design, however, it dried up. Tobias remained a collector. He refused to allow the digital design he made on Piczo to be part of his life in the same way it was for elaborators.

Two elaborators' use of brands

Henry was among the very first Piczo users in the class. He was highly productive and set up a number of pages, both alone and together with others. Henry took a keen interest in brands and consumer culture, an interest also clearly seen in his everyday school life. He referred to fashion magazines in class discussions, for example, and wrote essays about Britney Spears in class tests. He also dressed in typical fashion clothes. On his Piczo pages, brands formed part of his presentation of himself, his interests and favourites.

On a shared site, Henry and one of his friends proclaimed their aspirations for a future as fashion designers and models. Together with his friends, he recreated himself through advertising aesthetics on his pages, and allowed himself to be portrayed with branded clothes and personal effects. Brands were also found in his definition of the friends he made pages with. Many of the pages had brand names as their address and a variety of brands were continually commented on and rated through the design of his pages. Henry did not allow the brands on his pages to pass without comment, but evaluated them and made them carriers of meaning in the interaction taking place on his web pages. He was very productive and had a declared ambition to go on developing his digital design. This ambition found expression both in interviews and in the shoutboxes on the pages he created. He saw becoming a better designer as a long-term project.

Jenny was not one of the early Piczo adopters, but once started she soon produced more pages than anyone else in the group. Initially she presented a large number of texts she had written herself before becoming a Piczo user (e.g. an fictional interview with herself, a diary and various fictional stories), but gradually she went on to produce pages based on branded resources. This resulted in an extended use of branded resources, although brands in themselves did not interest her much.

Adding pages and making new sites at a very rapid pace, she soon asked for help and assistance from others in the local network: a network partly underpinned by other children's interests in the production on her various sites. Some of her pages were copied "as is" from the Piczo network or elsewhere on the web, but generally her use of commercially branded resources resulted in a production that gave her a role as creator of fun in the Piczo network. Basically, these roles were based on her ability to show the others how to be inventive in their engagement with commercially provided resources on the net. She was also generous in her role as provider of entertainment and fun. For example, after having produced a fan site for a young female actor, she finally gave it away to another girl in the network. Jenny engaged the others by taking on the role as editor of her own magazine, or as head teacher of her own Harry Potter inspired "Witch school". But she also received negative comments for these initiatives. For example, one anonymous commenter told her to stop her silly games and "get yourself a life". Another told her that her pages were full of girlish silliness.

It was her creativity Jenny wanted to present through her production of Piczo pages, not her consumer culture or use of brands. She also took an expressly critical view of a digital design based on simple collection of brands and branded resources. As Jenny gradually abandoned her own texts in favour of elaboration of branded resources, she simultaneously underwent a development that made the Piczo universe too limited and childish for her. She developed a digital design reminiscent of teenage social network sites such as Myspace. Her excellent expressive abilities allowed her to be productive in a continuous dialogue with visitors to her site:

From the shoutbox on one of Jenny's pages:

Anonymous commenter:

HOT OR NOT?: NOT: Fergie actually ISN'T hot any more, pink is out (white's in), big beads are definitely out, small ones are in if they're real. LoL is right out, NO ONE says LoL! Orlando Bloom is lukewarm, but Johnny Depp... Yummy! Emma Watson is as far out as it's possible to be, and she's no good as Hermione... Black dresses are in, but otherwise black is out.. Piczo is out, Facebook is in. Manga is out, only 10 year old boys read it... Swearing is out, no one likes girls who swear (OK at football matches, ONLY). HOT: Pamela is actually in, after showing up in Borat. Mika's Grace Kelly is the 2007s' it-sound. Daniel "Radcliffe" is in, especially after the nude scenes: D:D Smoking seems to be in, I'm afraid, my dear....

Jenny : You really don't need to care about what **I** think! Maybe **you** think something different: for example – some people are fans of My Chemical Romance and other not, whatever turns you on!! And I think Fergie's music is good, even if **you** don't. Not everyone needs to be like **you** for everything to be OK!

Social network sites have been regarded as a place where people can profile themselves through their tastes (Liu 2007), but Jenny's response was only one of the ways in which she defended her own taste judgements. She gave her interests and favourites value and the power of persuasion mainly through elaborating her own Piczo page design. A growing number of her friends connected to her pages. More are likely to come along now that she is developing pages in English as well as her Norwegian website.

Discussion

Through their use of branded space, texts and tools all the Piczo users in the study allowed marketing to penetrate their private sphere. Overall, lack of bodily presence coupled with distantiation in time and space means that brands can be given a more important and central place in self-presentation on Piczo pages than in real life or on the non-commercial website eLogg. In real life, bodily presence gives brands less room for play, since the most fundamental communicative resources, such as speech and body language, cannot be branded. eLogg offers only non-branded resources and text is the primary mode of expression. This allows only very limited scope for using brands and branded resources. On Piczo, on the other hand, brands become an integral part of the young people's production of self-presentations, and the branding of space, texts and tools is strengthened by simultaneous assertion on these three levels.

Goffman's starting point is self-presentation in face-to-face settings, not through new media. Goffman maintains that face-to-face impressions "are given and given off", which implies an asymmetry in the communicative situation. This asymmetry is created because in a face-to-face situation one cannot see oneself as the other does: one only controls the expression one *gives*, not the expression ones *gives off* (Goffman, 1959: 7). When the children in the study presented themselves to each other on Piczo, however, there was symmetry in the sense that the children, like everyone else, could consider their own mediated self-presentation and hence expressions both given and given off. They could thus present a "polished surface" as themselves with greater ease than in real life. Extended opportunities to assume control over the way in which one appears also allow greater scope for dissimulation and manipulation. From that point of view, the cynicism of which Goffman has been accused when he sees identity as (calculated) role-play (see e.g. Lyman & Scott, 1970) has greater latitude on Piczo than face-to-face. Absence of physical presence and distantiation of time and space attenuate the user's awareness of emotional ties and commitments and encourage a greater degree of callousness in the role-play Goffman describes.

The study shows that the opportunity to produce a self-presentation on Piczo depends on the pupils' social standing in the classroom. While the school-based website eLogg is structured and used in a way designed to prevent social exclusion, Piczo confirms and reinforces the dividing lines between the popular and less popular pupils in the class.

As confirmed on their pages and in interviews, the young people are Piczo users because they appreciate the freedom to make their self-presentations fun and cool in an easy and convincing way by consumption of the branded space, texts and tools they are offered. Consequently, through their presentations of themselves they are also presenting brands and thus taking on the role as advertisers in the Piczo network. Under the Piczo brand, young people present themselves in a spatial context that makes them compete for attention with the eye-catching strategies of professional marketers. In "Gender advertisements" (1979) Goffman shows how gender in the advertisement is displayed in frames so that the images used reflect gender relations in concentrated and idealised form. This style of presentation is designed to have greatest possible public appeal. Likewise on Piczo, young people are given access to branded text and tools allowing them to present themselves in the same idealised way.

For marketers, the self with the highest value is the self that calls for attention and identification among the highest number of consumers. This self typically belongs to athletes, models and artists from sports, music videos and TV series. Just as the most popular commodities become the bestselling commodities, the most popular selves become the bestselling selves. These bestselling and branded self-presentations are, to echo Goffman, ultimately allowed to "define the situation" in the Piczo network. Consequently, the children's use of branded resources to copy commercially produced fun and coolness enforced the social competition among them: "Just as not everyone can be upper class and not every one can have good taste, so not everyone can be cool. This isn't because some people are essentially cooler than others, it's because cool is ultimately a form of distinction." (Heath & Potter 2006: 196).

Yet while the young people in the study were all obliged to relate to the branded resources and commercial strategies with which marketers capture their attention and admiration, they did so in different ways. They can be divided into elaborators, who became skilful designers through persistent use of brands and branded resources on Piczo pages, and collectors, who did not. The elaborators produced self-presentations that allowed them to try out their aspirations as creators, models, designers and trendsetters in the interaction with their peers.

They related the commercially manufactured resources to their self-presentations in ways that increased their ability to, as Goffman puts it, "guide and control the response made by the others present" in their Piczo networks.

Both collectors and elaborators were held up to ridicule for their self-made texts but not for their choice of brands and branded texts. By their straightforward use of brands and branded resources, the collectors made their own creativity less visible than the elaborators did. It was the young people's non-commercial texts which were denigrated and ridiculed by other Piczo users, not the commercial and branded texts they used to present themselves. Being an elaborator raises the risk of being insulted online and elaborators must be self-confident enough to withstand this pressure.

Conclusion

By comparison with marketers, who are professional experts at filling extended time and space with fun and coolness, it was very demanding for the young people in the study to create texts with equally great appeal. Only a very few elaborators managed this, either by presenting themselves through their consumer culture or by being fellow-creators in the fictive pop-cultural universes the marketers offer. For most of the pupils, however, the collection of branded resources appeared simpler, more convincing and more unassailable than elaborating them in their self-presentation. There therefore arises a disparity between the wealth of attractive resources available on Piczo and the level of creativity displayed when young people use them. Although there are many more possibilities, social competition helps to reinforce a uniformity in the use of brands and branded resources that creates a higher threshold for the free expression of one's own creativity on Piczo than on eLogg.

Arguing for a positive correlation between "good video games" and learning, Gee (2003) emphasizes that gamers not only consume but also produce. On Piczo pages users consume in order to produce. If the production of playing "good videogames" is a positive thing, can the production of Piczo pages be understood in a similar way? Isn't Piczo simply an excellent opportunity for young people to choose brands which, as Holt (2002, p. 87) puts it, "provide the most original and relevant cultural material" for self-presentation? Presumably most people do not see any problem with this if marketers are working to combat famine in the third world or save the global system, but what if their products are unwanted or harmful? On the Piczo website young users are left with the responsibility of understanding and discerning the difference themselves. They are also left with the task of understanding the difference between selling a product and selling themselves. Although both possibilities are open, the choices made by the young people in this study show that in the dialectic between "impression management" and "brand management" it is much more challenging to grasp one's freedom than to be manipulated.

References

Banerjee, R. (2002) Children's understanding of self-presentational behavior: Links with mental-state reasoning and the attribution of embarrassment. *Merrill-Palmer Quarterly*, 48(4), 378–404.

Belk, R. W. (1988) Possessions and the extended self. *Journal of Consumer Research*, 15(2), 139–68.

Berger, J., and C. Heath (2007) Where consumers diverge from others: Identity signaling and product domains. *Journal of Consumer Research*, 34(2), 121–34

Buckingham, D. (2007) Selling childhood? Children and consumer culture. *Journal of children and media*, 1(1), 15–24.

Cook, D. T., and S. B. Kaiser (2004) Betwixt and between: Age ambiguity and the sexualization of the female consuming subject *Journal of Consumer Culture*, 4(2), 203–27.

Cova, B., and V. Cova (2001) Tribal aspects of postmodern consumption: The case of French in-line roller skaters. *Journal of Consumer Behavior*, 1(1), 67–76.

Fournier, S. (1998) Customers and their brands: Developing relationship theory in consumer research. *Journal of Consumer Research*, 24(1), 343–73.

Gee, J. P. (2003) *What Video Games have To Tell Us About Learning and Literacy*. New York: Palgrave Macmillan.

Giddens, A. (1990) *The Consequences of Modernity*. Cambridge: Polity Press.

Gladwell, M. (1997) The Coolhunt. *The New Yorker*. March 17, pp. 78–88.

Goffman, E. (1959) *The Presentation of Self in Everyday Life*. New York: Doubleday.

Goffman, E. (1963) *Behavior in Public Places: Notes on the Social Organization of Gatherings*. New York: Free Press.

Goffman, E. (1979) *Gender Advertisements*. London: The Macmillann Press.

Heath, J., and A. Potter (2006) *The Rebel Sell: Why the Culture Can't BeJjammed*. Capstone: Chichester.

Holt, D. B. (2002) Why do brands cause trouble? A dialectical theory of consumer culture and branding. *Journal of Consumer Research*, 29(2), 70–90.

Holt, D. B. (2004) *How Brands Become Icons: the Principles of Cultural Branding*. Boston, Mass.: Harvard Business School Press.

Klein, N. (2000) *No Logo*. London: Flamingo.

Liu, H. (2007) Social network profiles as taste performances. *Journal of Computer-Mediated Communication*, 13(1), 252–75. [http://jcmc.indiana.edu/vol13/issue/liu.html].

Lyman, S. M. and M. B. Scott (1970) *A Sociology of the Absurd*. New York: Appleton-Century-Crofts.

Meyrowitz, J. (1985) *No Sense of Place: The Impact of Electronic Media on Social Behaviour.* New York. Oxford University Press.

Muniz, A. M. and T. C. O'Guinn (2001) Brand community. *Journal of Consumer Research*, 27(4), 412–32.

Muñiz, A. M. and H. J Schau (2005) Religiosity in the abandoned Apple Newton Brand Community. *Journal of Consumer Research*, 31(1), 737–47.

Silverman, D. (2005) *Doing Qualitative Research: a Practical Handbook* (second edn). London: Sage.

Ries, A. and J. Trout (1980) *Positioning: The Battle for Your Mind.* New York: McGraw-Hill.

Schau, H. J., and M. C. Gilly (2003) We are what we post? Self-presentation in personal web space. *Journal of Consumer Research*, 30(3), 385–404.

Skaar, H. (2008) Literacy on a social networking site. In K. Drotner, H. S. Jensen and K. C. Schrøder (eds) *Informal Learning and Digital Media*, Newcastle, UK: Cambridge Scholars Publishing.

Østerud, S., T. Schwebs, L. M. Nielsen and M. Sandvik (2006) eLogg – et læringsmiljø for sammensatte tekster. *Digital Kompetanse: Nordic Journal of Digital Literacy*, 1(3), 214–26.

14
"Hello – We're Only in the Fifth Grade!!": Children's Rights, Inter-generationality and Constructions of Gender in Public Discourses About Childhood

Mari Rysst

Different understandings of childhood have developed throughout European history, from the medieval idea of children as 'minor adults', to the idea of children as 'incomplete human beings', to the present idea of children as the equals of adults in terms of rights (Maagerø and Simonsen 2008). This last idea is elaborated in the UN Convention on the Rights of the Child (1989), which was ratified in Norway in 1993. Among other rights, the convention underlines children's right to be heard in matters affecting the child (article 12), the right to be protected from sexual exploitation (34) and the right to rest and leisure, to engage in play and recreational activities (31). In this chapter, I show how these rights may be read in relation to consumption by children, particularly the first two.

Against this background, I discuss the relationship between inter-generationality and the construction of 'traditional' and 'modern' femininities in public discourses relating to pre-teen girls in Norway. I discuss gender constructions in relation to discourses about childhood, because how a 'girl' and a 'boy' are understood is directly related to how a 'child' and 'the good childhood' (*den gode barndom*) are understood in Norwegian society.

In the following section, I focus on how young girls' constructions of gender, for instance through fashion and clothes, are presented in public discourses, in official policy, in newspapers and fashion magazines, and elsewhere. How are 'traditional' and 'modern' ways of 'doing gender' reflected in these discourses? How are these ways of thinking illustrated in the girls' own constructions of gender? What do the terms 'traditional' and 'modern' related to gender and childhood actually imply in the Norwegian context? Is there an inter-generational discrepancy in how young girls' gendered bodies are understood? And finally, in what ways do Norwegian understandings of childhood in this area relate to the three rights mentioned in the UN Declaration?

Girls' points of view regarding how they 'do' gender do not form part of the public gender discourses just mentioned. Therefore, in order to highlight the relevance of 'inter-generationality', I go on to present examples of girls' descriptions, which I take from my PhD thesis on pre-teen girls in Norway, dating from 2002 to 2004.[1] Finally I elaborate on ways of doing young femininities in Norway today as examples of the new or modern, and show how consumption and material items are essential parts of these constructions of gender. I also describe the implications of discrepancies in interpretation (or the lack of them). The conclusion draws the discussions together and relates them back to the UN Declaration of the Rights of the Child.

Inter-generationality and public discourses about childhood

The term 'inter-generational' denotes the relationship between different generations or age groups – or more precisely, individuals or groups within different generations. It is important to bear in mind that generations are not homogeneous groups. Invoking inter-generationality means that the perspectives and relationships of different generations will be included in the analysis as one approach to studying cultural reproduction, continuity and change. For instance, anthropological studies of households often adopt inter-generational perspectives in studying life-cycles and household viability (see Rudie 1994). Regarding young girls' constructions of gender, parents (and sometimes grandparents) contribute with their ideas and opinions. These may or may not resonate with the daughters' views, and negotiations occur. I found an inter-generational perspective to be necessary in my research regarding interpretations of pre-teen girls' gender constructions. This was because my material revealed a discrepancy between young girls' understandings of how they do gender and the ways in which their presentations of self were referred to in public discourses. Material items play a vital role here.

For instance, Norwegian newspapers and other media have anxiously reported that young boys and girls are dressing and acting as if they were 'older than their age', fearing both the disappearance and the sexualisation of childhood. What they fear disappearing is the so-called 'good childhood'. Anne Trine Kjørholt describes the good Nordic childhood as associated with lots of freedom and spontaneous free play, being closely in touch with nature and having the ability to play outdoors in the neighbourhood. Childhood and nature are closely united, she writes (Kjørholt 2008). Building huts, climbing trees and living an outdoor life are viewed as important parts of children's culture. According to Kjørholt, the Norwegian child is associated with innocence, immaturity, play, emotions, spontaneity and nature, while the adult is associated with rationality, work, responsibility, logical reasoning, maturity and a lack of playfulness (ibid.). Jean Jacques Rousseau's philosophy has to a large extent influenced European ways of thinking on children and childhood: he was the first to stress, in Marianne Gullestad's words, 'the child's inno-cence and the corrupting influence of society as the only source of evil in children' (Gullestad 1996: 16). Rousseau was also one of the first to speak of children having 'special needs, desires and even rights' (James, Jenks and Prout 1998), ideas which have informed today's view of the child having equal rights with adults, as elaborated in the UN Declaration.

The good childhood must also be protected from the adult world of sex, drugs and violence. It is for this reason that public concern has been particularly directed at the new codes of clothing fashion for young girls, which are read as connoting eroticism rather than chastity: such clothes offend against the view that eroticism should not be associated with childhood (see Davis 1992). In January 2001, some Norwegian feminists argued that 'the connection between fashion and sex is apparent from the time girl-children are very small. Five-year-olds look like small pop stars' (*Dagbladet magasinet* 24/1-2001). That same year the distribution of a school catalogue for sweaters was stopped because it showed two girls in sexy poses: hands on hips, with half-open mouths and seductive eyes. The following year's catalogue was free of such pictures.

The Norwegian children's Ombudsperson (*Barneombud*) also expressed concern about sexuality and young girls and boys:

> The heavy focus on sexuality and the body that is aimed at ever younger age groups is upsetting. Repeated appeals to marketing agencies have not led to identifiable improvements. Therefore the children's Ombud calls for a debate and political efforts in order to combat the negative influences this industry is having on children and young people. (*Barndom pågår* 2001)

Evidence of the sexualisation of childhood has also regularly mobilised Norwegian politicians and feminists. In 2004, the bras and string briefs (thongs) for young girls that had appeared in some shops were withdrawn from the market following public criticisms. In March 2005 the Norwegian Minister for the Family made leading chain stores withdraw baby bikinis from their shops: 'It is the exact copies of grown women's bras that are the worst. This is children in adult women's clothes, a fact that changes *childhood into something different from what it is'* (Dåvøy in *Verdens Gang* 31 March 2005). In other words, such clothing challenges the notion of the good childhood. The minister does not want very young girls to wear clothes meant for women, indicating that the boundary between childhood and adulthood is to be upheld. A similar case emerged in February 2006, when *Cubus* (a low-price chain store) was criticised for selling underwear tops to three-year-old girls, which was interpreted as sexualising young girls and 'breaking down the boundary between adult women and children' (*Verdens Gang*, 10 February 2006).

All these examples from public discourses on childhood and gender represent attempts to resist what are seen as an erotic elements in children's dress – elements that may make children seem older than their culturally understood age. Such expressions may be read as reflecting the protection of traditional femininities, but they also reflect a governmental strategy to take seriously the UN Declaration on children's right to protection from sexual exploitation.

By contrast, the following citation from a designer of children's clothes only partly follows this protectionist attitude. She was interviewed by the Norwegian fashion magazine *Tekstilforum* because she had opened a new children's clothes shop for clothes she had designed herself. The article has the heading 'Angels in the street' (*Engler i gatebildet*):

> The clothes for girls are a good mixture of the cute and the tough, which are the best selling clothes. I want to make trendy clothes for children, clothes that are not too provocative (*utfordrende*), says the designer. In my latest collection there are many really short skirts with tucks sown down, and some people will surely think my clothes are provocative, but I am conscious about my clothes not being that. For instance, I avoid making clothes with bare midriffs, she says. Still, she does not oppose children having clothes in a fashionable, teenage-inspired style. Children want to look like teenagers, she says, and it is important that they are permitted to dress in clothes they enjoy wearing. These are clothes that both children and mothers like, says the designer (*Tekstilforum* December 2003).

This designer may be read as trying to combine something traditional with something modern in her design. However, the following extract from the same magazine, with the heading 'Snappy young girls' (*Snertne småpiker*), introduces something very *new*, namely the issue of sexy clothes for pre-teens:

> As soon as the kids have put away their nappies and their bulging stomach figure, they want clothes similar to the 'older children'. And the child garment producers meet their demands as best as they can. We know that some are provoked by the fact that sexy teenage fashion is being offered to 8-10-year-olds, but today it is a fact that children want to choose their wardrobe themselves (at a reasonable price, of course) and as far as possible look like their idols. And personally we think that next summer's combination of jeans and romantic corsets and blouses looks really nice on young girls. (*Tekstilforum* 2003)

As these quotes suggest, the designers are taking it for granted that younger children want clothes similar to older children, and want to look like their idols – although I doubt that children have been advisors either here or elsewhere when decisions on the design of children's clothes are made, contrary to what may be understood as the approach implied in the UN Declaration. The designers' opinions illustrate how the marketing industry works to create a new consumer group, the so-called *tweenagers* or *tweens*, just as *teenagers* were constructed in the US in a similar manner during the Second World War (Cross 2004). Of particular interest here is how marketing tries to convert pre-teens into more sexualized 'tweens'.

The above examples thus illustrate how adults typically contribute to children's gender constructions without children's voices being heard. The following utterances from the girls I came to know include examples of both traditional and new ideas on gender construction. They also indicate how these images are related to each other and how they are debated inter-generationally. According to Ivar Frønes (2004), the Norwegian family atmosphere is characterized by negotiation and diplomacy. This is apparent when the girls talk about the clothes they are allowed by their mothers to buy and wear. Oda recalled this experience from a shopping trip with her mother, her best friend Ellen and the latter's mother:

> Ellen and I were in a shop for clothes (*Popin*, a shop for women), and there were many clothes that fitted us, and then Mummy and Ellen's mother thought they were rather nice, but they didn't think

we should have them, because we became sort of too grown up – that it became *strange.*

Oda said this about what she is allowed to buy:

> I am allowed to if I need it, or if it happens that Mummy and I both like it. If, for instance, I think a pair of jeans is very nice and it has on it such weird things that Mummy thinks are weird, then she won't buy it, because *she thinks it is a bit scary, or something.*

According to Oda, her mother expresses dislike of her wearing clothes that violate her ideas of appropriate clothing for ten-year-old girls. The clothes make her daughter look older than her culturally understood age, a notion which is informed by a developmental discourse. The following quotation says something about the clothes the popular girls want to wear in the context of a conversation about *Bratz* dolls, a fashion doll, which they like because it has such *kul* clothes. (The *Bratz* are made with exceptionally big heads, big eyes with make-up, and short bodies. The shops also offer a *Bratz* wardrobe and other *Bratz* accessories, similar to the *Barbie* concept.)

> Mari: So what do you mean, then, by *kul* clothes?
> Marit: Jeans, and short sweaters, tee-shirts and skirts...
> Mari: So that some of your midriff is visible. Is that *kul?*
> Nina: Yes! (the other two agree)
> Marit: And also high-heeled shoes, everything we don't have is *kul.*
> Mari: All that you *don't* have is *kul...*? So if you were free to choose, you would like to wear such clothes? (like the Bratz dolls wear)
> Nina and Oda: Some of them, at least.

That the girls have opinions on what *not* to wear as well, as Nina and Oda also indicate, is underlined in the following conversation on a shopping trip with two girls who want to belong to the popular group and who share their interest in *kul* clothes:

> Mari: Did mummy say something about what clothes you shouldn't buy?
> Farou: No, or like, not such 'yucky' *(ekle)* clothes...
> Mari: But what are yucky clothes, then?

Farou: Clothes where you show a lot of body. But she didn't say that, but I know she thinks so, I'm only ten years old.

Mari: Yes...

Samira: I don't want to show much body either...

To sum up, these quotations from different generations offer examples of how traditional and new ways of doing gender are represented in public discourses and among girls themselves. They also illustrate processes of cultural reproduction, in that the girls show they have internalized their mothers' views on culturally acceptable ways of dressing for young girls – views which are informed by a developmental discourse. Farou says she cannot dress in certain clothes because she is 'only ten years old', implying that she will be able to when she gets older. In Paul Connerton's terminology, age-appropriate ways of dressing are practices incorporated through socialization, primarily in the social context of the family, but also in schools and among one's peers (Connerton 1989).

'Traditional' femininities

Many writers, myself included, tend to use the concept 'traditional' more or less synonymously with 'conventional' or 'conformist' when related to gender. I have done this so far in this chapter. It is easy to take its meaning for granted, particularly in research on one's own country of origin. However, I would now like to question the taken-for-grantedness of this term 'traditional' in relation to girls' constructions of gender. To this end I have been helped by the work of Paul Connerton, who argues that knowledge and practices become incorporated while growing up, becoming 'traditional' through repetition over time (Connerton 1989). Tradition can be seen as a form of knowledge passed from one generation to the next. In general, 'traditional' and 'modern' often work as very loose and broad descriptive or analytical concepts, in which 'traditional' generally depicts cultural continuity and 'modern' depicts something new, or change. However, I agree with Leif Selstad that tradition, like culture, is ambiguous and complex, and is better understood contextually (Selstad 1998). He argues that traditions are constantly influenced by socio-cultural processes – they are not static. In light of this, I view 'old' and 'new' ways of doing gender as *parallel* femininities. Something new seldom replaces what is already there: rather, old and new ways of doing gender may exist simultaneously as different femininity options, and even overlap. I prefer to view gender construction as something that is achieved through a kind of 'cultural circuit', bearing in mind the relationship between 'old' and 'new' ways of doing girl and accordingly between continuity and change in young girls' gender constructions.

According to much of the existing literature on childhood and girlhood (see Hey 1997, Thorne 1993), the most common associations with traditional femininities for young girls in many Western countries, including Norway, seem to be the following: girls are expected to be kind, sweet or cute, modest and a bit shy, to appear childlike or childish, to play with dolls and engage in other household activities like cooking, to like adornment and dressing up, maybe as a little princess, to have 'natural' long or shoulder-length hair, and most importantly, to be asexual and to embody chastity and innocence rather than eroticism. The sexuality aspect is the most important one in creating anxiety in public discourses about gender and childhood, not only in Norway, but throughout the western hemisphere. From the United States, Daniel Cook and Susan Kaiser underline the problematic nature of changing ways of doing gender for young girls. They write:

> What remains unresolved in the history of this age range for girls *is the ambivalence and anxiety regarding sexual innocence and agency.* The subteen, preteen and contemporary Tween seem to encode anticipatory statuses and identities to be acted out in the present, all the while preparing the ground for entry into a particular articulation of *heterosexual* female culture. They represent a coupling of everyday anxieties and pleasures with cultural discourses that blur age boundaries while also (strategically and commercially) aiming to define them. In this way, *middle girlhood has increasingly become a favoured political site for the understanding of femininity,* for discourses about vulnerability and 'lost childhoods' and for locating some of the evils of the consumer marketplace. (Cook and Kaiser 2004: 223, emphasis added)

This resonates with the Norwegian situation, illustrated by some of the examples first quoted above. As already indicated, the 'traditional' is usually associated with something that has existed for a long time. Sexuality is not one of the traditional, childlike ways of doing gender; and hence teenage-inspired clothes for children, clothes that suggest associations of eroticism rather than chastity, seem to be something new and thus an aspect of something 'modern'. In Norway and many other Western countries, it is believed that the spheres of childhood and adulthood should be kept apart. The less children know about adult matters, the more innocent they are. Bente Clausen has analysed Norwegian women's most important values in the life span between 1895 and 1960, arguing that both in homes and schools young girls were thought to be modest, devoted to family issues and care, obedient, hard-working, practising sexual abstinence before marriage and being silent in the company of adults. These values were intended to prepare the young girl for being the optimal perfect wife, mother and housewife (Clausen 2003). The associations many people make with traditional femininities can thus be traced back many decades.

In addition, I understand traditional femininities (and masculinities) to have a close relationship with gender stereotypes – that is, long-standing and dominant notions of femininity and masculinity. Gendered colours and different material items are examples of this: pink is associated with girls, light blue with boys; ribbons, laces, dolls, skirts and dresses with girls; cars, guns, soldiers and suits with boys. In other words, material items play an important part in the construction of gender as soon as a child is born. Already in the birth clinic, Norwegian baby cribs are decorated with traditional gender items such as pink or light blue ribbons or blankets. 'Traditional' femininities in Norway are also related to the childhood discourse of innocence and the good childhood (*den gode barndom*), which, as already mentioned, includes lots of play and sports activities, particularly self-governed outdoor 'free-play' associated with nature (Gullestad 1989, 1997; Kjørholt 2008). Likewise, Eva Maagerø and Birte Simonsen (2008) stress 'nearness to nature', in addition to equality and moderation, as being core Norwegian values. As such, 'nearness to nature' may be understood as informing the notion of the good childhood, and thus also traditional femininities.

Bente Clausen's research, already mentioned, on female values in the period 1895–1960 also shows that outdoor activities, sports and play are highly valued and followed in all generations (Clausen 2003). These activities were engaged in by both boys and girls, and it was particularly the father who initiated outdoor life during the holidays in both the working and middle classes. Other research from the same period reports the same. Harriet Bjerrum Nielsen and Monica Rudberg interviewed women from three generations, the first born in 1910, the second in 1940 and the last in the 1970s, and found that Norwegian girls in all generations had the option to be sporty on a par with boys. In addition, acceptable femininities also included being spirited, lively and unruly, even a bit wild (Nielsen and Rudberg 2006). As such, it seems that Norwegian pre-teen girls have a long history of outdoor play and sport, which thus make up a particular feature of traditional femininity. To this extent, girls in Norway might seem to have more options of 'doing girl' than, for instance, British girls. Emma Renold's research on pre-teens and Benedicte Carlsen's master's thesis from the UK show that it is not as acceptable or as common for girls there to engage in sports activities associated with boys, such as football (Renold 2005; Carlsen 2007; see also Thorne 1993).

These ideas of the good childhood are based on the notion that children become happier adults if they are allowed to be 'children' for as long as possible, for instance, by being encouraged and allowed to play instead of work. As such, the UN Declaration of the right of the child to rest and leisure, and to engage in play and recreational activities, resonates very well with the idea of the good Norwegian childhood. The emphasis on children being protected from the 'dangerous' world of adults has been most prominent in the higher educated social classes, and has over the years become the predominant official ideology on childhood, in both academia and politics. The manner in which the Minister for the Family reacted to the baby bikini suggests her internalisation of the idea of the innocent child, which is also reflected in several of the quotes first cited above. As we have seen, these understandings are also employed by girls themselves, albeit in different ways in different contexts.

'Modern' or new ways of doing gender

The work of Viveka Berggren Torell shows how the emphases on 'cute' girls and 'tough and cool' boys were visualized in Swedish women' magazines as far back as the 1930s. According to Torell, the cool boy existed in juxtaposition with the sweet and cute little girl (Torell 2007). In Norway today, however, 'cool' refers to both genders, and is a very important notion in the teenage-inspired constructions of gender by ten-year-old girls, as suggested in the conversation over the Bratz dolls. As such, 'cool' femininity represents something new, like the designer's notion of 'sexy', and I will interpret these ideas here as representing the 'modern'. The cool subject position is also at the core of the intergenerational gap in interpretation of young girls' gendered bodies.

The concept of coolness is widely shared in the younger generations in Norway (and probably in other countries imbued with a Western culture). Although the symbols of coolness and being cool have many variants and connotations depending on age, gender, socio-cultural background, class and subculture, in general the phenomenon can be read as being associated with youthfulness, teenage culture, consumption and fun.

Cross-culturally, the concept of cool has a long history, at least in English-speaking countries. Dick Pountain and David Robins (2000) argue that being cool suddenly became popular among children in the successful post-depression generation, as an expression of inter-generational rebellion and resistance to attempts at the revitalisation of morality. In their view, being cool is primarily a question of consumption. In a similar vein, Gary Cross underlines the gendered position of the cool:

> The images, goods, and rituals of a commercialized childhood led very subtly to a fantasy culture from which parents were excluded and which appeared to be anything but innocent. The first clear signs of the cool appeared among older boys in the 1930's with the appearance of dark science fiction stories and then in the 1960's and 1970's, when the cool look of Barbie and monster figures replaced baby dolls and Tinkertoys (Cross 2004: 17).

In Norway the term 'cool' has entered everyday speech through youth, popular culture and general commercialism, and is used to an increasing degree by all but the oldest generations and in connection with both girls and boys. The fact that both girls and boys define themselves by adopting a *kul* subject position may be interpreted as evidence of how femininities and masculinities overlap in new ways. Being *kul* is an option for both, inspired by marketing and consumerism, but has particular gendered expressions. As such, the *kul* subject position explicitly reflects the relationship between childhood, gender and the consumer society.

Today, the ten-year-old girls whom I got to know diverge from Cross's presentation of *Barbie* as *kul*: it is now the *Bratz* dolls who are *kul*, as indicated in the conversation with Nina, Marit and Oda. Being *kul*, as these girls defined it, includes elements such as making funny remarks, having good looks and a slim body, wearing lipgloss and make-up, not being childish, 'going out' (having a boyfriend), showing an interest in popular culture, wearing fashionable teenage-like clothes and, most importantly, being sporty and showing proficiency in sport.

This is not to imply that all girls share identical associations in their understanding of what is *kul*. This is particularly so when it comes to class and socio-cultural background. However, many of the girls I got to know shared most of these qualities, even though the associations between them were different, depending on situation and context. Most importantly, not all of these elements can be read as 'modern' or new compared to what were described as traditional femininities. How the 'old' and 'new' overlap is an empirical question, one that is activated in different social contexts. Thus, we saw that being sporty and displaying proficiency in sport were also among the associations connected with traditional femininities. As such, it may be argued that continuing importance of 'nearness to nature', such as living an outdoor life, activities and sports, represents a form of cultural reproduction between generations. The cultural models of 'nearness to nature' and 'the outdoor life' can thus be interpreted as being present in both traditional and new ways of doing gender, in that being *kul* includes outdoor activities such as skiing, football and so on. Types of sporting gear, particularly expensive branded items, play important parts in the construction of *kul* subject positions.

The preceding discussion of 'traditional' and 'modern' ways of doing gender has thus pointed to the difficulty in establishing clear lines of demarcation between the two. I would therefore propose that the concepts of 'girl-child' and 'teenager-girl' grasp better what is going on in young girls' gender constructions today. These concepts are based on the girls' points of view, and are situated along a continuum of identification with teenage culture: the girl-child at one pole, being childlike and showing minimal identification with teenage culture, and the teenager-girl at the other, being teenage-inspired in her construction of gender. The empirical presentations of actual girls' gender constructions fluctuate along this continuum depending on situation and social context (see Rysst 2008).

Inter-generational gaps in interpretation

However, it is important to note that the issue of sexuality, or of being provocative or sexy, was absent from these ten-year-olds' definitions of what is *kul*. Eroticism is the association that is activated by older generations when young girls dress in certain teenage clothes, as illustrated in the examples cited earlier, and particularly well expressed by a grandfather in the following quote:

> Every time I visit "Femmanhuset" (a mall in central Gothenburg) I see at least a dozen little children, eleven to thirteen years old, wandering about dressed in tight sexy clothes, and then I just wonder one thing.

Why let children be sex objects so that the clothing companies are able to make money? Clear away everything that can be attractive or offending to adults (from Gøteborgs-Posten, in Torell 2004).

But what about the girls themselves: do they include being sexy in their construction of *kul*? The associations of being *kul* for the ten-year-olds encompass elements of youth culture and a distancing from the world of children and childishness: being childish is definitely not *kul*. But the issue of sexuality seems to be a taboo theme, something 'yucky' and embarrassing, at least in the proximity of adults. Erik Erikson (1963/1993), later Gagnon and Simon (1973/2005) and lastly research done by Epstein and colleagues (2003) in Britain all suggest that pre-teen children's sexuality patterns are better understood as *play*, in that children's sex play 'occurs most significantly in social scripts that are manifestly not sexual (e.g. doctor-nurse)' (Gagnon & Simon 1973/2005:26). These researchers emphasise the importance of the interplay between biological and cultural forces in forming sexual practice. They argue that children are socialised and acquire cultural sexual competence through learning, experience and bodily practice. This implies that it is not enough to be taught theoretically about sex and sexuality. If the child is to understand the depth and implications of adult sexual words, it must experience the bodily practices. According to these authors, these practices become sexual as an adult knows them only through experience and conditioning (Erikson 1963/1993; Gagnon and Simon 1973; Epstein *et al.* 2003).

I therefore suggest that the ten-year-old girls and boys in my study do not understand sexuality in the same manner as adults because they lack the (older) sexual bodily experiences, both the maturation and the practice, behind the words and symbols. My interpretations are primarily based on the observation of interactions and talking to the children about these matters, particularly the focus-group interviewing of thirty girls and fifteen boys below the age of thirteen. Among other questions, I asked in these interviews if they knew the meaning of the word 'sexy'. Most of them answered in the affirmative, but said it was difficult to explain in words. They knew it had something to do with looking good and having a nice body. In a conversation with Mitha, she said this about being sexy:

I have an idea of what it is, but in general I don't think much about it. I don't think of 'sexy' as something I want to be or become in the future. The important thing is that the clothes are *kule*.

Mitha's statement is worth noting because she aspires very much to being teenage-like. Some of the other girls associated opposite-sex attraction to being sexy, such as Mona and Toril: "It is about somebody who likes you very much and things like that", This was also apparent in the conversation below between Nina, Marit and myself:

> Mari: So what does it mean then to be sexy?
>
> Marit: Maybe they want to show off?
>
> Nina: And if it concerns girls, they might want the boys to think they are *kul*, so that they fall in love with them.
>
> Mari: That the girls do such things so that the boys fall in love with them?
>
> Both: Yes.

Considering the strong position of Nina and Marit (and partly Mona) in the peer group, it is worth noting that they are aware of the connection between opposite-sex attraction, being *kul* and 'love'. None of the other children admitted that connection in so direct a fashion. The popular girls, in this case Nina, seem consciously to presume that a *kul* subject position increases the likelihood of getting a boyfriend and implies being popular. Nina's statement points to an awareness of a connection between being sexy and being *kul*, but most significantly, she translates the 'sexy' into the 'cool'. This suggests that the girls are primarily concerned about coolness, understood as flirting with a teenage-like appearance and activities, rather than sexiness per se, which they believe they are too young to engage in. This is illustrated in the following conversation between two other girls and myself, when I asked if being sexy was something they thought important:

> Helena: No…
>
> Mari: Not for you?
>
> Thale: Hello…come on…we are only in the 5th grade!!
>
> Thale said that in an angry voice, indicating to me how awfully 'far out' that question was.

In sum, these examples show a discrepancy in how individuals in different generations may interpret the same bodily representations: what the girls see primarily as fashionable and *kul*, the adults see as fashionable and sexually provocative. This gap in inter-generational interpretation does not sit easily with the UN Declaration of the right to protection from sexual exploitation – although whether putting provocative clothes on pre-teen girls actually increases the risk of sexual abuse by adults is another question.

Conclusion

In this chapter, I have discussed young girls' gender constructions in the light of children's rights, consumption and inter-generationality. The discussions underline the importance of an inter-generational perspective in the study of children's gender constructions, both traditional and modern, here exemplified by the design of young girls' clothes. In accordance with the UN Declaration, it can be suggested that children's voices should be taken into consideration when decisions about new, possibly provocative aesthetics are taken, both to ensure their right to their voices being heard, and to protect them from sexual exploitation. Because the sexual interpretation is not the girls' intention, the designers have a particular responsibility in making clothes that avoid this possible misunderstanding – that is, assuming that our society wants to remain with the currently dominant version of the good childhood.

The preceding discussions suggest that the Norwegian notion of the good childhood is well in line with the provision laid down in the UN Declaration of the child's right to leisure and play, but is less clear and more ambiguous concerning the right to be heard and the right to protection from sexual exploitation. However, the present idea that children have equal rights to adults makes inter-generational negotiations necessary in future constructions of childhood. On the whole, there are reasons to believe that future public discourses about childhood will continue to favour the gender constructions of ten-year-old girl-children rather than those of teenager-girls.

Note

1. The title of the PhD thesis is ' "I want to be me. I want to be kul": an anthropological study of Norwegian preteen girls in the light of a presumed "disappearance" of childhood'. The thesis is based on ethnographic fieldwork in two Norwegian school settings between 2002 and 2004. A total of 71 ten-year-old children were included in the study, which was grounded in 'experience-near' methodology. The overall aim was to highlight the children's points of view and describe how they understand and live their everyday lives (Rysst 2008).

References

Barneombudet (2001) (Children's Ombud): *Barndom pågår*. Oslo: Barneombudets årbok 2000/2001.

Carlsen, A. B. (2007) 'Our world? Our world!' Social Identities in an English Boarding School. Master Thesis in Social Anthropology. The University of Oslo.

Clausen, B. (2003) På sporet av den tapte fremtid. Autobiografier som kilde til kvinners verdier. Master Thesis in Ethnology, The University of Oslo.

Connerton, P. (1989) *How Societies Remember*. Cambridge: Cambridge University Press.

Cook, D. T. and S. B. Kaiser (2004) 'Betwixt and be tween: age ambiguity and the sexualization of the female consuming subject'. In *Journal of Consumer Culture*, 4(2), 203–27.

Cross, G. (2004) *The Cute and the Cool*. New York: Oxford University Press, Inc.

Davis, F. (1992) *Fashion, Culture and Identity*. Chicago and London: University of Chicago Press.

Erikson, H. E. (1963/1993) *Childhood and Society*. New York: W. W. Norton and Company

Epstein, D., S. O' Flynn and D. Telford (2003) Silenced Sexualities in Schools and Universities. Stoke-on-Trent: Trentham Books.

Frønes, I. (2004) *Moderne Barndom*. Oslo: Cappelen Akademisk Forlag

Gagnon, J. H. and W. Simon (1973/2005) *Sexual Conduct*. London: AldineTransaction.

Gullestad, M. (1989) *Kultur og Hverdagsliv*. Oslo: Universitetsforlaget A/S.

Gullestad, M. (1996) *Imagined Childhoods*. Oslo: Universitetsforlaget AS.

Gullestad, M. (1997) 'A passion for boundaries'. In *Childhood*, Vol.4(1):19–42.

Hey, V. (1997) *The Company She Keeps: An Ethnography of Girls' Friendship*. Buckingham: Open University Press.

James, A., C. Jenks and A. Prout (1998) *Theorizing Childhood*. New York: Teachers College Press.

Kjørholt, A. T. (2008) Retten til lek og fritid. In Høstmælingen, N., E.S. Kjørholt and K. Sandberg (eds): *Barnekonvensjonen. Barns rettigheter i Norge*. pp. 219–32. Oslo: Universitetsforlaget.

Maagerø, E., and B. Simonsen (2008) *Norway: Society and Culture*. Kristiansand: Portal Books

Nielsen, H. B., and M. Rudberg (2006) *Moderne jenter: tre generasjoner på vei*. Oslo: Universitetsforlaget.

Pountain, D., and D. Robins (2000) *Cool Rules: Anatomy of an Attitude*. London: Reaktion Books, Ltd.

Renold, E. (2005) *Girls, Boys and Junior Sexualities*. London: RoutledgeFalmer

Rudie, I. (1994) *Visible women in East coast Malay Society*. Oslo: Scandinavian University Press

Rysst, M. (2008) I want to be me. I want to be kul. An Anthropological study of Norwegian preteen girls in the light of a presumed 'disappearance' of childhood. PhD thesis, The University of Oslo.

Selstad, L. (1998) Konstruksjon, diskurs, tradisjon. In *Norsk Antropologisk Tidsskrift*, 4.

Thorne, B. (1993) *Gender Play*. New Jersey: Rutgers University Press.

Torell, V.B. (2007) *Folkhemmets barnkläder*. Gøteborg: Bokforlaget Arkipelag.

15
"One Meets Through Clothing": The Role of Fashion in the Identity Formation of Former Soviet Union Immigrant Youth in Israel

Dafna Lemish and Nelly Elias

The study described in this chapter examines the role of fashion in the lives of immigrant children and adolescents from the Former Soviet Union (FSU) in Israel. It is part of a more extensive, ongoing research project concerned with the role of media in the lives of immigrant children and youth, as they explore their new environment and also look back at the life they have left behind (Elias and Lemish, 2008a; 2008b, 2008c). While fashion was not an original focus of this study, it emerged in the interviews as a site where immigrants are constructing hybrid identities, as well as re-affirming old ones, in the realms of gender, adolescence, Russianness and Israeliness. Accordingly, the aim of this chapter is to present a grounded analysis of these aspects of the interviews and to highlight the unique roles that fashion preferences serve as a facilitator of young immigrants' search for collective and individual identities, as well as for communicative means of expressing them.

Israel provides fertile ground for examining the integration of immigrant children, as a wave of one million immigrants from the FSU arrived in Israel during the 1990s. This situation has provided us with opportunities to investigate the roles of popular culture and mass media, as well as fashion, in Israeli, Russian and transnational cultures. Fashion provides a lens through which we can view the process of young immigrants' adaptation to a new society, the preservation of their original culture, and their development of a new social identity.

The sociology of fashion

Appearances are closely related to presumptions about one's individual "essence"; and clothing, as one of the most visible forms of appearance, performs a major role in the social construction of identity (Crane, 2000). As Tseelon (1995) observes in her historical analysis of fashion and clothing, an appearance code "is a dynamic site of struggle for control of the power to define selves and situations" (p. 122). Clothes have been used throughout history as a means to define people's role, status, and gender identity. In the previous century, with the strengthening of individualism, people's unique clothing choices were increasingly used to mark out individual diversity in relation to social categories such as "femininity," "youth" or "religiosity". Fashion and clothing are communicative phenomena that carry deep social and cultural meanings, as they are used to indicate social worth or status, to convey moral values regarding the body (such as issues related to modesty, sexuality and promiscuity), and to promote social and even revolutionary agendas. Furthermore, clothing codes are means of expressing relationships within and between social groups, and constructing and communicating a group's identity to its members as well as to outsiders. They are also profoundly political, as they represent and reproduce inequalities and at the same time are sites of struggle and resistance in which challenges to authority are advanced (Barnard, 1996, 2007; Crane, 2000; Hendrickson, 1996).

If fashion changes can involve a search for meaning and a "new look" at both the individual and collective levels (Lynch and Strauss, 2007), then examining clothing choices may be especially important during the crisis caused by immigration to a new society. Indeed, Turner refers to clothing as "the social skin," suggesting it is "the symbolic stage upon which the drama of socialization is enacted" (1980, in Hendrickson, 1996: 2). With such understandings in mind, we turn now to dramas enacted on the symbolic stage of fashion in the lives of young people who have migrated from the FSU to Israel.

The study

Our study was based on semi-structured, in-depth interviews conducted in 2005 with 93 immigrant adolescents aged 12–18, 37 boys and 56 girls. The sample was solicited through a combination of two non-random sampling methods – snowball and quota. The sample was equally divided between residents of the urban center of Israel and the periphery (in this case smaller towns in the southern part of the country), and between the more veteran immigrants who had lived in Israel for 3–5 years and newcomers who have been living in the country between six months and two years. The interview questions asked the young people to discuss a variety of topics concerning the role of media in their lives, as well as various aspects of their social and cultural identity and their integration in Israel.

The in-depth interviews were tape-recorded, transcribed verbatim, and submitted to a grounded analysis as is customary in qualitative studies (Lindlof and Taylor, 2002). In-depth analyses of various aspects of the interviews are discussed elsewhere (Elias and Lemish, 2008b, 2008c). Here we focus on the surprising centrality of clothing and fashion as it emerged, unexpectedly, from the grounded analysis. The interviewees' names have been changed to protect their anonymity. The information provided in parenthesis follows this format: M or F – for gender; age; and length of stay in Israel. For example, Oleg (M, 17, 1.5) is a 17-year-old male who immigrated to Israel a year and a half prior to the interview.

Findings

Information about the local Israeli youth fashion was of particular concern for many interviewees even prior to immigration and became even more acute following their arrival in Israel, as the "proper" style of dressing turned out to be an important "ticket for entry" into the circle of native-born teens. Above all else, the findings suggest that local fashion played a central role in forming interviewees' opinions about the host culture and local residents, as many recalled their feeling of cultural shock after encountering Israeli teens' codes of behaviour and style of dress. Oleg (M, 17, 1.5) shared such painful experiences as follows:

> You know, "one meets through clothing." This is what exactly happened here. You have to dress according to the fashion, to look good, and not fall behind your friends... Here I look all the time at how people are dressed. For example, a religious-Israeli will always wear a clean white shirt, a solid business suit, pants down to the ankles and a tie, of course. But in the case of a person who is not religious – then it is jeans, t-shirt, sport-style. I never dressed like this in the Ukraine. I always wore a suit, tie, shirt, I had six suits. But here I don't dress like this because it will be strange, inappropriate. Since I am not religious, I can't wear suits, so I started wearing jeans and t-shirts. Sometimes I really feel like wearing a suit. There, in the Ukraine, I always went to school in a suit, because I was the head of the class. I went often to see the principal, and I knew the entire administration. You can't walk into the principal's office dressed in a t-shirt. But here I am an ordinary student. Schools here are underde-

veloped. Full of neglected areas. Much worse than it was over there. The people here also are not something either, they like to curse us [*Russian immigrants*]. I don't feel at home here, I don't have that feeling of lightness, easiness… It is hard here, I wish I could go back. […] When I came to school the first time I felt awful. I was the only one dressed in a suit and I felt like an idiot because all the other boys wore t-shirts. Here I took off my tie and became an entirely different person. I became much less serious. In the past when someone said something wrong I would correct him. But here I know that no one will listen to me anyway. I am dressed in a much freer way but I feel a lot less sure of myself. It is so much nicer to wear an ironed shirt and polished shoes […]. Recently I passed a store and saw a white suit there, and I wanted to buy it, badly. But where will I wear it?

Oleg's account presents many of the functions served by fashion. It provides him with a social categorization system through which to distinguish between religious and non-religious Israelis, immigrants and non-immigrants, those with and without status. For him, his current style of clothing represents estrangement – "I don't feel at home here." Changing one's fashion style is perceived as a matter of personal transformation: "Here I took off my tie and became an entirely different person." At the same time, the external adoption of the local fashion style does not guarantee a change in self-worth, as he confesses: "I am dressed in a much freer way but I feel a lot less sure of myself." Oleg's opening sentence summarizes it all: "One meets through clothing." This statement is a paraphrase of a well-known Russian expression that states: "One meets through clothing, but departs based on intelligence."

The theme of social categorization through clothing is also prominent in the following quote from the interview with Sveta (F, 16, 3), who we see is involved in trying to figure out Israel's ethnic structure. In doing so, she ascribes a different style of dress to different ethnic groups:

In Israel everyone dresses differently. The Moroccans have a particular dress style and the Russians have a different one. The Moroccan girls like low-cut or long wide skirts. That's not the kind of skirts we used to wear in Russia. There it had to be elegant, mini, and tight. Here it is all the way down to the floor, to swipe the sidewalks.

The term "Moroccans" was used frequently in the interviews to refer to the more general social category of Israeli Jews of Middle Eastern origin, clearly distinguished by their darker skin in comparison to European Jews, as well as by other social and cultural aspects of "otherness," including clothing styles. Pinpointing youth of Moroccan origin as the negative reference group out of the entire rich ethnic mosaic of Israeli society is by no means accidental. It is important in this context to note that Israel's social stratification overlaps to a large degree with its ethnic composition, with Jews of European origin ("Ashkenazim") occupying the top of the hierarchy and Jews originating from the Middle Eastern, Arab world ("Mizrachim") mostly below them. Immigrants from the FSU enter Israeli society through its lower socio-economic strata and are often perceived by the veteran Mizrachim as a threat to their employment and housing, and as reinforcements of the hegemony of European Jewry. At the same time, the new immigrants perceive them to represent an inferior culture to their superior European one. No wonder that these complicated relationships are also expressed through fashion, as one of the most obvious sites of cultural struggle.

Thus, the juxtaposition of "us" versus "them" came across very clearly in many of the interviewees' free-flowing accounts, suggesting that clothing serves as a means to identify the "other" as the one who does not belong. Interestingly, the disciplined, regulatory "gaze" related to appearance and clothing is not uni-directional, from the local youth to the immigrant "other," but rather a reciprocal process. Both groups – immigrants and local youth alike – serve as "others" to one another, and both stigmatize one another based on clothing styles, ignoring their common interests (for example, in making friends, media, school, and the like). This tension between the competing forces of inclusion and exclusion can be detected in the following quote:

> When I arrived, I looked around at people at school and I was shocked. They dress as they wish and they behave accordingly. Everyone can wear whatever he feels like and the teachers don't care. Me, even when I wear jeans I try to look solid – dark jeans and white t-shirt, even a jeans blazer. I try to wear solid colours, so it will look as if it is a suit. Israelis don't like the way I dress, but Russians, Indians, Argentineans [*other immigrant groups*] do, and compliment me. But Israelis belittle me with all kinds of unpleasant comments about my clothing, because I do not dress like the others. If one of them leaves his shirt out, then everyone else does. And then they will say to me: "Why are you so tidy?" I don't react well to such comments. I can even strike at them, because I have the right to wear what I like. It

is not right that they humiliate someone just because of something minor like clothing. But Israelis do look at it and they don't care what the person is like inside (Danil, M, 16, 3).

The strong sense of estrangement, anger, humiliation and pain apparent in these interviews was tied together with strong criticism of the host society and local youth culture, both of which were perceived as being inferior – that is, too "oriental," "untidy" and "loose" – in comparison to the culture of the homeland, perceived as more European, superior, and advanced. As Danil's comment exemplifies, degrading comments about appearance are emotionally hurtful enough to provoke an aggressive reaction, as they pose a threat to one's identity and self-worth. Rapoport and Lomsky-Feder (2010a) suggest that immigrants are particularly sensitive to the ways they are perceived by local residents as well as to signifiers that identify them as immigrants. Clothing, as a central form of visibility (along with many other observable phenomena such as physical appearance, skin colour, language and accent, mannerism, smell, movement, haircut, and so on) receives particular scrutiny in the case of "white" European immigration, since skin colour cannot be counted on to define otherness (as it can, for example, in the case of the dark-skinned Ethiopian immigrants to Israel).

In a manner similar to the boys, female interviewees made it clear that their difference in appearance became a significant obstacle in making friends with local peers, and consequently created a strong feeling of estrangement and embarrassment. Oxana (F, 13, 3), for example, said:

People [*immigrants*] here want to be like everyone else. They do not want to stand out, because they might be laughed at, and pestered, and put down, just because they don't have money to buy nice clothes. So no one wants to feel different and become a victim of pestering.

Ilana (F, 12, 1) reinforced the same perception:

Here both boys and girls do not respond well if you are not dressed fashionably. They won't be your friends because of fashion. It hasn't happened to me, but it did happen to my neighbour. She used to wear the kind of pants that no-one has been wearing here for a long time, so other girls would say that it is shameful to be around her. You have to make an effort if you want to have friends.

As these examples suggest, fashion is a major mechanism for determining, maintaining and blurring the boundaries of collective social identities within and between local and immigrant youth subcultures. As a result, the need to strike a balance between immigrants' two identities – old and new – is particularly evident in their attempts to preserve their original style of clothing and/or to adopt the local one. These efforts reflect the tension between cultural resistance and adjustment, as we highlight in the next two sections.

Fashion as a site of social resistance

Negative sentiments aroused by being stigmatized as "different" were particularly evident in the responses of the boys we interviewed, who were often quite open about their harsh criticism of local youth culture and their various degrees of resistance to what they perceived to be Israeli conformity. An example of such strong language came from Alexei (M, 17, 4), who refused outright to accede with local norms:

> I don't want to be like the Israelis. Russian youth dress in a much more modest manner. It is because of their education. You won't see their underpants or untied shoelaces. I too do not exhibit my underpants and I tie my shoelaces. Only Russians who came here many years ago, who are becoming like Israelis, walk around with their underpants showing, because they have a different education. I don't want to be like the Israelis, I just don't want to [...] And also with girls, I don't like it when one can see their bulging fat. It is not pretty. She needs to cover up her defects. And with men, when they dress fashionably, I don't like it either, because they dress like homos, kind of feminine, transparent t-shirt, pink shirt. No Russian will ever dress like this. No one! I don't get along well with Israelis, because they are dumb. Our interests are entirely different. Come to think of it, I don't even know what interests them. Perhaps to buy an even pinker shirt? I am interested in studies, friends, the computer, high-tech.

Alexei, like many other boys in our study, reverses the situation by expressing his contempt for Israelis and their dress codes, as well as towards those who have adopted Israeli norms. He ridicules them for not being "man enough" ("homos") or not "feminine enough" ("bulging fat"), and for generally being "dumb." He clearly disassociates himself from their company – while they may be dumb and interested in frivolous things (such as buying pink shirts), he is a serious young man with depth, interested in studies, friends, computers, and high technology.

Clearly, these quotes indicate that immigrant youth were very critical of the appearance of their local peers and often looked down on them, thus resisting their positioning as less powerful. In some cases they openly rejected attempts to "pass," and in doing so demonstrated their unique identity, as in the case of Roman (M, 17.5, 2.5):

> In our class the fashionable boys are all Israelis. The Russian boys dress regularly, like normal people, that is – not fashionable. The personality of the fashionable boys is disgraceful. They behave awfully, they abuse the teacher, and they are also dumb, completely retarded. They behave nicely only to those from their circle, but not to us... I don't want friends like this. And I don't want to look like them or behave like them, ever. I didn't like their style from the start, as soon as I saw the low-cut pants. It is not nice. So Israeli fashion – there, and me – here. At first I wore only the clothes we brought with us, but I grew and I can't wear the same jeans any longer. So for a long time we looked for a normal pair of jeans and couldn't find any. We ended up buying low-cut jeans. I wore them and I was miserable. So I ended up buying myself a belt and lifted the waist line with it. I know it is kind of inappropriate to wear them like this, but I don't care... I want the jeans I had in Latvia.

According to Roman, resistance to a particular clothing style clearly represents resistance to (and complete disengagement from) an entire behavioural and personality style associated with local peers, who, in his view, are dumb and disgraceful. Yulia (F, 14, 3), who expressed a more refined form of resistance, accepted some popular Israeli youth fashion, but set a limit to how far she was willing to adjust. She told us:

> In Uzbekistan, everyone in my home town dressed simply. It was only important to dress neatly. It was impossible to wear a long sleeve shirt underneath a short sleeve shirt. But here it is OK. There it was not pretty, but here it is pretty. There, nobody wore torn jeans, but here – they do. If I would dress like this there, they would just think that my jeans are overused. I got used to things here, so I dress like this as well, but there are things here that I still cannot accept. I can't do piercing in my face. I barely pierced another hole for an earring in my ear. At school there, you were not able to dress the

way you wished – there was a uniform for everyone, but here it is OK. I like this. And you can also dye your hair. What I like here is the fact that there is a huge selection, but the problem is that people here dress too vulgarly, with non-matching colours. What is most important for them is that it is fashionable, and they don't care if it is beautiful or not. Fashion here is too loose. In our class, the Israeli girls who are the most fashionable have piercing on their faces and those are the ones that are really vulgar. They don't do their homework; they are rude to the teacher. Maybe we are less fashionable, but we are attentive and disciplined. I wouldn't want friends like that. [...] I don't have a common language with Israeli girls, and the worst are the Moroccan ones. They are very aggressive...

Yulia also associated a particular fashion style which she perceived as vulgar with unacceptable behavioural patterns, and she too, preferred to disassociate herself from such peers. At the same time, she has become accustomed to local fashion, according to her own statement, but has drawn a line about how far she would go in accommodating.

Similarly, Lena (F, 14.5, 1.5) complained about her nickname, "Grandma," and about difficulties in school that stemmed in her view from the conservative clothes she wore and her refusal to wear low-waist jeans, as was required by the "fashion law" of her Israeli counterparts:

I can't really say that I have become integrated here. I don't get along with the Israeli girls or the Russian girls, because they are a lot more veteran than I am. [...] At school they call me "grandma" because I am unwilling to wear what they are wearing. I am not willing to wear jeans or a low-cut skirt because in my opinion it is not pretty at all. I continue to wear the pants I wore in Russia, but they don't like them. They laugh at me because of that. So what, let them laugh. I know I am better than they are, no matter what I wear. I am who I am. [...] I cannot find clothes for myself in the stores here; I need to be forced to wear them. It is too exposing. I would be ashamed to wear them like this.

Lena was determined to hold on to her own views and thus was willing to accept the Israelis' ridicule. She decided to stick to her own preference for a more conservative, disciplined feminine appearance, one that did not cause her embarrassment. In doing so, she reconfirmed her self-worth: "I know I am better than them, no matter what I wear." She even co-opted her nickname, and in so doing she committed a subversive act: she appropriated the insulting title used by others to demean and to deprecate her, to assert herself and to redefine her situation.

Standards of fashion, beauty, and physical appearance also served as an important means to reinforce a sense of "Russian" superiority over local residents. Hence, some female interviewees claimed there were profound differences between their European physical appearance and sophisticated sense of style and that of local teenage girls. Interestingly, such a difference was usually described as being at the stage of irresolvable confrontation. When the female young immigrants chose to retain their original standards of beauty, they used the media – and the Internet in particular – as the most available and even the most trustworthy source of information. It was this that enabled them to access what was happening on the international scene (what they referred to as "proper" fashion), and to strengthen their self-esteem as immigrants of European origin, who chose to confront and challenge local values and models of behaviour by affirming different models of beauty and fashion.

Fashion as a site of social adjustment

The alternative strategy identified in the analysis involved the adoption of local fashion. In explaining this strategy, we draw upon the suggestion that immigrants, in an everlasting effort to erase the border between themselves as stigmatized others and the hegemonic society, are constantly engaged in "visibility work" (Rapoport and Lomsky-Feder, 2010a). Such practices include the application of strategies such as impersonation, concealment and imitation, among others, in order to "pass" in the new society. Previous studies have documented how immigrants relinquish traditional clothing as a means of discarding their previous identities and establishing new ones (for example, Crane, 2000; Dwyer, 1999). Rapoport and Lomsky-Feder (forthcoming b), for example, relate the experiences of Jews who, upon emigrating from Europe, shed their anachronistic and old fashioned clothes in adoption of the "Israeli" look.

Indeed, we too found that some of our interviewees made special efforts to adapt to the local fashion, willingly or reluctantly. They did so by adopting normative signs of appearance (such as low-waist pants) while at the same time concealing stigmatised ones (for instance, discarding Russian suits). Mila (F, 14, 2) admitted to this process quite openly:

> Fashion is very important here. It helps me feel popular. I don't want to look like a stranger. I don't want people to look at me like this. The

first day at school I wore a jumper. No one was dressed like this. I felt very uncomfortable. What did I wear the next day? I can't remember, but definitely not such a dress. I went immediately with my mother to the stores to search for local clothes so I would look like Israelis.

Katya (F, 15, 2.5) was willing to compromise her health and comfort in order not to stand out:

In what ways am I different from Israelis? For example, they don't like to wear a coat. And it always creates a problem for me because I am used to it, I feel cold. But I, too, do not wear a coat because I want to look normal. Because if no one wears one and only I do, it doesn't look good. I prefer to suffer but not to wear a coat. Israeli girls run in the rain wearing only a shirt and they don't care. Several times it was cold and I wore a coat, so immediately they commented saying 'what's wrong with you? What's the coat for?'. What else is different? I can't go out to the street with slippers, but they don't care, they can go out like this. In Russia no one would even dare think about it.

While some girls interviewed clearly identified the different fashions that distinguished them from the local youth culture, others expressed enthusiasm in adopting the local fashion, displaying sincere interest and preference for it. Such, for example, was Ilana's (F, 12, 1) account of the conscious efforts she made for personal transformation and adaptation to the new society with the help of a local friend (expressed, as well, in her voluntarily replacing her original Russian name with a Hebrew one):

I prefer living here and I also like the clothes here more. In the Ukraine there were only regular clothes, but here it is oriental clothes with lots of colourful stones and palettes. I like it a lot. In the Ukraine people dress simply, but here both at school as well as in the street, people look at how you are dressed, and if it is inappropriate, they laugh at you. Once I wore pants I brought from the Ukraine and walked outside like that, and my friend laughed heartily. It is fine to go out into the street dressed as you do in the Ukraine, but here, they treat you according to what you wear. So I am accepted. I have an Israeli friend who gives me advice on what to wear. She herself wears torn jeans, and I really like it.

Similarly, Ira (F, 15, 4) also went through a phase of adjustment to the local fashion that included learning to distinguish between "there" and "here" according to dress codes, and in doing so developed a strong preference for Israeli fashion:

> When I arrived it was really strange for me to see clothes in such shining colours, with all kinds of beads. In Russia you might be wearing this for some party, but here it is for everyday. First it seemed very strange to me, but since then I have gotten used to it, and today I like it. It is more festive, happier. Today the colours that I like are pink, orange, and turquoise. It has to be light and happy. But over there it's more solid, grey, black, white. I really like Israeli fashion.

It is important to note that what sets the immigrant girls who like the Israeli fashion apart from other immigrants is the fact that they have been integrated relatively well in other realms of life in Israel and that they are pleased with the move to the new homeland. It is no coincidence that they interpret the local clothing style as "cheerful" and "festive" and are quick to adopt it, as it seems to reflect their internal sentiments. It is therefore evident that the adoption of local fashion goes hand-in-hand with a relatively smooth social integration.

Discussion and summary

These findings demonstrate that visibility and appearance are related to power relationships and processes of exclusion and inclusion, as immigrant youth and local peers, both deemed foreign and thus threatening, gaze at each other as they evaluate and compare their social and cultural capital. The study reveals that fashion was a very useful resource that facilitated different aspects of immigrant adolescents' identity formation; while at the same time, adolescents used fashion to reinforce their self-image and confirm their personal qualities as immigrants when comparing themselves to the new peer group. In a situation in which there is an absence of valuable resources for personal growth and empowerment, during a critical period of material and social disadvantage, fashion seems to occupy a central role both in "trying on" new social roles and in reinforcing old ones. We have seen that in this process clothing and fashion serve as a form of cultural capital and a regulating force. Immigrant youths' adoption of a particular style also signifies cultural and social choices. As a result, fashion can be regarded as a site of struggle between competing identities in the lives of immigrant youth, as they strive for a happier new life.

The illustrations provided above also reveal that estrangement, adaptation and resistance are not mutually exclusive: rather, they work hand-in-hand and balance one another. One can adjust on one level, but at the same time resist the power of assimilation and preserve one's homeland identity on another level. It seems that each teenager drew a personal line between these competing forces and, literally, displayed it on his/her body for others to see. This led to numerous forms of identity negotiation: low-cut jeans – but with a belt that pulls them up; colourful oriental clothes – but no facial piercing; refraining from wearing suits – but paying attention to matching dark jeans pants and a jeans blazer. Fashion battles seem to take place daily on immigrant teenagers' "social skin," with personal compromises and "treaties" being negotiated, agreed upon, and resisted in a dynamic process of adaptation and resistance.

As in the findings of Rapoport and Lomsky-Feder (2010b), in our study several gender differences were evident. Girls, on the whole, were less resistant to the fashion demands placed on them and more open and positive about experimentation and adaptation. This partly reflects the over-emphasis society puts on external appearance as the most central characteristic of female "essence." This is a particularly relevant issue for female immigrants from the FSU who are often framed as "sluts" and mistreated accordingly (Lemish, 2000). No wonder, then, that female interviewees in our study appropriated the local "look" as an important resource for their self-definition, during this key period of their lives as developing, and respectful, young women: they mostly appreciated the freedom of choice and the variety (of shapes, colours, styles, fabrics, and so on) that local fashion offered them.

At the same time, a substantial argument can be made for the notion of fashion as a bricolage of styles, through which the teenage girl can create and recreate new appearances that are meaningful to her (Crane, 2000). This can also be perceived as an act of transformation by which an original individual style challenges the dominant youth culture (Muggleton, 2000). In our study, the mixing of homeland and host-country styles by the girls seemed less a form of blunt resistance than an act of appropriation and integration that was positively reinforced by the peer group.

In summary, our study reveals that fashion serves as a "metaphoric" realm of cultural exchange, similar to what we have found in regards to popular music (Elias *et al.* forthcoming). It seems that the trauma and crisis involved in immigration is so deep and overpowering, that it surfaces in every social and cultural aspect of these youngsters' lives. What is unique about fashion, though, is that the struggle is visible and takes place, literally, out in the open. It cannot be hidden like musical taste, nor can it be investigated in the privacy of one's identity games, as in the context of Internet surfing. The "social skin" of the young immigrant is out there, constantly scrutinized by peers, serving as an identity card, a declaration of cultural war, or an exhibit of personal and social transformation. As Oleg observed so rightly, when immigrant youth and Israeli peers encounter each other, they "meet through clothing". No wonder that clothing serves as such a fruitful site for studying young people's identity formation.

References

Barnard, M. (1996) *Fashion as Communication*. London: Routledge.

Barnard, M. (ed.) (2007) *Fashion Theory: A Reader*. London: Routledge.

Crane, D. (2000) *Fashion and Its Social Agendas: Class, Gender, and Identity in Clothing*. Chicago, Ill: The University of Chicago Press.

Dwyer, C. (1999) 'Negotiations of femininity and identity for young British Muslim women', in N. Laurie, C. Dwyer, S. Holloway and F. Smith (eds) *Geographies of New Femininities*, pp. 134–52. Essex: Pearson.

Elias, N. and D. Lemish (2008a) 'Media uses in immigrant families: torn between "inward" and "outward" paths of integration', *International Communication Gazette* 70(1): 23–42.

Elias, N. and D. Lemish (2008b) "Internet and immigrant youth hybrid identities: the case of Former Soviet Union immigrant adolescents in Israel", in I. Rydin and U. Sjöberg (eds) *Mediated Crossroads: Identity, Youth Culture and ethnicity*, pp. 173–92. Göteborg University: Nordic Information Centre for Media and Communication Research.

Elias, N. and D. Lemish. (2008c) "When all else fail: the Internet and adolescent-immigrants", in K. Drotner (ed.) *Informal Learning and Digital Media*, pp. 139–57. Cambridge: Cambridge Scholars Press.

Elias, N., D. Lemish and N. Khovorostianov (forthcoming) "Britney Spears remained in Russia": dynamics of musical preferences in the integration of immigrant adolescents', *Journal of Ethnic and Migration Studies*.

Hendrickson, H. (ed.) (1996) *Clothing and Difference: Embodied Identities in Colonial and Post-Colonial Africa*. Durham, NC: Duke University Press.

Lemish, D. (2000) "The whore and the other: Israeli images of female immigrants from the Former USSR", *Gender and Society* 14(2): 333–49.

Lindlof, R. T. and B.C. Taylor (2002) *Qualitative Communication Research Methods*. Thousand Oaks, CA: Sage.

Lynch, A. and M.D. Strauss (2007) *Changing Fashion: A Critical Introduction to Trend Analysis and Meaning*. Oxford, UK: Berg.

Muggleton, D. (2000) *Inside Subculture: The Postmodern Meaning of Style*. Oxford, UK: Berg.

Rapoport, T. and E. Lomsky-Feder (2010a) 'Introduction', in T. Rapoport and E. Lomsky-Feder (eds) *Visibility in Immigration: Body, Gaze, Representation,* pp. 11–42. Jerusalem, Israel: Van-Leer Institute. (Hebrew).

Rapoport, T and E. Lomsky-Feder (2010b) "The transformation of the " migrating body in the journey from Russia to Israel: The "body on alert", "an upright body", "the resettling body", in T. Rapoport and E. Lomsky-Feder (eds)*Visibility in Immigration: Body, Gaze, Representation,* pp. 69–98. Jerusalem, Israel: Van-Leer Institute. (Hebrew).

Tseelon, E. (1995) *The Masque of Femininity: The Presentation of Woman in Everyday Life*. London: Sage.

Index

abandoned flat study   104–5
accoustemology   97
acculturation
adaptation   256
adolescents *see also* divorce research;
   teenagers
   appropriation of space   166
   bedroom decoration   167–70
   room culture   165–6
adult pleasure, through
   children   23–4
adult supervision   88
adults
   fully socialized   68
   implications of changing
      perceptions of childhood
      27–9
advertising
   aimed at parents   20
   appeals to selfishness   29
   changing perspectives on   17
   for children   21
   deregulation   21
   and gender   224
   immersive   118–19
   targeting   113–14
   voluntary restraint   20–1
advertising trade cards   50–1
African-American children   73
agency
   of children   42–3
   range of   90
   and sexual innocence   235
   and structure   6
   and technology   172–3
anti-consumption rhetoric   20
archiving, digital   106
Ariès, Philippe   27
autonomy   4, 18, 88–9

babies' rooms   102
babies, safety   154–5
babyhood   151–2

Barbie   41
Baudrillard, Jean   90
becoming and being   9
   changing meanings   89–90
   as events   82–3
   as intertwined   87–9
bedrooms   102, 167–70
being and becoming   9
   changing meanings   89–90
   as events   82–3
   as intertwined   87–9
Berggren Torell, Viveka   237
birthday parties   75
Bjerrum Nielsen, Harriet   236
Boltanski, Christian   100–1
Bottomley, Paul   11–12
boundaries, adults and children
   231
Bourdieu, Pierre   37
boys, cool   237
brand attachment   202
brand control   140–1, 143
brand equity   133–4
brand loyalty   132–4, 143
Brandchild   3
branding   12, 133
brands
   and identities   212
   Piczo study   218–23
Bratz   42, 233
broadcasting, Bubble Books   56–7
Bubble Books   8, 46, 47, 49 *see also*
   phonograph records
   advertising   50
   appeal to mothers   52–6
   avoiding controversy   57–8
   broadcasting   56–7
   cultural impact   58–9
   educational content   54
   marketing strategies   50–1
   parties   57
   as quasi toys   52–3
Buchli, V.   104–5

Captain Sabertooth   10
   appealing to girls   137
   brand control   140–1, 143
   brand loyalty   133–4, 143
   characters   136–7
   as cultural phenomenon   131–2
   as cultural practice   134
   inclusion   136–40, 143
   indirect marketing   139–40
   origins   130–1
   settings   136
   spin-offs   131
   synergies   134–6, 143
   targeting adults   138–9
car culture   5
catalogues   96
categorization, and limitation   90–1
cell phones   103–4
'child-centredness'   37
child consumers, constructing   2–4
child development   64–5, 178
child market, fragmentation   137–8
child mortality   25–6
child safety   154–5
childhood
   ambivalent view of   18–19
   assumptions about   5
   changing perspectives on   32
   commercial   132–3
   construction of   38
   ideological view of   43
   materialism, self-esteem and socio-
      economic status   197–9
   as not existing   90–1
   permissive view of   24–5
   plurality of   73–4
   psychological perspectives on   65
   public discourses   229–34
   separate from adulthood   236
   sexualization   229–31
   understandings of   23, 228
childhood studies   63, 104–6
children
   active and knowing   74
   as actors   65, 81
   as agents   42–3
   centrality in marketplace   46
   changing image of   25–6
   discourses of   80
   influence on parents   50
   rationality   19–20
   treatment as consumers   82–3
   voices   242
   white middle class as 'ideal'   73
children as consumers, types of
      construct   2, 3–4, 9
children's consumer studies,
      perspectives on children   63–4
children's rights   37–8, 230
Chin, Elizabeth   73–4
China
   consumer revolution   11, 181
   economic growth   178
   growth in children's
      consumption   178
   parental attitudes to
      consumption   179
China research study
   children's need for guidance and
      protection   183–6
   concerns for future   187–8
   Dao of consumer
      socialization   190–2
   effects of economic, social and
      cultural changes   186–8
   methods   180–1
   parental views on consumer
      influence   182–3
   preparing for future   188–90
   technology   187
choice, increased opportunities
      for   88
Church, attitudes to children   27
class stratification, and
      consumption   37
Clausen, Bente   236
clothing   12, 230–2
   age appropriate   232–3
   and construction of identities   245
   fitting in   248–50
   kul   233–4
   and sexualization   230
   and social categorization   247–8
cognitive development   65–6
cognitive psychology, critiques of   65
Collins, Caitlin   10–11
colours, associated with
      babies   150–2

commercial childhood 132–3
commercial enculturation 8, 64, 69–73, 76
commercialization 1
communities of parenthood 152–3
competence 4
concupiscence 20
conflicting values 205
Confucianism 191
Connerton, Paul 234
consumer acculturation 70
consumer culture 31–2, 147–8
consumer groups, creating 232
Consumer Involvement scale 202
consumer orientation 202
consumer revolution, China 11
consumer socialization 8, 64–7, 71–2
  critiques of theory 68
  Dao of 190–2
  reasons for putting aside 75–6
  use of term 69
consumer subjectivity 8
consumers, as unmanageable 89–90
consuming, learning 74–5
consumption
  broad definition 72
  and class stratification 37
  controlling 19–23
  foci of research 150
  Norwegian state's attitude 38
  and technology 170
Cook, Daniel 3, 8, 31–2, 50, 52, 55, 235
cool 26–7, 29, 216–17, 238
cool boys 237
cool femininity 237
coolness 216–17, 237–8
crazes 10, 132–3
critical theory 4
Cross, Gary 7, 42
cross-promotion 136
cult of the child 20
cultural capital 37
culture of the cool 19
cultures
  adolescent room culture 165–6
  motherhood 147–8
curatorial play 102
cute girls 237

Dao of consumer socialization 190–2
Daston, L. 94
debates, polarization 2
deep memory 106–7
deliberate remembering 98–9
deprivation, materialism and wellbeing 11–12
deregulation, advertising 21
desire
  of adults 23–4
  children as valves of 18–19, 23–9
desiring child 25–6
diet 187
digital archiving 106
digital media, debates about 211
Disney 57, 116, 140
diversity, Proper Toys 39
divorce 10–11
  changing identities 165
  children's experiences 166–7
  reframing of objects 165
divorce research *see also* adolescents; teenagers
  agency and technology 172–3
  bedroom decoration 167–70
  'fun' vs. 'not fun' 170–1
  incentives/one upmanship 171
  methods 167
  relations of property 175–6
  sense of displacement 175
  technology and consumption 170
  technology and time allocation 173–5
  views of parents and home 170–2, see
  virtual connectedness 171–2
Dohring, Doug 118
dolls 102
Dream Worlds 150

economic deprivation, and materialism 11–12, 196
economic rationality 68–9
Edison, Thomas 47–8
Edwards, Elizabeth 95, 99
Ekström, Karin 69
Elias, Nelly 12–13
elitism 4
Ellis, Liz 150–1

eLogg   214, 216, 217
empowerment, and marketing to
        tweens   3
enculturation, diverse forms   73–5
eroticism   230, 239–40
estrangement   256
exhibitions   150

families, negotiation and
        diplomacy   232–3
family, as context of
        consumption   188–90
family roles, and marketing   52
fashion
   as bricolage of styles   256
   codes of dress   246
   experiences of migrants   246–55
   functions   246–7
   and identities   255
   and immigrant identities   250
   immigrants   12–13
   and integration   255
   as site of social resistance   250–3
   and social acceptance   248–50
   and social adjustment   253–5
   sociology of   244–5
   tweenage girls   12
Federal Drug Administration
        (FDA)   22
Federal Trade Commission (FTC)   21
femininities
   cool   237
   traditional   234–7
   traditional and modern   228
festivals, commercialization and
        infantilization   24
films, rating   28
Formanek-Brunell, Miriam   57
Formoe, Terje   131, 133, 135, 136,
        137, 140, 141
fragmentation, of child
        market   137–8
frames   214
free agency   17
'fun' vs. 'not fun'   170–1

Ganz Toys   121–2 *see also* Webkinz
Garvey, Ellen Gruber   50–1
gaze, reciprocal   248

gender
   adult roles in children's
        construction   231–2
   and advertising   224
   as negotiated construction   229
   new ways of doing   237–9
   and sport   237
   stereotypes   236
   traditional and modern
        views   229–34
gender construction   228–9, 235,
        242
generational order   8
Girard, Gilbert   48–9
girl-child   239
girls, cute   237
global self-esteem   198
Goffman, Erving   211–12, 213, 223,
        224
good childhood (*den gode
        barndom*)   229–30, 234–7
good consumers   67–9
Goode, J.   165
Growing up in Montreal   105

Hagen, Ingunn   10
Hart, J.   95, 99
hegemony, adult   40, 43
Hjemdahl, K. M.   131
Hodder, Ian   104
home consumption, defining   163
homes, material culture,
        consumption, and
        identity   164–5
Hooley, William F.   48
hopelessness   198
human becomings   80
human beings, concept of   81

identities   12–13
   adolescents after divorce   163
   bedroom decoration   167–70
   and brands   212
   changed by divorce   165
   and clothing   245
   and consumption   32
   and fashion   255
   and home consumption   163–4
   hybrid   12–13

immigrants 250, 255
  as parents 146
  ready-made 71
  transformation as new
    parents 147–8, 154
ideology
  Neopets 119–20
  Proper Toys 36
  Webkinz 124
immersive advertising 118–19
immigrants
  estrangement, adaptation and
    resistance 256
  fashion 12–13
  identities 250, 255
immigration, trauma of 256
impression management 215–16
inclusion 136–40, 143
information, at Baby Show 153–6
Inglehart, Ronald 196
innocence 17–18
integrated marketing 135
integration, and fashion 255
intergenerationality 228–34
International Council for Children's Play
    (ICCP) 34
internet
  data gathering 127
  as marketing tool 114–15
  self-presentation 213–14, 223–4
Israel
  immigration 244
  social stratification 247–8
Israel research study
  discussion and summary 255–7
  estrangement, adaptation and
    resistance 256
  findings 246–50
  methods 245–6
  social acceptance 248–50
  social adjustment 253–5
  social resistance 250–3

Jacobson, Lisa 46, 58
James, A. 74
Janning, Michelle 10–11
Johansson, Barbro 8–9
John, Deborah Roedder 65–7,
    68, 73

juvenile records *see* phonograph
    records

Kaiser, Susan 235
Key, Ellen 31, 37
Kirkham, Pat 95
Korswald, Tora 7
kul 238–9, 240–2

Leach, William 57
learning, and video games 225
learning to consume 74–5
Lee, Nick 89
Lego 41–2
Lemish, Dafna 12–13
life phases, and subjectivity 80
life stories, ways of telling 163
Lindstrom, Martin 3
local fashion, adopting 253–5
lost wonder 23–4
love, and consumption 23
Lucas, G. 104–5

males, changing concept of
    maturity 28–9
mapping 101
market research, Neopets 120–1
marketing
  changing perspectives 32
  and family roles 52–6
  integrated 135
  targeting 113–14
marketing discourse, focused on
    children 3
marketing strategies
  Disney, Walt 57
  indirect marketing 139–40
  storybook strategy 55
  for tweens 3
  virtual worlds 126
Marshall Plan 38
Martens, Lydia 10
material culture 9
material dissatisfaction 202–3
Material Values Scale 195
materialism
  in adulthood 195–7
  and attitudes to parents 203–4
  and economic deprivation 196

materialism – *continued*
  new 104–6
  and self-esteem 195–6
  self-esteem and socio-economic
      status 197–9
  use of term 194
materiality 95, 100
maturity 27–8
Mayhew, Ralph 49
McVeigh, Susan 125
media 2, 28, 57–8, 229–30
media culture, studying 113–14
memory work 97–9
memory writing 98
metadata 106
Mickey Mouse Club 21
migration 19
Mitchell, Claudia 9
modern childhood 18
Montgomery, Kathryn 114–15
moral panics 26–7
morality 20, 157, 179
Mosco, Vincent 114
motherhood 147–8, 153
mothering, diversity of
      experience 147
mothers, marketing to 52–6

Nairn, Agnes 11–12
Nakken, Øivind 10
nature, nearness to 239
Neopets 9, 116–21
new materialism 104–6
Nordic countries, traditions of
      play 35
Norway
  cool 238
  good childhood (*den gode
      barndom*) 229–30
  women's values 236
nostalgia, Proper Toys 36, 39–40
nursery rhymes 54

obesity 5
objects
  approaches to study 106–7
  ephemerality 106
  and gender construction 236
  gendered 95–7

in study of material culture 94–5
and visual culture 99–104
online social worlds 9
ontology of flow 91
oral tradition, Bubble Books 54–6
organizational networking 136
Ormrod, Johanne 11–12
othering 80–1
otherness 248
Others, children as 80–1
outdoor activities 236–7, 239
outdoor play 237

Pacifier Heaven 139–40
pacifism, Proper Toys 36–7
packaging 95–7
parental authority 88
parental rights 19, 22
parenthood
  communities of 152–3
  morality 157
  pleasures of early 150–1
parents, influence of children 50
parents, new 146–7, 153–4
peer groups 26
Penaloza, Liza 70
persuasive intent 72–3
philanthropy, Webkinz 124–5
phonograph records 7–8 *see also*
      Bubble Books
  children's media
      entertainment 46–7
  history and development 47
  performers 48–9
photographs 99–100
Piczo study 211
  branding 214–15
  collectors and elaborators 217–18,
      224–5
  collector's use of brands 218, 220
  conclusions 225–6
  coolness 216–17
  creativity 222
  discussion 223–5
  elaborators' use of brands 221–3
  methods 214
  production modes 219
  use of brands 224–5
  users and non-users 215–16

Pink, Sarah   95, 167, 168
Pirates of the Caribbean   144
play
  outdoor   237
  traditions of   35
political economy approach   9
political economy of media   114
political pressure   4
Postman, Neil   27
Pountain, Dick   238
poverty   203
power relationships, visibility and
     appearance   255
Pre-school Pedagogue   36
preparation and protection, children
     as consumers   179
productive remembering   97–9, 106
projection   7, 23–5
Proper Toys   7, 31
  adult consumers   42
  children's rights   37–8
  foundation of   33–5
  overview of case study   32–3
  pedagogical aims   35
  political and economic
       context   35–6
  properness   38–40
  selection of toys   39, 40, 43–4
  significance of name   34
  vision, ideology and
       morality   35–7, 40–1, 43
properness   38–42
protection   19
  of good childhood   230
  from sexual exploitation   231
protection and preparation, children
     as consumers   179
Prout, A.   74
Pugh, Allison   26, 73–4

quality, Proper Toys   39
quantitative research   194–5
quasi toys   52–3

referencing   101
regulation, of childhood
     consumption   19–23
remembering, deliberate   98–9
research

autobiographical dimension   148–9
  quantitative   194–5
resistance   256
responsibility, sharing   87
restraint, in advertising   20–1
Riggins, Stephen   101–2
rights, of children   37–8, 230
Riktige Leker (Proper Toys) *see* Proper
     Toys
Robins, David   238
Rosenberg Self-Esteem Scale
     (RSES)   198
Rousseau, Jean-Jacques   230
Rudberg, Monica   236
Rysst, Mari   12

safety   38, 154–5
Schor, Juliet B.   46, 53, 198, 199
Seiter, Ellen   52, 53–4, 130
self-control   19
self-determination   88
self-esteem   195–6, 197–9, 204 *see
     also* well-being
self-presentation, internet   213–14,
     223–4
selfishness   29
Selstad, Leif   234–5
senses, appeal to   134–5
sensory ethnography   95
serial purchasers   50–1
sexual exploitation, protection
     from   231
sexuality, understanding of   240–2
sexualization   12, 229–31, 239–40
Seybold, Patricia   3
Skaar, Håvard   12
Smith, Jacob   7–8
smoking   22–3
social acceptance   248–50
social adjustment   253–5
social categorization, and
     clothing   247–8
social contexts, of children's
     consumption   10–11
social democracy   37–8
social networking   12, 211 *see also*
     Piczo study
social resistance   250–3
social skin   257

socialization, as competent
    agents   17
socio-economic status   197–9, 204 *see
    also* well-being research
Sofaer, Joanna   106–7
Sofaer, Joshua   106–7
sounds, of toys   96–7, 103
space, appropriation by young
    people   166
Spencer, Len   48–9
spending, restricting   18
spoken word, limitations   104
sport   237, 238
staging   98
standard adult   89
stereotypes, gender   236
stigmatization   250
storybook strategy   55
structure, and agency   6
subjectivities
    aspects of production   80
    of consuming child   83–7
supervision, by adults   88
Sutton-Smith, B.   43
synergies   134–6, 142

Talking Machine World   50–1
technology   170, 172–5, 187
teenage cool   29
teenager-girl   239
teenagers *see also* adolescents; divorce
    research
    implications of changing
        perceptions of childhood   27–9
television, marketing to children   46
The Baby Show   10, 148–50
    as celebratory   156–7
    as community of
        parenthood   152–3
    as fun and practical   157
    as information conduit   153–6
    orchestration   150–2
    the cute   151–2, 157
Therborn, Göran   38
time, allocation after divorce, and
    technology   173–5
tobacco advertising   22–3
toy packaging   95–7

toys   34–5, 38–40, 42, 96–7, 103
"Toys That Teach" articles   53–4
traditions of play   35, 54–6, 234–5
trans-toying   53
tweenage girls, fashion   12
tweenagers   3, 232, 235

UN Convention on the Rights of the
    Child   228, 242
US consumer culture, relations
    between children and adults   7

values   43, 205, 236
valves of desire   18–19, 23–9
Victor Phonograph Company   7–8,
    46
video games   28, 225
violence in media, and maturity   28
virtual worlds *see also* Neopets;
    Webkinz
    analysing   125–6
    business models   115–16
    critiquing   126–7
    data gathering   127
    defining   114–15
visual ethnography   101–2
visual, materiality of   100
voices, of children   242
vulgarity   28

Wærdahl, Randi   11
Ward, Scott   64
Warner, Marina   99
Wasko, Janet   9–10
Webkinz   9, 121–5 *see also*
    Ganz Toys
well-being   1, 194 *see also* self-esteem
well-being research
    disappointment   204–5
    discussion and conclusions   204–6
    methods   199–200
    research tools   198
    results   200–4
Williams, Rosalind   150
wise consumers, children as   4
wondrous innocence   23, 27–8

Youth Materialism Scale (YMS)   197